ROY BENNETT

ƒORTISSIMO!

D1460845

CAMBRIDGE
UNIVERSITY PRESS

Published by the Press Syndicate of the University of Cambridge
The Pitt Building, Trumpington Street, Cambridge CB2 1RP
40 West 20th Street, New York, NY 10011-4211, USA
10 Stamford Road, Oakleigh, Melbourne 3166, Australia

First published 1996

The moral right of the author has been asserted

Printed in Great Britain at the University Press, Cambridge

A catalogue record for this book is available from the British Library

Student's Book   ISBN 0 521 56923 0
Teacher's Resource Book ISBN 0 521 56924 9
Set of 4 Compact Discs   ISBN 0 521 56925 7

Cover illustration by Helen Manning
Cover photograph: Tribal Drummers with Dancer, Burundi, Ninga,
by Bruno de Hogues © Tony Stone Images

Contents

Acknowledgements

We are grateful to the following for permission to reproduce photographs:

p. 9 Sonoton (photograph by Paul Mulcahy); p. 12 Redferns (David Redfern); p. 25 Vasily Kandinsky *Accompanied Contrast*, March 1935. Oil with sand on canvas 197.1 x 162.1cm. Solomon R. Guggenheim Museum, New York. Gift, Solomon R. Guggenheim, 1937. Photograph by David Heald, copyright The Solomon R. Guggenheim Foundation, New York FN37.338; p. 28 Culver Pictures Inc.; p. 32 Camera Press (The Rolling Stones); p. 32 Topham Picturepoint (stalactites and stalagmites, Nerja caves, Andalusia, Spain); pp. 32/33 Zefa (fireworks); p. 33 A–Z Botanical Collection (bryony berries, Maurice Nimmo); p. 33 The Image Bank (gem stones, Peter Frey); p. 37 Rheinisches Bildarchiv, Wallraff-Richartz-Museum, Köln; p. 38 Christine Osborne Pictures; p. 51 Rex Features (David Hancock); p. 54 cliché Bibliothèque Nationale de France; p. 54 Frank Spooner Pictures (skydiving, Gamma/Ward); p. 54 Oxford Scientific Films (reflections of reeds on water, Mike Birkhead); p. 55 Frank Spooner Pictures (Liz Young, showjumper, Gamma/Pugliano/ Liaison); p. 55 Tony Stone Images (Balinese dancer, James Palmer); p. 55 Telegraph Colour Library (rollercoaster, P. Beney); P. 70 Sonoton (photograph by Paul Mulcahy); p. 74 Sonia Delaunay *Rythme Syncopé, dit Le Serpent Noir*, cliché Ville de Nantes, Musée des Beaux-arts – H. Maertens, Inv. 8806; p. 76 Robert Harding Picture Library (Wells Cathedral, Somerset, Philip Craven); p. 76 The Natural History Museum, London (fluorite); pp. 76/77 James Davis Travel Photography (New Orleans jazz musicians); pp. 76/77 Science Photo Library (iridescent soap bubble, Dr Jeremy Burgess); p. 77 Oxford Scientific Films (Red Admiral butterfly, Larry Crowhurst); p. 79 *below left and right* The Trustees of The British Museum 1987. As 1.94; and 1966. As 1.69; p. 80 Rui Vieira/Panos Pictures; p. 84 Peter Hodges; p. 95 *above* The Hutchison Library; p. 95 *below* Aspect Picture Library (Brian Seed); p. 97 The Hutchison Library; p. 100 The Image Bank (Neuschwanstein Castle, Bavaria, Peter Grumann); p. 100 The Science Museum/Science & Society Picture Library (mechanical works of clock at Wells Cathedral); p. 101 Science Photo Library (Grand Canyon, Simon Fraser); pp. 100/101 Paul Mulcahy (Japanese print); p.101 Robert Harding Picture Library (fountain pieces, Pompidou Centre, Paris); p. 105 Robert Harding Picture Library; p. 117 Supraphon/Josef Kalousek (Paul Mulcahy); p. 120 Chinese and Japanese Special Fund, courtesy of Museum of Fine Arts, Boston *Clear Weather in The Valley* 13th century, Anonymous (formerly attributed to Dong Yuan) China, Jin Dynasty or slightly later. Handscroll: ink and light colour on paper 37.5×150.8cm; p. 122 Telegraph Colour Library (moonlight on sea and rocks); p. 122 Winstanley Sixth Form College, year 11 student's work (Caroline Wardle, Shell Bay); pp. 122/123 Tony Stone Images (waves breaking, H. Richard Johnston); p. 123 The Natural History Museum (Chinese dinosaur remains - Tuojiangosaurus); p. 131 Winstanley Sixth Form College (Kathleen Smith, bark study); p. 144 Oxford Scientific Films (magnified jellyfish/plankton, Peter Parks); p. 144 Science Photo Library (magnified snowflakes, Scott Camazine); p. 145 The Image Bank (Autumn trees & reflection, B. Atkins); p. 145 *above* Winstanley Sixth Form College (Kathleen Smith, varied weaving techniques); p. 153 P. O'Reilly; p. 165 Leslie E. Spatt; p. 170 Rex Features (The Police); p. 170 The Image Bank (rap dancers, Kim Keitt); pp. 170/171 Tony Stone Images (tribal drummers & dancer, Burundi, Ninga, Bruno de Hogues); p. 171 Redferns (Indian dancer, Dankaj Shah); p. 171 Rex Features (Mexican street musicians, Nadia Senepart); p. 174 Reg Wilson; p. 178 Collections (Ben Boswell); p. 186 *left* The Bridgeman Art Library (Pope Innocent X, Diego Rodriguez de Silva Velasquez, Palazzo Doria Pamphili, Rome); p. 186 *centre* City of Aberdeen Art Gallery & Museums Collections; p. 186 *right* Städtische Kunsthalle Mannheim (Marlborough Fine Art London Ltd.); p. 190 Tony Stone Images (light trails); p. 190 Wilfred Grove (Fountains at Breda, Holland); p. 190 Winstanley Sixth Form College (screaming face, photo Paul Mulcahy); pp. 190/191 ScotRail (The Forth Bridge, Gordon Smith); pp. 190/191 Telegraph Colour Library (raindrops on water, D & J Gleiter); pp. 190/191 Winstanley Sixth Form College (Kathleen Smith, study of natural forms in machine embroidery – insets); p. 191 Winstanley Sixth Form College (Erica Roby, snarling head); p. 199 Robert Harding Picture Library; p. 215 Scala/Accademia Venezia; p. 220 Redferns, (Herbert Kuehn); p. 221 Oxford Scientific Films (daffodil, G.I. Bernard); p. 221 RCA (Cathy Berberian performing Berio's *Recital I*); p. 221 Science Photo Library (DNA double helix, National Institute of Health); p. 225 *inset* John Garner; p. 230 A Schöenberg, *Alban Berg*, Historisches Museum der Stadt Wien; p. 243 Jackson Pollock, *Convergence*, 1952, oil on canvas 93.5 x 155", Albright-Knox Art Gallery, Buffalo, New York, Gift of Seymour H. Knox, 1956; p. 250 Collection of Whitney Museum of American Art, New York (photo by Geoffrey Clements). Mobile by Alexander Calder, *Pomegranate*, 1949. Copyright © 1995; p. 250 Paul Mulcahy (dice & coin); pp. 250/251 Science Photo Library (printed circuit board, Simon Fraser); p. 251 Science Photo Library (total solar eclipse, Dr Fred Espenak);

We are grateful to the following for permission to reproduce poems:

p. 101 A. P. Watt Ltd on behalf of Michael Yeats for 'He Wishes for the Cloths of Heaven' from William Butler Yeats's collection of poems entitled 'The Wind Among the Reeds' (1899); p. 163 Sinclair Stevenson for Edith Sitwell's poem 'Tango' from 'Collected Poems'.

Every effort has been made to reach copyright holders; the publishers would like to hear from anyone whose rights they have unknowingly infringed.

Introduction

Fortissimo! is a music course structured in thirty chapters. Each of these explores one or more structural or expressive elements of music, concepts, or composing devices. Throughout, you will find opportunities for Performing, Composing, Improvising, and Listening.

The Listening material consists of varied pieces and extracts of music from different musical periods (from the 13th century to the 1990s), of different types and styles (classical, jazz, blues, rock, folk, traditional), and from a variety of cultures and traditions – both Western and non-Western.

All musical terms and phrases are usually explained upon their first appearance in the book. A full Index is given on pages 252–6.

Throughout the course, there will be opportunities for you to critically evaluate (appraise) your own compositions and performances, and also those of others – including the work of fellow students, and of established composers and performers. In the Teacher's Resource Book there are photocopiable question sheets. The questions are intended to help and guide you in the process of evaluating a composition or an instrumental or vocal performance.

However, in the case of your own work, it is important that you think of evaluating as an *ongoing* activity, and not as just a question of formally evaluating your finished composition or performance. You need to evaluate the process leading to the finished, refined product:

- *at every possible stage* during the creating of a **composition** ('Is this the way I want it to sound?')
- *continuously*, while **practising** or **rehearsing** ('Am I playing/singing the right notes, at the right time, in the right way?').

At regular intervals throughout this book there are double-page spreads displaying visual, and occasionally verbal or musical, material. Although the items have been chosen to link to musical elements and ideas explored in preceding chapters, they are intended to serve – in any interpretation you may choose – as springboards or stimuli, to spark off ideas for Composing or Improvising.

World Map

This map shows some of the countries/cultures whose musics are represented in this course.

RUSSIAN FEDERATION

Budapest
HUNGARY ROMANIA
          •Bucharest
Sofiya BULGARIA
GREECE   Ankara
  •Athens TURKEY

Beijing   N. KOREA   JAPAN
             S. KOREA   •Tokyo

E A S T   A S I A
CHINA

New Delhi

SOUTH ASIA
   INDIA
Bombay   •Hyderabad

THAILAND
•Bangkok

SOUTH-EAST
   ASIA

I N D O N E S I A

PACIFIC

OCEAN

AFRICA

Desert

INDIAN

OCEAN

Jakarta
•   BALI
JAVA

Dodoma
TANZANIA

SOUTHERN
AFRICA

MOZAMBIQUE
•Maputo

A U S T R A L I A

•Canberra

A possible strategy for creating a piece of music

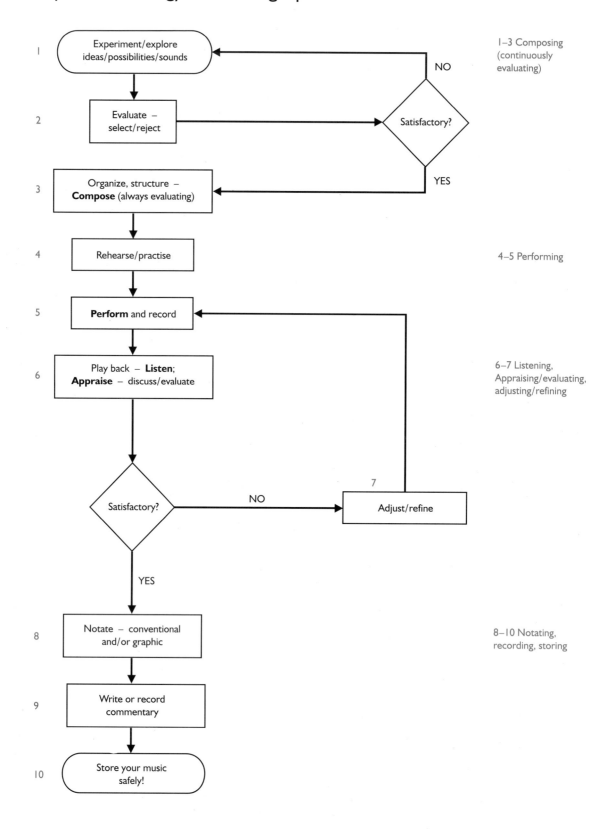

CHAPTER I

Rhythm (1)

Listening

Listen to a colourful piece from Korea called *Tiger Dance*. This was specially composed by Moon Pyung Hwang for the 1988 Olympic Games, which took place in Seoul. The tiger is the national emblem of Korea. The instruments taking part include:

- *hyangp'iri* – a double-reed wind instrument
- *taegŭm* – a bamboo flute
- *haegŭm* – a two-string fiddle
- drums
- cymbals
- gong

The music gradually builds up. Then listen for four occasions when the percussion players dramatically stop, and then start off again. In each of the four gaps, a solo player improvises:

 hyangp'iri *taegŭm* *haegŭm* cymbals

Several musical elements, or ingredients, combine to make *Tiger Dance* sound vivid and exciting. They include:

- the colourful and contrasting sounds of these Korean instruments;
- the melodic lines played by the three melody instruments;
- perhaps most important of all – the **beat** and the **rhythm**.

Tiger Dance

Listening

Now listen to part of the *Prelude* to the opera *Carmen* by Bizet. The extract begins with the march-tune of the Toreador's Song, which is immediately repeated. Then it ends with another march-tune: the Entry of the Toreadors.

Listen to the extract a second time. It begins with eight steady chords played by trumpets and trombones (see the music below). Then the tune is played by the strings.

As you listen, wait for the tune to begin – then clap or tap (with fingertips, or with your foot on the ground) in time with the music. Go on doing this until the music ends.

Was your clapping or tapping steady and even throughout? If so, you were marking the basic **beat**, or **pulse**, of the music. This provides a steady framework – the 'heart-beat' of the music. It is against this framework that the ear measures other musical events.

Clap this row of crotchet beats, saying each number out loud. Keep your clapping and counting steady and even – taking care that you don't get quicker or slower.

A single beat is a basic unit of musical time. Beats are grouped together to make a repeating pattern – made up either of twos, or threes, or fours.

The repeating pattern of beats gives us the **metre**, or the **time**, of the music.

Each repetition of the beat-pattern is called a **bar**, or **measure**. In printed music, the bars are separated by vertical lines called **bar-lines**.

Some beats carry a stronger accent than others. The first beat of a bar usually carries the strongest accent.

Performing

Clap again the twelve crotchet beats (above). Then clap them as shown on the opposite page, where they are now grouped into three different metres, or beat-patterns. Strongly accent the first beat of each bar with a loud clap. Make all the other beats unaccented by clapping them more softly.

(a) **Duple metre** – two beats to a bar

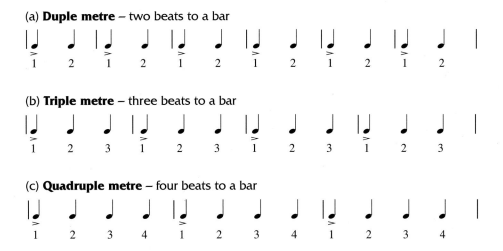

(b) **Triple metre** – three beats to a bar

(c) **Quadruple metre** – four beats to a bar

Composers show what kind of metre, or beat-pattern, is being used by writing a **time signature** at the beginning of the music. This is made up of two figures, written one above the other. The top figure gives the number of beats to each bar. The bottom figure indicates what kind of note is taken for the beat. This is shown as a fraction of a semibreve (or whole note).

In each of the metres (beat-patterns) you have just clapped, the beat was a crotchet. Here is the time signature for each one:

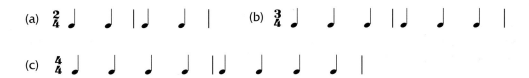

In each of these, the bottom figure indicates a crotchet beat, since a crotchet is a quarter of a semibreve. (See charts 2 and 3, page 13.)

Performing

Form a group of three musicians, each with a contrasting percussion instrument. Perform the following, all beginning together, but each of you starting with a different line (A, B or C). Before you start, one person must set the basic beat (pulse) by steadily counting '1, 2, 3' – then all begin. Keep a steady beat, and strongly accent the first beat of each bar. Decide how many times you will play it through – then everyone ends on the first beat of the next line.

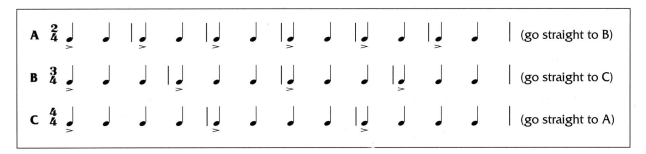

The metre, or repeating beat-pattern, in a piece of music serves as a steady framework. It is against this framework that the ear measures **rhythm.**

Rhythm is the grouping of long and short sounds into patterns, within the metre. Rhythm is characterized by:

- accent, and non-accent;
- duration: the lengths of notes, long or short, in relation to each other;
- and also – silence.

Chart 1, opposite, gives the names of the different notes, and how they are written. For each note there is a corresponding sign called a **rest**, which indicates an equivalent length of silence.

Listening

Listen to the beginning of *Running in the Family* by Level 42 (Mark King – vocals and bass guitar, Mike Lindup – keyboards and vocals, Phil Gould – drums, Boon Gould – guitar). The drum kit emphasizes the $\frac{4}{4}$ metre. Against this strong beat-pattern, rhythm – with its own accents and varied note lengths – flows freely on other instruments, and voices.

Listen to the music again, and concentrate your listening, low down, on the sound of the bass guitar. Is this supplying the steady *beat* (like the drum kit) – or is it moving along freely in *rhythm*?

Listen a third time – and mark the steady beat, along with the drum kit:

As you mark the beat-pattern in this way, listen carefully to how the rhythms are moving freely against the beat.

Level 42

1 Notes and rests

Name	Note	Rest	Value when each beat is a crotchet
semibreve			4 beats
minim			2 beats
crotchet		or	1 beat
quaver			$\frac{1}{2}$ (2 to a beat)
semiquaver			$\frac{1}{4}$ (4 to a beat)
demisemiquaver			$\frac{1}{8}$ (8 to a beat)
hemidemisemiquaver			$\frac{1}{16}$ (16 to a beat)

A dot after a note or rest makes it half as long again. For example:

♩ = 1 beat;   ♩. = 1 + $\frac{1}{2}$ = 1$\frac{1}{2}$ beats

2 Time-values of notes in relation to the semibreve

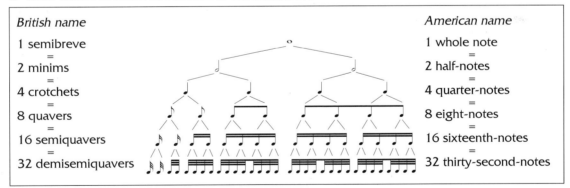

British name		American name
1 semibreve		1 whole note
=		=
2 minims		2 half-notes
=		=
4 crotchets		4 quarter-notes
=		=
8 quavers		8 eight-notes
=		=
16 semiquavers		16 sixteenth-notes
=		=
32 demisemiquavers		32 thirty-second-notes

3 Simple time signatures

	Note-value of each beat			Number of beats to each bar
	♩ (minim)	♩ (crotchet)	♪ (quaver)	
duple	$\frac{2}{2}$ or ¢	$\frac{2}{4}$	$\frac{2}{8}$	2
triple	$\frac{3}{2}$	$\frac{3}{4}$	$\frac{3}{8}$	3
quadruple	$\frac{4}{2}$	$\frac{4}{4}$ or C	$\frac{4}{8}$	4

Improvising

Join up with a partner. Choose a percussion instrument each. Then choose a metre:

$$\frac{2}{4} \qquad \frac{3}{4} \quad \text{or} \quad \frac{4}{4}$$

Performer 1 begins by steadily marking the beat-pattern of the metre. Slightly accent the first beat of each bar.

Performer 2 joins in and improvises rhythm patterns, including rests, against the steady beat.

After a while, swap parts. Try a different metre.

Performing

Form a group of four musicians. Together, clap this rhythm. (On the second beat of bar 3, ♪♪♪ is a **triplet** – three notes to be performed evenly in the time of two notes of the same kind.)

Try the rhythm several times until you can perform it absolutely steadily and accurately.

Now perform it as a 'rhythm round'. Performer 1 begins. Then after one bar, performer 2 begins; and so on. Decide how many times you will play it through – and how you will end the round.

Try the round again, this time using four contrasting percussion instruments.

Composing

On your own or with others, compose your own 'rhythm round'. Decide upon the basic metre, and then create the rhythm against it. Make sure that no two bars have the same rhythm.

Organize a performance of your round. (You may find that some adjustment or refining is necessary.)

When you are satisfied, make a recording of your round, and then listen to it. Judge how well the rhythm patterns fit against each other, and against the basic beat.

Improvising

Rhythmic dialogues

In twos, each of you with a percussion instrument, try this:

1   Performer A chooses a metre ($\frac{2}{4}$, $\frac{3}{4}$, or $\frac{4}{4}$) and improvises a rhythm pattern two bars long. Without pause (keeping the beat) B copies exactly. A improvises another two bars, B copies; and so on.

2   Swap parts. Performer B now leads, choosing a different metre.

3   Performer A leads again – but B now answers each time with a *different* rhythm pattern.

4   Swap parts again.

.5   Try stages 3 and 4 again, but this time consider:

- sometimes playing more loudly, sometimes more softly;
- sometimes adding crisp and firm accents;
- changing the metre after every eight bars.

Listening

Listen again, twice, to the Korean *Tiger Dance* (page 9). Listen for the different rhythm patterns which are used – repeating, combining, contrasting, changing. Listen also for strong accents.

1   What is the metre, or beat-pattern, of this music? Would the time signature be:

$\frac{2}{4}$ (duple); $\frac{3}{4}$ (triple);   or $\frac{4}{4}$ (quadruple)?

2   Are all the 'gaps' (when the soloists improvise in turn) of exactly the same length?

Now try this...

Form a group of four musicians – three of you with contrasting percussion instruments, and the fourth serving as conductor.

Create an exciting piece of rhythm music, based on the way in which *Tiger Dance* is structured:

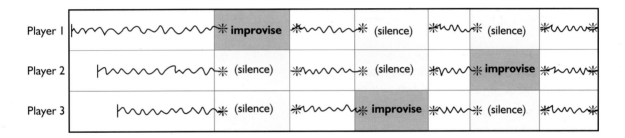

Players start one after another with contrasting rhythm patterns – often repeating, sometimes changing, sometimes returning. The conductor must keep the beat (pulse) steady, and continue to conduct throughout – even during the improvised sections.

Experiment with different rhythm patterns in combination on all three instruments. Judge how well they sound together. You could try some of the ones below – and/or make up others of your own.

Decide how long (how many bars, or beats) each improvised section is to be. Decide also how the conductor will (silently) signal, or cue, players to end cleanly to mark the beginning of each improvised section. For example:

Now try out the piece. When all three percussionists are playing together, make the music forceful, sometimes with punchy accents, so that there is a strong contrast with the solo improvised sections.

Give your piece a suitable title.

Make a recording of your piece. Then listen to it and discuss it. For example, how effective are:

● the contrasting rhythm patterns, and the accents;

● the stops and starts before and after the improvised sections;

● the solo improvisations;

● the balance between the sounds of the instruments (is any too loud? should any be played more loudly?)

Develop this by trying another version of the piece, this time with a conductor and *six* instrumentalists: three playing percussion, and three playing melody instruments. The melody instrument players improvise melodic patterns against the percussion rhythms – and each, in turn, improvises a solo as everyone else stops.

Linked listening

Sousa: March – *The Stars and Stripes Forever*, for military band
Elgar: *Pomp and Circumstance Marches* 1 and 4 (described in 'Enjoying Music' Book 2)
Vaughan Williams: *March Past of the Kitchen Utensils* from *The Wasps*
Richard Rodgers: *March of the Siamese Children* from the musical *The King and I* (described in 'Adventures in Music' Book 4)
Encina: *Triste España* (recorded on 'Enjoying Early Music' cassette)
Renaissance dances such as the basse danse and the pavan (several described in 'Enjoying Early Music')
Dances in $\frac{2}{4}$ time – e.g. *Trepak* from *The Nutcracker* by Tchaikovsky, *Tango in D* by Albéniz
Dances in $\frac{3}{4}$ time, such as minuets from symphonies and chamber works by Haydn and Mozart; waltzes by the Strauss family; waltzes, mazurkas and polonaises by Chopin
Dances in $\frac{4}{4}$ time – e.g. *Dance of the Rose Maidens* and *Sabre Dance* from the ballet *Gayaneh* by Khatchaturian (melody-line scores are included in 'Musical Forms: Listening Scores')
Dances by the Cuban composer Ernesto Lecuona ('Adventures in Music' Book 3)
Carl Orff: songs from *Carmina burana*
Varèse: *Ionisation* (described in 'Enjoying Modern Music')
Stockhausen: *Kreuzspiel*, for oboe, bass clarinet, piano, and three percussionists
Steve Reich: *Music for 18 Musicians*, *Clapping Music*, and *Music for Pieces of Wood*
Recordings of African drumming
Interlocking rhythm patterns in Balinese gamelan music
Duke Ellington: *Echoes of the Jungle* ($\frac{4}{4}$ time)
Louis Armstrong's recording of *Mack the Knife* by Kurt Weill – $\frac{2}{2}$ time; steady minim beat marked by plucked bass, crotchets on drum kit
The Beatles: *When I'm Sixty-four* ($\frac{2}{2}$ time)
Prince: *Purple Rain* ($\frac{2}{2}$ time)
The Moody Blues: *Minstrel's Song* (especially the chorus) – rhythms overlaying basic $\frac{4}{4}$ beat
Records of rapping – rhythmic word-patterns above a steady beat
Elmer Bernstein: title music to the film 'The Magnificent Seven' – flowing tune above a very rhythmic accompaniment.

CHAPTER 2

Shaping melodies

To many people, **melody** is the most striking element, or ingredient, in music. When getting to know a piece of music, it is usually the melody which we remember the best.

A melody (or melodic line) moves in two ways. It moves:

- forwards, in *time*, and also
- up and down, in *pitch* – its individual notes are higher or lower than each other.

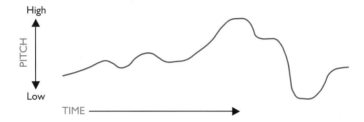

The shape or **contour** of a melody – the way it curves along, rising and falling in pitch – is very important.

Investigate some contrasting melodies. First, the folk-song *O Waly, Waly*. (The Scottish word *waly* is an exclamation of sorrow.) Occasionally in this melody, a note is immediately repeated. Otherwise, the notes move mainly **by step** – to a 'next-door' note, just a step higher or lower in pitch.

Performing

Play the melody of *O Waly, Waly* (if possible, on a keyboard). Discover – by playing, looking, and listening:

- when notes are immediately repeated;
- and especially, when they move by step (to a next-door note on the keyboard).

The melody of *O Waly, Waly* is structured in four **phrases** – shown by the curved lines, called **phrase-marks** or **slurs**. A phrase is a group of notes giving the strong impression of 'belonging together'.

Play *O Waly, Waly* again. Then *sing* the melody (to 'ah' or 'lah').
Shape each phrase. Sing each phrase in a single breath.

Another important characteristic of a melody is its **range**. This is the distance in pitch between its lowest note and its highest note. The range of *O Waly, Waly* is one octave, from D to D. (An *octave*, meaning 'set of eight', is the distance between any note and the next note with the same letter-name, either higher or lower.)

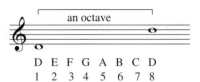

	D	E	F	G	A	B	C	D
	1	2	3	4	5	6	7	8

The second melody is from the famous waltz *The Blue Danube* by Johann Strauss II. Again, notes are sometimes immediately repeated. Otherwise, the notes move almost entirely **by leap** – which may be narrow, or wide.

[original key: D]

Performing

Play this version of Strauss's melody, which covers a range of almost two octaves. Select a voice on your keyboard such as violin, or strings. By playing, looking and listening, discover answers to these questions:

1 In which bars of the melody is there a leap of an octave?

2 In which bars do you play any leap which is wider than an octave?

3 Which bars contain the widest leap?

4 Which is the only bar where the notes move by step?

The melody of *O Waly, Waly* moves mainly by step. Strauss's melody moves mainly by leap. Most melodies, however, move by a balanced mixture of step and leap, perhaps also including some repeated notes.

Listening

Now listen to *Bess, You is My Woman Now* from Gershwin's opera *Porgy and Bess*. This melody is written in the bass clef. (If you are not familiar with this, see the diagram opposite.) The small curved line joining two notes of the same pitch in bars 7 and 8 is called a *tie*. The effect is a single sustained sound which lasts for the value of both notes added together (in this case, seven beats).

As the recording is played, look and listen for notes moving by step, and by leap. Discover where, on two occasions, Porgy sings an expressive leap of a 9th (one step greater than an octave).

Many melodies make use of **repetition** of musical ideas. The repetitions give shape to the melody, and also make it more easy to understand and remember. Sometimes, to add interest, a repetition is slightly **varied** in some way – what we might call 'repetition with a difference'. For example, the pitches might remain the same, but the rhythm is varied. Or the same rhythm might be repeated, but with variations of pitch.

Listening

Listen to the well-known melody from the slow movement of Dvořák's Ninth Symphony (*From the New World*).

There are several repetitions of melodic and rhythmic patterns – sometimes two bars long, sometimes a single bar, sometimes shorter still. For example:

- bar 3 is a repetition of bar 1;
- bars 7 and 8 are a repetition of bars 5 and 6;
- there are many repetitions of this short rhythmic figure: ♪♪ ♩ ;
- bar 9 is a varied repetition of bar 1 (how is it varied?).

Listen to the melody two or three times, and spot other repetitions – and varied repetitions.

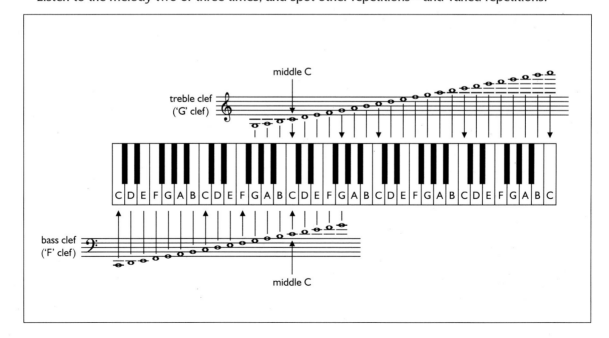

Characteristic features of a melody include:

- its shape or contour – the way the notes rise and fall as they curve along in musical time and space;
- whether it moves mainly by step, or by leap, or by a balanced mixture of both (perhaps also with some repeated notes);
- its range – which may be wide, medium, or narrow;
- its phrase-lengths (long, or short, or varying) and structure – perhaps involving repetition and variation of melodic and rhythmic patterns;
- the speed at which it moves;
- a sense of direction – and, perhaps, a climax (a 'high-point');
- the kind of scale on which its notes are based – major, minor, pentatonic, or perhaps some other kind of scale;
- metre, rhythm and accent;
- often, a particular mood – which may be created by some of the above features.

Composing

1 Compose or improvise a short melody which moves mainly by step. Match this rhythm (or make up one of your own).

Now compose or improvise a short melody which moves mainly by leap. Give your melody an interesting rhythm.

Is there any difference in mood between your two melodies?

2 Compose a longer melody in which you use a balanced mixture of step and leap, and perhaps also some repeated notes.

Decide whether your melody will be for voice or an instrument – the range of an average voice is not as wide as that of most instruments. As you shape your melody, carefully consider the contour.

Use some repetition, and varied repetition, of melodic and rhythmic patterns. Some repetition will give *unity* to your melody. Using varied repetition, or bringing in a fresh idea, will add *variety*.

Write down your completed melody, and add phrase-marks.

Perform your melody (or ask someone else to perform it) and make a recording of it. Afterwards, listen back, and judge whether you need to make any adjustments or alterations to refine your melody.

Improvising

With a partner, each using voice or a melody instrument, build up a long, unfolding melodic line by improvising phrases in turn. Performer 1 leads, then 2 responds – sometimes with:

- a repetition of the same phrase;
- a varied repetition of a phrase;
- a phrase which contrasts in some way – for example, by using mainly steps instead of leaps (or the other way around), or shaping a falling/rising contour instead of a rising/falling contour.

Performing

Sing or play these six melodies from different parts of the world. Investigate them, and discover:

- the main differences between them – but also any similarities;
- repetition, and varied repetition, of melodic and rhythmic ideas;
- movement by step, by leap, or a mixture of both; use of repeated notes;
- the phrase structure of each melody (how many phrases? how many bars in each phrase?);
- whether a particular mood is created;
- any other interesting features.

(If you are using electronic keyboard – experiment, and discover what you think is a suitable voice for each melody.)

1   Tanzania, East Africa: *Dance*

2   China: *Lotus Blossoms*

3   Java: *Little Father Horse-washer*

4   India: *Weaving Dance*

5   Navajo (North American Indian): *Happy Song*

6   Hungary: *The Bold Hussar*

Composing

Try one or more of these ideas. Whichever you choose, store your music by writing it down in any suitable way. Then practise it, and perhaps make a recording of it. Store your music safely.

1   Compose a melody, in any style you choose, for voice or instrument, in which the phrases vary in length.

2   Compose a melody in which you aim to express a particular mood. Give your melody a suitable title.

3   Compose a melody in which the pitches are limited to five or six notes only. Choose your notes carefully, and consider how you can achieve variety in your melody.

4   Compose a rhythmic melody for a dance. When you have completed your melody, add a percussion accompaniment.

5   Compose a melody for a special occasion – for example, a theme-tune which will be heard several times during a weekend athletics meeting.

6   Form a group of musicians, and compose a melody for a TV jingle. Decide:

  ●   what kind of product your music will advertise;

  ●   which sounds – instruments and/or voices – will be most suitable;

  ●   whether to add a backing on percussion instruments.

Your music should last for just thirty seconds, and must make an immediate impact and appeal.

7   Compose a 'float-and-flutter' melodic line – shaped by long-held notes, each followed by a group of decorative swift notes. For example:

(and so on)

Your music could be:

- in **strict time** – with a steady beat; or,
- in **free time** – freely flowing, without beat or metre.

Performing

Give a performance of your music to the rest of the class. As others perform theirs, listen for some of the characteristic features of melody, given in the box on page 20.

Linked listening

Listen to, and compare, some of these melodies, and assess their characteristics. Which kind of melody appeals to you the most?

Melodies moving mainly by step

Plainchant: *Hodie Christus natus est* (the music is printed in 'Enjoying Early Music')
Josquin des Prez: partsong, *El grillo* (The cricket)
Beethoven: theme from the last movement of Symphony No. 9 ('Choral')
Tchaikovsky: opening of *Pas de deux* from the ballet *The Nutcracker* – expressive use of downward scales
Francis Lai: theme from the film 'Un homme et une femme'

Melodies featuring leaps

Pugnani, arranged Kreisler: *Praeludium* for violin and piano
Wagner: *The Ride of the Valkyries* ('Enjoying Music' Book 1)
Mahler: first movement of Symphony No. 10 – as the violins enter, expressive leaps, covering $2\frac{1}{2}$ octaves in just over three bars
Berg: *Schliesse mir die Augen beide* – compare the version Berg made in 1925 (mainly leaps) with the version he made in 1907

Balanced mixture of step and leap (perhaps with repeated notes)

Mozart: *Lacrymosa* from Requiem in D minor (music printed in 'Musical Forms: Listening Scores')
Brahms: Hungarian Dance No. 5
Prokofiev: *Montagues and Capulets* from *Romeo and Juliet* (melody-line score printed in 'Musical Forms: Listening Scores'); Gavotte from the *Classical Symphony* ('Musical Forms' Book 2)
Schoenberg: Theme from *Variations for Orchestra* ('Enjoying Modern Music')
Bernstein: *Tonight* and *Somewhere* from *West Side Story*

Melodies featuring repeated notes

Sibelius: Trio from the third movement of Symphony No. 2
Khatchaturian: *Sabre Dance* ('Musical Forms: Listening Scores')

Melodic line and contour

Villa-Lobos: *New York Skyline Melody* – created by copying a photograph onto graph paper, then converting the resulting lines into musical pitches and durations. (Try a similar idea yourself?)

CHAPTER 3

Timbre (1)

Musicians use the word **timbre** to describe the characteristic and distinctive sound – the tone-quality, or tone-*colour* – of an instrument or voice.

A violin, a guitar, a saxophone, a horn, a xylophone, an Indian sitar, a Chinese *cheng*, and a great many other instruments, can all play exactly the same note – yet each will sound different from the rest. Each has its own characteristic *timbre* or 'colour of sound'.

Listen to the three instruments (string, brass, and woodwind) recorded on the compact disc. Each of them plays the note A above middle C.

Can you hear the difference in timbre between the three instruments?

Can you identify each instrument?

The characteristic timbre of an instrument is the result of several factors. These include:

- the size and shape of the instrument;
- the materials from which it is made;
- the method by which it produces its sounds (e.g. strings, a reed);
- the way in which its sounds are made to resonate (e.g. the hollow wooden body of the violin);
- the way in which each sound actually begins;
- harmonics.

The most important of these is **harmonics**. When a length of stretched string, or the air in a length of tube, is made to vibrate, it not only vibrates as a whole, but also in two halves, three thirds, four quarters, and so on – all at the same time. Our ears pick up most strongly the vibrations of the whole, and so we decide what note is being sounded. But this main note is only the lowest, or *fundamental*, in a whole series of pitches, called the **harmonic series**. The vibrations of the halves, thirds, quarters, and so on, are at the same time producing higher, fainter pitches which 'colour' the tone of the main note. These are called *harmonics*.

If the stretched string, or the tube, is of such a length that the main note (the fundamental) being sounded is C below the bass stave, then the first sixteen pitches of the harmonic series will be as shown below. The main note (the fundamental) is counted as the first harmonic. (The four notes marked with a cross are not in tune with any normal scale in use.)

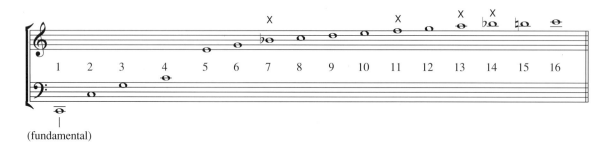

(fundamental)

A different fundamental would of course offer another series – but with exactly the same pattern of pitch-distances between the notes.

Some instruments produce more harmonics than others. And different instruments stress different harmonics. It is the relative strengths of the harmonics, and the way they mix together, which mainly decide the distinctive timbre of an instrument, and also the brilliance (or lack of brilliance) of its sound. Whereas some instruments have a characteristically bright, penetrating timbre, others have a darker, richer timbre.

Listening

Compare the timbres of various instruments of the orchestra as you listen to *Scene* and the first part of *Gypsy Song* from Rimsky-Korsakov's colourful *Spanish Caprice*. Several instruments are featured solo. (Drawings of all the instruments taking part are shown on page 115.)

Listen for these 'events' in the music:

(1) snare drum roll + a fanfare for trumpets and horns (with trumpet playing the top line);

(2) solo violin (snare drum roll continues, softly);

(3) a rhythm on percussion, joined by the strings of the orchestra, alternately bowed (*arco*) and plucked (*pizzicato*) – then a tune on flute and clarinet (a mixture of timbres);

(4) kettledrum roll + solo flute;

(5) cymbal roll (with sponge-headed sticks) + solo clarinet;

(6) solo oboe + three strokes on triangle;

(7) triangle roll + solo harp;

(8) loud stabs on clashed cymbals, trombones and tuba, + violins, leading into the *Gypsy Song* for full orchestra – combining a wide variety of timbres . . .

> 'Timbre in music can be compared with colour in painting.'
>
> (The American composer, Aaron Copland)

A painting by Wassily Kandinsky called 'Accompanied Contrast'

Listening

Now investigate the very different timbres of an instrumental ensemble from Thailand, playing a piece called *Ricebowl* by Pichit Paiboon. This music depicts the joy and fun of the Thai rice harvest. Instruments are often featured solo, against a percussion accompaniment, with other instruments throwing in musical 'comments' between the phrases.

Besides drums, instruments which you will hear include:

- *ching* – small hand cymbals of thick metal
- *pi morn* – a type of shawm (woodwind instrument with a double reed)
- *pi nai* – a larger shawm with a quadruple reed made from dried palm leaf
- *ranad ek* – a high-pitched xylophone
- *ranad thume* – a lower-pitched xylophone
- *gong wong lek* – a high-pitched gong-chime (set of knobbed gong kettles of different sizes)
- *gong wong yai* – a lower-pitched gong-chime

Listen to *Ricebowl*, noticing the distinctive timbres of the Thai instruments.

Then listen again, and see if you can match the timbres you hear to the brief descriptions of the instruments, given above.

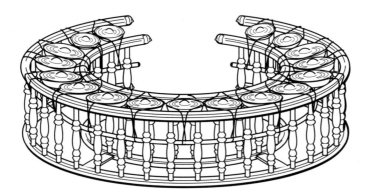

gong wong lek – the player sits or kneels inside the circular frame and uses disc-ended beaters

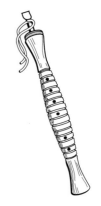

pi nai

The characteristic timbre of an instrument may vary according to the way in which it is played. The instruments of the string section of the orchestra may, of course, be played with a bow, or the strings plucked with the fingertips (an effect called *pizzicato*). The timbre can be altered in other ways – for example, by using a **mute**, a small comb-like device which is clipped onto the bridge. This dampens the vibrations and brings a hushed, veiled quality to the tone.

violin mute

Mutes of various shapes and sizes can also be used to change the timbre of brass instruments. For instance, a 'straight' mute, wedged into the bell of a trumpet, can make the tone sound mysterious and distant in quiet playing, and harsh and sinister if the trumpet is blown forcefully.

Many percussion instruments can vary their sounds considerably according to how firmly – and where – they are struck, and also the particular kind of stick or beater being used.

'straight' trumpet mute

Listening

Listen to the first part of *Popular Song* from Walton's *Façade*. In this music, the string section plays *pizzicato* throughout.

First listening

Compare the colourful and contrasting timbres of the wind instruments which Walton features. Here is a plan showing how the music begins:

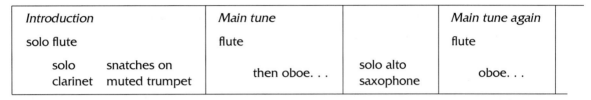

Introduction	Main tune		Main tune again
solo flute	flute		flute
solo snatches on clarinet muted trumpet	then oboe. . .	solo alto saxophone	oboe. . .

Second listening

This time, focus on the varied timbres of the percussion. Listen for:
Introduction – snare drum;
Main tune – cymbal played very quietly with soft-headed stick. . .
  and then more firmly with wood stick. . .
Main tune again – cymbal with soft-headed stick, then wood stick;
Short link – solo snare drum struck 'on the wood' (rather than on the skin). . .
  then triangle struck with wood stick (rather than metal beater);
Main tune, third time – snare drum, played normally (on the skin). . .
  cymbal struck with wood stick. . .

Composing

1 Choose a percussion instrument. Experiment, and discover a range of different qualities of sound – interesting shades of timbre, various 'colour' effects – that you can get by playing your instrument in different ways. For example, if you choose a cymbal, try striking it:

  ● with various kinds of stick or beater;

  ● gently, more firmly, very firmly;

  ● at different places – on the edge, very near the centre, at different points between the two;

  ● letting the sound ring on and die away, or quickly grasping the edge so that the vibrations are immediately damped (stifled).

2 Join up with a partner. Listen to each other's range of varied sounds and 'colour' effects. Select the ones you each find most interesting. Then organize your chosen sounds to create a short composition – by juxtaposing sounds, alternating them, sometimes combining them, repeating some of them – and perhaps also including, at certain points, an expressive (even dramatic) use of silence.

Performing

Practise your piece. Make a recording of it, then listen to it and discuss it.

  Give a performance of your piece to the rest of the class. As you listen to others performing theirs, judge how varied the different shades of timbre are, and whether the sounds (and silences) are arranged and presented in an interesting and effective way.

Listening

Now listen to Benny Goodman's recording of *Stompin' at the Savoy*. This piece is in a smooth and danceable style of jazz called **swing**, which originated in the 1930s (the years 1935–1945 are known as the 'swing era'). Swing was 'composed' jazz – but opportunities were usually given to soloists to improvise. The music was played with polished precision, yet with a rhythmic 'swing'.

The jazz bands which played swing were known as big bands. They included trumpets, trombones, clarinets, saxophones of various sizes, and a rhythm section. The music was carefully arranged, with frequent contrasts in timbre between brass (trumpets and trombones) and reeds (clarinets and saxophones), and between soloists (in the foreground) and supporting instruments (in the background).

Benny Goodman was nicknamed 'The King of Swing'. When he recorded *Stompin' at the Savoy* in 1936, his band included thirteen players:

Brass 3 trumpets 2 trombones *Reeds* 1 clarinet (Goodman himself) 3 saxophones (various sizes)	*Rhythm section* piano double bass guitar drum set

Stompin' at the Savoy is based on a 32-bar pattern. This pattern is made up of four 8-bar sections, giving the structure A A B A – see the plan, opposite. Each playing of this chord pattern is called a **chorus**. (In chorus 4, however, the second A section is omitted.)

Benny Goodman, in 1944, with the brass section of his band which had then increased to seventeen players

The main musical idea of *Stompin' at the Savoy* is a two-chord motif. It is first played on muted brass, answered each time by a phrase on saxophones:

brass
(muted):

saxes:

First listening

As the recording is played, follow the outline plan below. (There is a short introduction before chorus 1.) Listen for the two-chord motif, played many times.

Second listening

Listen for contrasts of timbre:

⬤ between muted brass and saxophones, and

⬤ between soloists (in the foreground) and supporting instruments (in the background).

	A	A	B	A
Chorus 1 (32 bars)	chord motif on muted brass saxes respond	chord motif on muted brass saxes respond	saxes (muted brass in background)	chord motif on muted brass saxes respond

	A	A	B	A
Chorus 2 (32 bars)	chord motif on saxes muted brass respond	chord motif on saxes muted brass respond	clarinet solo, improvised (saxes in background)	chord motif on saxes muted brass respond

	A	A	B	A
Chorus 3 (32 bars)	trombone solo, improvised (saxes in background)	trombone solo, improvised (saxes in background)	tenor sax solo, improvised (accompanied only by rhythm section)	trombone solo, improvised (saxes in background)

	A	B	A
Chorus 4 (24 bars)	muted brass and saxes	clarinet solo, improvised (encouraged by saxes **and** brass)	chord motif on muted brass saxes respond

Improvising

Choose a melody instrument. Using the note D only, but at any octave, explore the various changes and shades of timbre you can obtain.

Now form a group of musicians, and improvise a piece called *Colours from a Single Note*. All performers play the note D, with various changes of timbre – sudden changes, gradual changes – so that there are contrasts of timbre *between* instruments, and also *within* instruments.

The note could sometimes be:

- sounded on a single instrument;
- passed from instrument to instrument – perhaps with some overlapping;
- sounded simultaneously on two, or more, or all instruments, so that there is a mixture of timbres.

You could sometimes play your note D:

- by sustaining it (holding it on);
- by repeating it – in long or short values, regularly, irregularly, or in a definite rhythm.

At all times, be sensitive to the sounds other members of the group are making. Decide when, and how, to play – and whether to aim for a blend or a contrast of timbres.

Record two versions of your piece. Then listen and compare them. How different are they? Which do you think is the more effective? For what reasons?

Afterwards, if possible, listen to the Italian composer Scelsi's *Four Pieces* for orchestra (1959) – 'each one based on a single note'.

Composing

Use timbre to structure a piece of music. For instance, you could build up the music in several short sections, each one featuring a certain kind of timbre or combination of timbres – so that the structure of the piece is brought out by changes and contrasts of timbre. You could link some, or all, of the sections together with a brief recurring refrain, perhaps on percussion. Decide whether any of the sections should occur more than once.

Afterwards, listen to the second movement, *Giuoco delle coppie* (The game of the couples), from Bartók's *Concerto for Orchestra* (1943). See if you can identify the instruments which are featured in turn. How does Bartók use timbre to bring out the structure of this piece?

Now try this...

Do you have **synaesthesia**? This rather long word is used to described the ability to link one of the senses with another. For example, some people have 'colour-hearing' – they link the sound (timbre) of different instruments with certain colours.

1   Listen once more to *Stompin' at the Savoy*. The different colours printed on the chart (page 29) are intended to match the qualities of the timbres of the instruments. Do you agree with each choice of colour? If not, which colour(s) would *you* choose?

2   Now listen, two or more times, to one of these pieces. In each one, timbre plays a very important part.

Stravinsky: *The Infernal Dance of King Kastchei* from *The Firebird*
Khatchaturian: *Sabre Dance* from *Gayaneh*
Webern: the fourth of *Five Pieces for Orchestra*, Opus 10

Create a picture or abstract design in which you use appropriate colours and shades –
bright/dark, vivid/muted, clashing/blending – to correspond to the various contrasting timbres
presented in the music.

Linked listening

Britten: *The Young Person's Guide to the Orchestra* – for familiarizing with the timbres of the instruments
of the orchestra (the music, and the instruments, are described in 'Enjoying Music' Book 3)
Ted Heath: *The Instruments of the Dance Orchestra*
Ravel: *Boléro* ('Enjoying Music' Book 2)
Mahler: Song No. 5 from *Das Lied von der Erde* (The Song of the Earth)
Delius: Prelude to *Irmelin*
Debussy: *Prélude à l'après-midi d'un faune* ('Enjoying Modern Music')
Schoenberg: *Farben* (Colours), No. 3 of *Five Pieces for Orchestra*, Opus 16 – changing combinations
of timbres
Bartók: second movement (especially the central section) of Piano Concerto No. 3 ('Musical Forms'
Book 2)
Webern: *Five Movements for Strings*, Opus 5; *Five Pieces for Orchestra*, Opus 10 ('Enjoying Modern
Music') – often featuring sounds from successive instruments of contrasting timbre
Copland: *Hoe-down* from *Rodeo*; *Variations on a Shaker Song* from *Appalachian Spring* – if possible,
compare the orchestral version with the original version for thirteen instruments
Tippett: first movement from *Concerto for Orchestra* ('Enjoying Modern Music')
Milhaud: *La création du monde* ('Enjoying Modern Music')
Boulez: *Le marteau sans maître* for alto voice and 6 instrumentalists
Earle Brown: *Available Forms 1* for eighteen performers
Chávez: *Toccata* for percussion ensemble
Takemitsu: *November Steps* for *biwa* (Japanese plucked lute), *shakuhachi* (bamboo flute) and orchestra
Compare the combination of timbres in pieces played by brass band (brass and percussion), military
band (woodwind, brass and percussion), symphonic band (a development and extension of the
military band), and full orchestra
Examples of early and traditional jazz – sharply contrasting the timbres of cornet/trumpet, clarinet,
trombone
Duke Ellington: *Mood Indigo; Hot and Bothered*
Mike Oldfield: *Tubular Bells* (especially the first half); *Tubular Bells II* (1992) – including
percussionists, guitarists, keyboard players, a pianist, vocalists, and sixteen Scottish pipers
Pieces played by Latin-American dance bands, with characteristic, varied and colourful percussion
The characteristic instrumental timbres of a variety of musical traditions – e.g. Balinese (see page 38),
Indian (page 52), Chinese (page 118), Japanese (page 96), Korean (page 9), South American (page
46)

CHAPTER 4

Tempo and dynamics – expressive effects

Listening

Listen to this music by the Italian composer, Vivaldi (1678–1741). It is the beginning of his Violin Concerto called *Autumn*, from *The Four Seasons*.

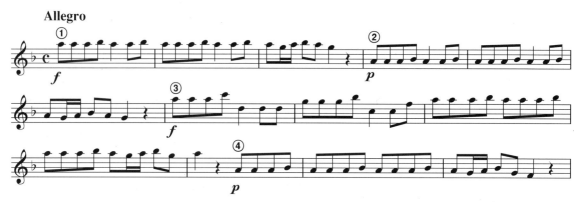

Vivaldi gives two clues which show how the music should be performed.

At the beginning, he gives a **tempo marking** – indicating the speed or pace at which the music should move: *Allegro* (fast).

And here and there, he adds **dynamic markings** – indicating different degrees of volume, or loudness: **f** (short for *forte* – loud); and **p** (short for *piano* – soft).

Listen to the music again. There are four phrases, each ending with a one-beat silence (shown by a crotchet rest).

How is phrase 2 related to phrase 1? How is it different?

How is phrase 4 related to phrase 3? How is it different?

Tempo and dynamic markings are two kinds of **expression markings**. Italian composers were the first to write performance directions into their music in this way. When composers of other nationalities took up the idea, they also used Italian. And this is still mainly the case, four centuries later.

This chart shows the most commonly used **tempo** markings:

Italian term	Meaning
Lento	slow
Largo	broad, slow
Adagio	slow, leisurely
Andante	at an easy walking pace
Moderato	moderate
Allegretto	fairly fast (but not as fast as Allegro)
Allegro	fast
Vivace	lively, brisk
Presto	very fast
Prestissimo	extremely fast

A composer may create an expressive effect in the music by marking a **change of tempo**. Here are the main terms which are used:

Italian term	Meaning
accelerando (*accel.*)	getting faster
rallentando (*rall.*) } *ritardando* (*rit.*) }	gradually slowing down
ritenuto (*riten.*)	immediately slowing down
meno mosso	less moved, less quickly
più mosso	more moved, quicker
a tempo or *tempo primo*	return to the original speed

Among the most important expressive effects a composer can use are **dynamics** – the varying degrees of loudness and softness at which the music is played or sung. For convenience (and also for cheaper cost in music printing) abbreviations and signs are commonly used instead of the full Italian words:

Abbreviation	Italian term	Meaning
p	*piano*	soft, quiet
pp	*pianissimo*	very soft
mp	*mezzo piano*	moderately soft
mf	*mezzo forte*	moderately loud
f	*forte*	loud
ff	*fortissimo*	very loud
cresc.	*crescendo*	getting louder
dim. or *dimin.*	*diminuendo* } *decrescendo* }	getting softer
decresc.		

These signs (commonly called 'hairpins') are often used to mean *crescendo* and *diminuendo*:

A composer may increase the number of 'p's or 'f's. For example: ***ppp***, 'extremely soft'; ***ffff***, 'as loud as possible'.

To many of the markings given above, other words may be added, such as:

meno, less (e.g. *meno forte*, less loud)

più, more (e.g. *più piano*, more softly)

poco a poco, little by little (e.g. *poco a poco dim.*, getting softer little by little)

subito, suddenly (e.g. *subito* ***pp***, suddenly very soft)

sempre, always, still (e.g. *sempre cresc.*, still getting louder)

molto, much, very (e.g. *molto più mosso*, much quicker)

Composing

Create a melody, or a short piece, which makes a feature of contrasting just two dynamic levels: soft and loud.

Write down your music, and write in the dynamic markings. Write each marking immediately below the first note where the dynamic level changes.

Which tempo marking best suits the speed of your music? Write it in, at the beginning.

Are there any points during your music where you need to write in any markings to indicate a *change* of tempo?

Make a recording of your music, and then listen to it.

Other expression markings indicate the **articulation** of notes – how they are to be attacked, sustained, or released; whether they are to be smoothly joined together, or disconnected from each other.

Here are the main markings which are used:

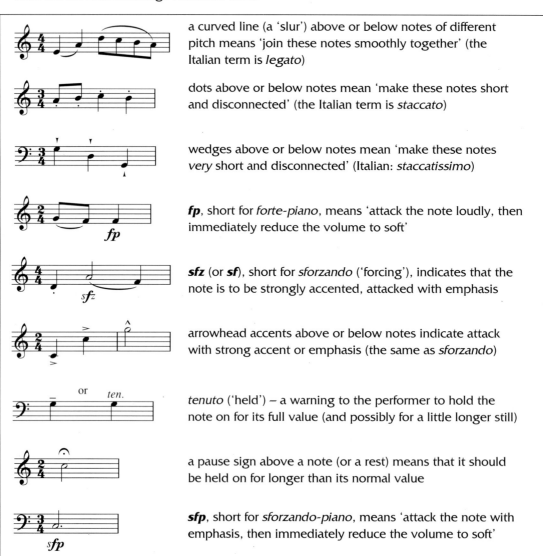

a curved line (a 'slur') above or below notes of different pitch means 'join these notes smoothly together' (the Italian term is *legato*)

dots above or below notes mean 'make these notes short and disconnected' (the Italian term is *staccato*)

wedges above or below notes mean 'make these notes *very* short and disconnected' (Italian: *staccatissimo*)

fp, short for *forte-piano*, means 'attack the note loudly, then immediately reduce the volume to soft'

sfz (or **sf**), short for *sforzando* ('forcing'), indicates that the note is to be strongly accented, attacked with emphasis

arrowhead accents above or below notes indicate attack with strong accent or emphasis (the same as *sforzando*)

tenuto ('held') – a warning to the performer to hold the note on for its full value (and possibly for a little longer still)

a pause sign above a note (or a rest) means that it should be held on for longer than its normal value

sfp, short for *sforzando-piano*, means 'attack the note with emphasis, then immediately reduce the volume to soft'

Dynamic contrasts in music can be compared with light and shade in painting. 'Still Life with Musical Instruments' by the 17th-century Italian painter, Baschenis.

Performing

1   Perform this melody – for the moment, keeping *all* the notes at the same dynamic level (say, moderately soft).

2   Now perform it again – but this time, vary the dynamics according to what you think sounds most musically effective.

3   Copy out the melody, and add expression markings to show how *you* think it would sound best:

   ● add your dynamic markings;

   ● add a tempo marking (and, if necessary, markings to indicate any changes in the tempo);

   ● also add any other expression markings which you think are necessary – such as slurs for *legato*, dots for *staccato*, and so on (see the chart opposite).

4   Ask someone else to perform your melody, obeying all your expression markings. Then perform *their* version. Discuss the differences between the two versions.

Listening

Strong contrasts in both tempo and dynamics are a striking feature of Balinese gamelan music. Gamelan is the general name for an Indonesian orchestra or instrumental ensemble (for example, from Bali or Java). The different kinds of instruments most often included in gamelan are:

- metallophones
- xylophones
- suspended and horizontal gongs of various sizes and pitches
- gong-chimes – sets of knobbed gong kettles
- double-headed drums, and cymbals
- zither (plucked string instrument), and two-string spike fiddle
- also, sometimes, bamboo flute

Here is a gamelan piece from Bali called *Desa Life*, by Wayan Udayana. The music depicts a colourful Balinese market scene.

First, listen to *Desa Life* simply to enjoy the vivid and varied timbres of the Balinese gamelan. Then, as the music is played two or three times more, listen for these expressive effects:

- changes in *dynamics*: loud   soft   *cresc.*   *dim.*
- changes in *tempo*: fast   moderate   *accel.*   *rall.*
- the effect of *combining*: *cresc. + accel.*   *dim. + rall.*

A Balinese gamelan

Sometimes, besides a word showing the speed of the music, a tempo marking includes one or more other words to indicate the style, mood, or expression. For example: *Allegro appassionata*, fast and passionate; *Lento misterioso*, slow and mysterious. Such words can also be written at appropriate places throughout the music. Here is a selection.

agitato, agitated, excited	*misterioso*, mysterious
appassionato, passionate	*pesante*, heavy, weighty
arco, bowed	*pizzicato*, plucked (cancelled by
cantabile, in a singing style	*arco*, bowed)
con, with (*con brio*, with vigour;	*rubato* ('robbed'), at a
con fuoco, with fire;	flexible speed
con sordino, with mute)	*scherzando*, joking, playful
dolce, sweet, gentle	*senza*, without (*senza rall.*,
doloroso, sorrowful, sad	without slowing down; *senza*
energico, energetic, powerful	*sordino*, without mute)
espressivo, expressively	*smorzando*, dying away (becoming
grazioso, graceful	softer, usually also slower)
legato, smooth, flowing	*sostenuto*, sustained
leggiero, lightly	*sotto voce*, 'under the voice' –
maestoso, majestic, stately	with subdued tone
marcato, marked, accented	*staccato*, short, disconnected, detached
mezza voce, 'half voice' – half power	*tranquillo*, tranquil, calm

Improvising

With a partner, each using voice or a melody instrument, build up a musical dialogue by improvising phrases, or brief sections of music, in turn. Performer 1 goes first; then performer 2 replies, as differently as possible.

Performer 1 – make your music:
- mainly calm, *legato* and flowing;
- moving at a fairly slow tempo;
- keeping to a dynamic range of **pp**, **p** and **mp**.

Performer 2 – make your music:
- more excitable than 1's, more *staccato* and spiky;
- moving at a faster tempo;
- keeping to a dynamic range of **mf**, **f**, and **ff**.

For example:

Performer 1   Performer 2   Performer 1

Andante   Allegro   Andante   (and so on)

p   *f*   accel. *sfz*   *pp* *mp* rall.

Afterwards, swap parts, and build up another musical dialogue.

Listening

Listen to *Tempus est iocundum* – a song about love in springtime, from Carl Orff's *Carmina burana* (Songs from Beuron). The song is written for soprano and baritone soloists, boys' choir, a mixed choir of men and women, and orchestra.

You will hear many changes of tempo, and contrasts in dynamics. Here is a plan of the first half of the song:

Chorus (mixed choir)	Allegro *f*	*p*	*f*	*p*

Verse 1 (solo baritone)	Più lento *p*
	(+ choir) *f*

Chorus (women's voices)	Allegro *f*	*p*	*f*	*p*

Verse 2 (solo soprano and boys' choir)	Più lento *p*
	(+ women) *f*

Chorus (men's voices)	Allegro *mf*	*p*	*mf*	*p*

1   In the choruses, how does Orff use his instruments to emphasize the contrasts between *f* and *p*?

2   What happens at the very end of each chorus?

3   How does Orff build up excitement during the music of each verse?

Composing

Look carefully at the painting on page 37. In art, the balance of light and shade in a picture, especially when they are strongly contrasting, is called *chiaroscuro* (Italian: 'bright-dark').

On your own, or with other musicians, create a piece of music called *Chiaroscuro*. Use as many expressive effects of musical light and shade as you like. For example, you could experiment with:

● strongly contrasting dynamics – and subtle changes (shadings) in dynamics;

● contrasts in tempo – and gradual changes of tempo;

● combining *crescendo* with *accelerando* (louder *and* quickening), and *diminuendo* with *rallentando* (softer *and* slowing down);

● contrasts of *legato* (smoothly-joined) sounds, and *staccato* (short, disconnected) sounds;

● differences in pitch (high/medium/low), and in rhythm (e.g. gentle and flowing, energetic and jerky);

● changes of timbre (tone-colour);

● and perhaps also, here and there, the expressive use of *silence*.

Looking again at the items in the boxes on pages 35 and 36 may give you further ideas.

When you have experimented with various expressive effects of musical light and shade, decide which ones you will use, and organize them into the best order. Write down your music in any suitable way, and include expression markings.

Practise your piece.

Performing

Perform your piece called *Chiaroscuro* to the rest of your class. When you listen to others performing theirs, decide how the expressive effects of light and shade are being created in the music.

Linked listening

Other pieces featuring expressive contrasts and changes in tempo and dynamics

Musorgsky: *Bydlo* from *Pictures at an Exhibition* – the whole piece is built upon the plan of:

Rossini – the last part of almost all his overtures includes a gradual and exciting *crescendo*; for example, bar 377 to the end of the Overture to *The Thievish Magpie* (a melody-line score is printed in 'Musical Forms: Listening Scores')

Grieg: *In the Hall of the Mountain King* from *Peer Gynt* – a gradual, exciting *crescendo* coupled with *accelerando* and rise in pitch

Gabrieli: *Sonata pian' e forte* (1597) – the first known piece to indicate contrasts of *piano* and *forte*

Handel: the four short choruses from *Messiah* beginning with: 'Since by man came death' – contrasting in tempo and dynamics

Beethoven: opening of Piano Sonata No. 8 in C minor (the *Pathétique* Sonata) – sudden contrasts of **p** and **ff**, and also expressive use of **fp** and **sfz**

Sir Henry Wood: *Hornpipe* from *Fantasia on British Sea Songs* – *accelerando* (when performed at the last night of the Proms, the audience can't resist joining in)

Barber: *Adagio for String Orchestra* – subtle shadings of dynamics; at about three-quarters of the way through, *crescendo* (with rising in pitch) to a powerful climax, followed by a pause, then **pp**

Schoenberg: the last of *Six Little Piano Pieces*, Opus 19 – Schoenberg restricts himself to dynamics ranging from **pppp** to **p**

Holst: from *The Hymn of Jesus*, the section beginning 'Glory to Thee, Father!' (about $4\frac{1}{2}$ minutes from the start) – varied dynamics, **pp** to **ff**, for the contrasting choral groups

Tippett: opening chorus, *The World Turns on Its Dark Side*, from the oratorio *A Child of Our Time* – expressive dynamics in the orchestral parts (especially brass – sometimes muted) and the voice parts

Lutosławski: first movement from *Jeux vénitiens* (Venetian games) – in short sections contrasting tempo, dynamics, and timbre; the start of each section is marked by a loud chord for percussion (recorded on the CD: item 2.13)

Messiaen: third piece from *Et exspecto resurrectionem mortuorum* (for woodwind, brass and metallic percussion) – including contrasting dynamics, silences, and two terrifying rolls (**pp** to **fffff**) on low gong and large tam-tam

'Cast Your Fate to the Wind' by **Sounds Orchestral** – changes in tempo and dynamics

Icelandic rock star **Björk's** recording of 'It's Oh So Quiet' (1996) – strong contrasts between *andante* **ppp** and *allegro frenetico* **fff**

CHAPTER 5

Major, minor, and pentatonic

Play or listen to these eight bars of music. The signs ⫶‖ and ‖⫶ ⫶‖ (below) mean 'repeat'.

Theme

In France, this well-known tune is called *Ah, vous dirai-je, maman*. Mozart once wrote a set of twelve variations for piano on this tune. Play or listen to the first eight bars of the eighth variation in the set:

Variation 8

The Theme is in the **major** key – in this case, C major.
In Variation 8, Mozart puts it into the **minor** key – C minor.

Play each of these melodic outlines, listening for the difference between them:

The Theme is built from the notes of the **major scale**. (*Scale* is from a Latin word meaning a ladder, staircase, or flight of steps.) A **scale** is a succession of single notes, arranged in order of pitch – moving upwards, or downwards.

The major scale is a mixture of tones and semitones. On the keyboard, the step from any note to its nearest neighbour is a **semitone**.

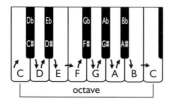

A step of two semitones is a **tone**. For example, from C to D, or D to E. (But E to F is a semitone.)

In the major scale, the tones and semitones are arranged according to a strict pattern:

tone, tone, semitone, tone, tone, tone, semitone

Here, for example, are the scales of C major and G major. (T = tone, S = semitone.)

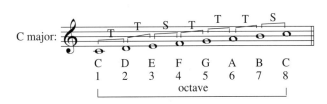

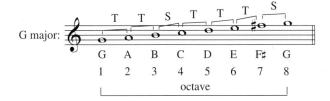

The music of Variation 8 (opposite) is built from the notes of the **minor scale**. To change a major scale into a minor scale, lower (flatten) the 3rd and 6th notes by one semitone:

Here are these two scales again, in their usual written form. Each is now given its **key signature**. (For a chart of key signatures, see page 44.)

In the major scale, the interval (distance in pitch) between the 1st and 3rd notes is a *major* 3rd. In the minor scale, it is a *minor* 3rd. (See the chart of intervals on page 44.)

Similarly, in the major scale, the interval between the 1st and 6th notes is a *major* 6th. In the minor scale, it is a *minor* 6th.

Naming the notes of a scale

The notes (or degrees) of any major or minor scale can be referred to by their technical names, or by number (using Roman numerals):

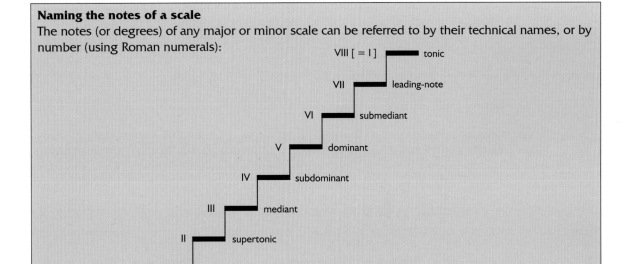

Key signatures

In each of the examples below, the white note shows the tonic of the major key, and the black note shows the tonic of the relative minor – the minor key which shares the same key signature. The leading-note of each minor key is shown in brackets. (This is 'extra' to the key signature and, where necessary, needs to be written in the music as an accidental.)

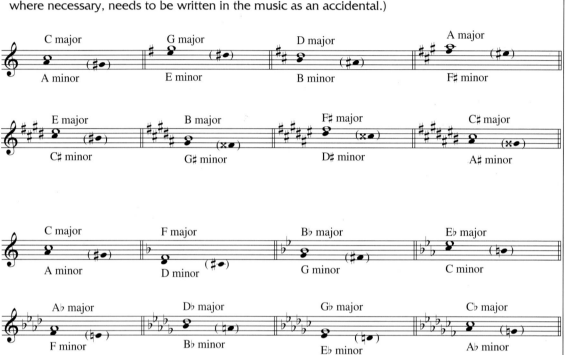

Intervals

An interval is the distance, or difference, in pitch between two notes. The notes may be sounded together, or one after another. (Top and bottom notes are included in the count).

major 2nd (tone)   minor 2nd (semitone)   major 3rd   minor 3rd   perfect 4th   perfect 5th   major 6th   minor 6th   major 7th   minor 7th   perfect octave

If perfect or major intervals are increased by a semitone, they become **augmented** ('made larger').If perfect or minor intervals are reduced by a semitone, they become **diminished** ('made smaller').

perfect 4th   augmented 4th   perfect 5th   diminished 5th

Performing and Listening

Try this experiment:

1 Play or sing the French tune *Frère Jacques*. Here it is, in the key of C major:

2 Now change the tune into the *minor*. Lower (flatten) the 3rd and 6th notes of the scale by a semitone:

- instead of E, play or sing E♭;
- instead of A, play or sing A♭.

3 Join up with one or more other musicians, and play or sing the tune as a round – in the minor key. What difference is there in mood when the tune is changed from major to minor?

4 Afterwards, listen to the beginning of the third movement of Mahler's Symphony No. 1.

Listening

Play these, alternately, several times:

Now listen to the fiery and rhythmic opening of Dvořák's Slavonic Dance No. 8. The music switches between minor and major.

In which minor key does the music begin?
When the printed music ends, the recording continues for another eight bars (repeated). Are these bars in the major, or the minor?

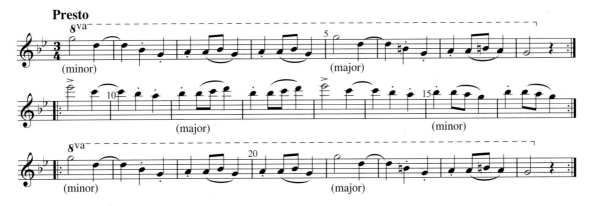

Listen to *The Fool on the Hill* by Lennon and McCartney. Spot when the music slips from major into minor, then back into major again.

Composing

Compose some music which makes a feature of contrasting major with minor. For example, you could:

- sometimes follow a phrase in the minor key with the same, or a different, phrase in the major key;
- follow a phrase in the major with just a part of it repeated in the minor;
- compose a melody in the major key – then follow it with the same melody, changed into the minor key (or the other way round);
- structure your piece in short sections, alternating between major and minor;
- compose a song in which the verses are in the minor and the chorus is in the major.

As you compose your music, also consider:

- tempo (speed, or pace) – and, perhaps, changes of tempo;
- the use of varied dynamics (degrees of loudness).

When you are satisfied with your music, write it down, and then practise it.

Performing

Perform your music to the rest of the class. As others perform their music, listen for shifts between major and minor, and judge how effective they sound.

Listening

Listen to a colourful and rhythmic folk-dance called *Achachikala* from Bolivia in South America. The instruments you will hear include:

- *charango* – a plucked string instrument, similar to a guitar
- *ch'ajchas* – goat's hooves
- *quenas* – notched end-blown flutes of the Andes Mountains
- *bombo* – a large double-headed drum, struck with a mallet

1.14

Listening

First you will hear the *charango*. Then listen for other instruments to join in one by one. (You will certainly notice the *bombo!*)

The melody of *Achachikala* is built from a scale which has only five different notes. This is called a **pentatonic scale** (*pent* meaning 'five'):

The pattern of this particular pentatonic scale is made up of tones + minor 3rds. Play the scale several times, alternately ascending and descending. Then listen again to *Achachikala*.

Composing

Play each of the pentatonic scales printed on the opposite page. Play each one ascending, then descending. (The first one uses just the black notes on the keyboard.)

Some of these scales are constructed from tones + minor 3rds. Others use tone + semitones + major 3rds.

Choose the scale whose mood or 'flavour' appeals to you the most. Then compose or improvise a melody or a short piece built from the notes of your chosen pentatonic scale. Make sure you use *only* the notes of the scale – but you can, of course, use them at any octave.

As you create your music, consider:

- shape and contour – the rise-and-fall of your melodic line;
- range – wide, medium, or narrow;
- the best-sounding note for your melody to end on.

If you are using electronic keyboard, experiment and select a suitable voice to match the mood of your music.

Linked listening

Major/minor
Mozart: Minuet and Trio from Symphony No. 40 in G minor (melody-line score in 'Enjoying Music' Workbook 2)
Beethoven: Scherzo and Trio from Piano Sonata No. 2 in A major ('Musical Forms: Listening Scores')
Schubert: *Die Forelle* (The trout) – third verse in the minor; *Der stürmische Morgen* (The stormy morning) from *Winterreise*
Brahms: Hungarian Dances 3 and 5
Grieg: Norwegian Dance No. 3 – in three sections, A B A, with the tune of A used also for B, but slower, quieter and in the minor; *Solveig's Song* from *Peer Gynt*
Bix Beiderbecke: *At the Jazz Band Ball* – first half of the 32-bar chorus in the minor, second half in the major
Duke Ellington: *East St Louis Toodle-oo* – C minor/E♭ major

Pentatonic
The Skye Boat Song – the melody is pentatonic throughout; the harmony is major for the chorus, minor for the verse
Debussy: *Pagodes* from *Estampes*
Ravel: *Laideronette* from *Mother Goose* Suite
Bartók: *Pentatonic Melody* from *Mikrokosmos* Book 2
Stravinsky: *Chinese March* from the symphonic poem *The Song of the Nightingale* (beginning at around 2′ 24″ from the start)
Tippett: settings of spirituals from *A Child of Our Time* – *Steal Away; Go Down, Moses; O, By and By; Deep River*
Pentatonic scales form the basis of much European folk-music, particularly Celtic and Scottish (e.g. the well-known tune, *Auld Lang Syne*), and also of the music of many other cultures – e.g. China (page 21, based on scale 1, above, on F), Japan, Bali (recorded example, page 38, based on scale 3, above), Thailand (page 26), parts of Africa (page 80), and American Indian music (page 22)

CHAPTER 6

Music with a drone

Listening

Listen to a 13th-century dance, called *Danse royale*, played by David Munrow on a simple type of bagpipe. The player blows air through the blowpipe into the bag. Squeezing the bag with the arm forces the air through reeds into the pipes. The melody is played on the chanter, which has finger-holes. At the same time, the dronepipe sounds a single, low, continuous note.

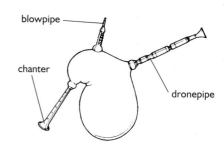

The low note you heard sounding continuously on the dronepipe is called a **drone**. Play or listen to these different kinds of drone:

As you have just heard, a drone can be a single note – which may be held on (as in Example 1, opposite), or persistently repeated (2), or repeated in a rhythmic pattern (3).

Or a drone can be made up of two (sometimes three) notes, usually making the interval of a 5th or an octave. The notes may be sounded together (Examples 4 and 5), or separately (6).

Listen again to part of *Danse royale* played on the bagpipe. Which of the kinds of drone, shown opposite, matches the one you hear?

Sometimes in a piece of music, a composer deliberately imitates the sound of a bagpipe. Listen to part of the Overture *Tam o'Shanter* by the 20th-century composer, Malcolm Arnold. The music is based on a poem by the Scots poet, Robert Burns.

Tam, riding home through a violent storm after a heavy night's drinking, passes the old ruined church. Seeing lights flickering inside, he staggers from his horse and investigates. A gruesome sight meets his eyes – upright coffins with their lids removed, each corpse holding a lighted candle, while in the midst, witches and warlocks dance wild strathspeys and reels to tunes played by the Devil himself.

For the dance music, Arnold uses a two-note drone (as Example 4) played by bassoons, trombones and tuba, and 'whooping' horns.

Haydn's Symphony No. 82 in C, composed in 1786, is nicknamed 'The Bear'. The last movement begins with music which suggests a bear dancing to the accompaniment of a bagpipe – a sight which would have been fairly common in Haydn's time.

Haydn uses a variety of drones, changing in pitch:

● first, in the bass:

p (cellos and basses) *(etc.)*

● later, in the treble, and the bass:

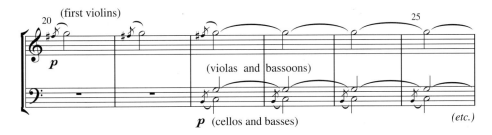

(first violins) 20 25

p

(violas and bassoons)

p (cellos and basses) *(etc.)*

● and then an octave drone in the treble:

33

f (oboes, violins, violas) *(etc.)*

Listen again to the music by Haydn. Besides the main drone notes, what other touches does he add to the music to suggest the sound of a bagpipe?

Composing and Performing

1   On your own, or with a partner, try out different kinds of drone against this tune. Experiment, and choose the best. Then practise your piece, and make a recording of it.

2   Try the same thing with the Christmas carol *Good King Wenceslas* – which originally was a 13th-century dance-song with a lively beat.

3   Compose a melody of your own, trying out different kinds of drone against it. Choose the best, then write down your music.
    Perform your piece to the rest of the class. As others perform their pieces, identify the different kinds of drone being used, and judge how well they suit the melody.

Listening

Investigate a piece based on a rhythmic drone. The music is played on a didjeridu – an instrument of the Aborigines of northern Australia. It is a long wooden trumpet made from a eucalyptus branch which has been hollowed out by termites.

The player vibrates his lips as he blows into the tube, and produces a low-pitched drone. In order to produce a continuous sound, the didjeridu player uses 'circular breathing'. He stores air in the mouth, using the cheek muscles to push the air out, while at the same time breathing in through the nose.

While blowing, the player may also:

● add other pitches above the drone by singing or humming into the instrument:
● give rhythm to the sound by making movements of the tongue, and by flicking the tube with a finger or tapping it with a stick;
● vary the timbres, by changing the shape of the mouth cavity;
● suddenly interject other vocal sounds – perhaps croaks, gurgles, grunts, and imitations of birds and animals (such as the dingo, the native wild dog of Australia).

Listen to the recording, two or three times.

1   Which of the various sounds and playing techniques, mentioned above, does the didjeridu player include in this music?

2   The player introduces some distinctive rhythms, which are heard several times. Which of the following does he *not* include?

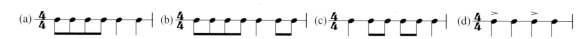

Now try this...

Listen once more to the music played on the didjeridu. Then form a group of three musicians. One will play electronic keyboard. The other two will play contrasting, but 'dry' sounding, percussion instruments, such as xylophone and claves, or snare drum and woodblock. Improvise a piece based on a rhythmic drone, like the music you heard on the didjeridu.

Player 1   First, repeating the note C below middle C, experiment and select a suitable 'voice' (such as trombone, or tenor sax, or one which you think sounds even more effective).
    Throughout the piece, improvise a rhythmic drone – changing and alternating your rhythmic patterns, like the didjeridu player.

Players 2 and 3   Once player 1 has started, begin to improvise fairly short rhythmic fragments above the drone – alternating with each other, rather than playing simultaneously, but sometimes overlapping.

Throughout the piece, listen carefully to each other – and *respond* to each other, so that there is a musical give-and-take of rhythmic ideas, and also of dynamics.

Any or all of the players could, now and then, add vocal sounds of various kinds.

It is the responsibility of player 1 to signal the end of the piece, so that all three players end neatly and at the same time.

Afterwards, try another version of the piece – this time swapping parts.

The didjeridu, together with clapping sticks, is used to accompany singing and dancing

Listening

Investigate a short piece from north India, called *Sitar Ecstasy*. Almost all Indian music is sung or played to an accompanying drone. One of the most often used drone instruments is the tamburā, which has four metal strings. The player holds the instrument upright, and continuously strums the strings, one after another. In this piece, the drone notes are D, A, and D – with two strings tuned to top D.

Drone notes:  played:

The other instrument taking part is the sitar. This has seven metal strings which the player plucks with a wire plectrum, worn on the forefinger. Five of these strings are melody strings, and the other two are drone strings. Beneath the main strings there are about a dozen more strings, and these vibrate 'in sympathy' when the main strings are sounded.

Usually, an Indian piece is mainly, if not completely, improvised. The music is based upon a chosen **raga**. A raga is a series of pitches, in ascending and descending patterns, which are used as a basis for improvisation. The music of *Sitar Ecstasy* is based on a raga called *Kalyan*:

Kalyan raga:
ascending · descending

As *Sitar Ecstasy* is played, listen for:

● the 'twangy' sound of the tamburā, which starts the drone and then continues throughout;
● the way the sitar player improvises upon the pitches of the raga, including decorations and repeated notes, and sometimes sliding from one pitch to another.

Listen to the piece again. After a while, the music changes. In what ways?
Does the music change again?

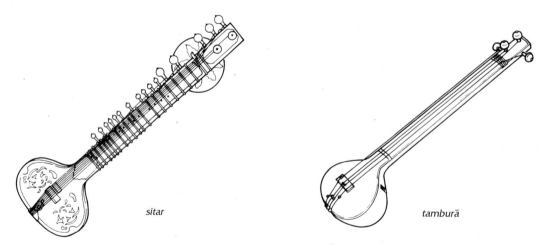

sitar   *tamburā*

Composing

Listen once more to *Sitar Ecstasy*. Then, with a partner, build up a drone piece based on Kalyan raga. Decide who will play the drone, and who will improvise the melody.

For the drone, play the notes D, A, and D – alternating slowly (as shown opposite). Play them on an instrument such as: bass xylophone; guitar, with the lowest string tuned down to D; piano, with the pedal pressed down; or electronic keyboard. (You may be fortunate enough to have access to a keyboard which includes sitar in its selection of voices! If so, try also the effect of stereo chorus.)

Improvise the melody, using notes from Kalyan raga (printed opposite). You could:

- select various groups of notes from the raga – sometimes from the ascending part, sometimes from the descending part;
- for variety, make the groups of different lengths;
- use some repeated notes;
- sometimes repeat a group of notes;
- sometimes repeat a group of notes – and add on one or more notes.

As you build up your piece, discover:

- which melody notes clash with the drone, making a **discordant** effect;
- which notes match well with the drone, making a **concordant** effect.

Which note, or group of notes, seems best for the melody to end on?

Listening

Listen to an Indian pop-disco piece called *Bombay at Night*. It is played by a mixed group of Indian and Western instruments. The Indian instruments include sitar, and tablā – a pair of hand-played drums of different sizes. Which popular Western instruments do you hear? (Listen also for the drone!)

Linked listening

As you listen to some of these pieces, describe the kinds of drone being used.

Other pieces of Indian music, structured against a drone
The medieval dance-song *Winder wie ist nu dein Kraft* by Neidhart von Reuental (recorded on 'Enjoying Early Music' cassette – you could try a group performance of this piece)
Haydn: Symphony No. 88 in G – the Trio of the third movement
Chopin: Mazurka in C (Opus 56 No. 2) – in the first and last parts, the music imitates the Polish bagpipe called the *dudy*
Tchaikovsky: *Farandole* from Act 2 of the ballet, *The Sleeping Beauty* (described in 'Adventures in Music: Ballet')
Prokofiev: *Classical Symphony* – the Trio of the third movement
Within You, without You, from the Beatles' album *Sgt Pepper's Lonely Hearts Club Band* (which instrument plays the drone?)
On the Road Again, by Canned Heat
Scotch on the Rocks, played by the Band of the Black Watch

CHAPTER 7

Chords and chord patterns

Performing

Using a keyboard, play the melody of the Afro-American spiritual, *My Lord, What a Morning*. (At the end of the third stave, *Da capo al Fine* means 'repeat from the beginning, then end at the word *Fine*'.)

Da capo al Fine

This melody, in G major, can be harmonized with just three different chords. A **chord** is a group of notes sounding at the same time. Many chords have three notes, and are known as **triads** (from Greek, meaning 'three'). A chord like this is built upon a main note, which is called the *root*, plus the notes which form a 3rd and a 5th above it. For example, build up a triad on G, like this:

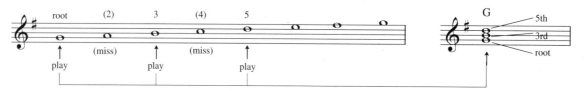

Now build up a triad on D (remember that in G major, F is sharp):

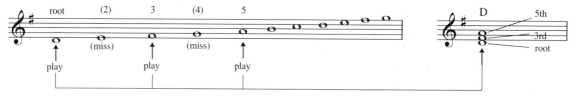

Do the same for a triad on C.

Here are the three triads, or chords, that you have built up in the key of G major. Each can be called by various names:

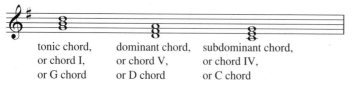

tonic chord,   dominant chord,   subdominant chord,
or chord I,   or chord V,   or chord IV,
or G chord   or D chord   or C chord

The **tonic chord** (chord I), **dominant chord** (chord V), and **subdominant chord** (chord IV) are the three most important chords in any key. These chords are known as **primary chords**.

The three notes of a triad can be used to build up a fuller-sounding chord by **doubling** (duplicating) one or more of the notes at another octave. For instance, all these chords are built from just the three notes (G B D) of the G major triad:

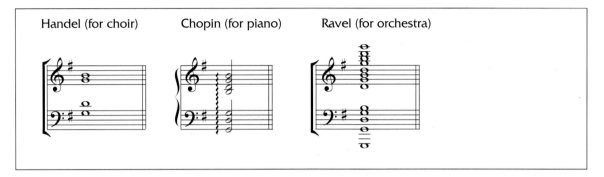

Now, as you play (or as someone else plays) the melody of *My Lord, What a Morning*, accompany it with chords. On the music below, two kinds of chord-symbol are given – above the melody, and below it. Change chord, or repeat a chord, as indicated by the chord-symbols.

Devise your own way of building up the chords from the three triads, or, if you are using electronic keyboard, play

G   D   C

in the bass register with the chord facility switched on, and you will get chords I, V and IV in G major.

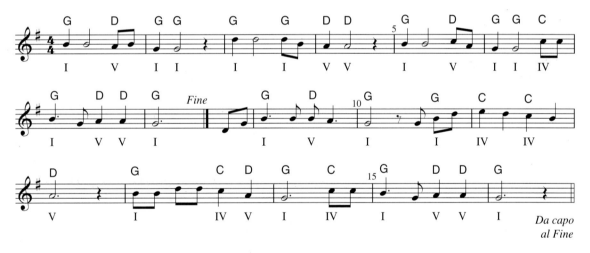

Very often, the dominant chord (chord V) has an extra note added to it, a 7th above the root. The chord then becomes a **dominant 7th**. For example, in G major:

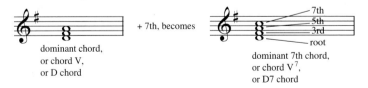

Again play *My Lord, What a Morning* – but instead of D chords, play D7 chords. (If you are using the chord facility on a keyboard, check your manual to find out how to finger a 'seventh chord'.)

Listening

Listen to part of *Black and Tan Fantasy*, recorded by Duke Ellington and his Orchestra in 1927. Ellington has been described as 'the finest composer in jazz history'.

This music is based on a typical **12-bar blues** pattern – a pattern or *progression* of chords lasting for 12 bars (three lines of four bars each):

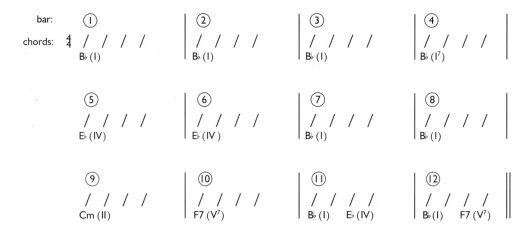

This extract from *Black and Tan Fantasy* is in the key of B♭ major. Besides using the dominant seventh (V^7 or F7: F A C E♭), this chord pattern also uses the tonic seventh (I^7 or B♭7: B♭ D F A♭).

Play the basic chord pattern on which this extract from *Black and Tan Fantasy* is structured.

Listen to the recording, following the plan of the music outlined in the box below. You will hear some interesting muted brass sounds, and also 'growl' – a rasping effect sometimes aimed for, especially when using a plunger mute. During the music, the basic chord pattern is repeated – though sometimes, for variety, some chords may be altered. Each playing of the chord pattern is called a **chorus**. In chorus 5, the 12-bar pattern is interrupted after ten bars. This plan shows how the music is structured:

12-bar chorus:	1	cornet, with plunger mute
	2	cornet, with plunger mute
	3	piano solo (Ellington)
	4	trombone, with plunger mute
	5	muted cornet, interrupted at the end of bar 10 by:
	Coda:	(4 bars) based on the best-known motive from Chopin's *Funeral March*

Chord-symbols

1   A chord can be called by its technical name, or by number – using a Roman numeral as a chord-symbol:

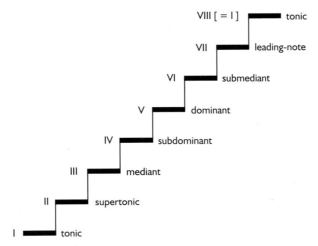

The particular name or number refers to the note of the scale on which the chord is built. This note will be the *root* of the chord. For example:

- the tonic chord, or chord I, is built on the first note of the scale;
- the dominant chord, or chord V, is built on the fifth note of the scale;
- the subdominant chord, or chord IV, is built on the fourth note of the scale.

In G major, for instance:

  I   = the chord of G (G B D),

  V = the chord of D (D F♯ A),

  IV = the chord of C (C E G).

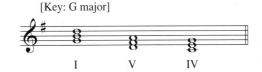

A chord or triad may be built on any note of the scale.

2   In popular music and jazz, however, a chord is usually referred to by the actual letter-name of the note on which it is built. This note is the *root* of the chord.

    Here are the chord-symbols for some of the chords which can be built on the note C (C = the root):

In these chord-symbols:

- a small 'm', standing for minor, refers to the *3rd* of the chord, and so it will be a minor chord – otherwise, the chord is understood to be major;
- 'maj', standing for major, refers to the *7th* of the chord – otherwise the 7th is understood to be a minor 7th (see the chart of intervals on page 44).

Now try this...

Form a group of musicians. The 12-bar blues pattern below is in the key of C major. It uses these chords:

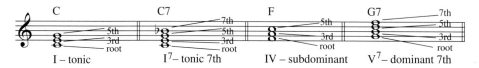

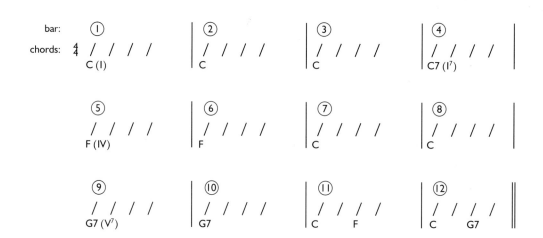

1   Listen to the chord pattern played through twice. Listen for when the chords change. The rate at which the chords (harmonies) change is called the **harmonic rhythm**.

2   The blues pattern is now played five times in succession – beginning with a one-bar lead-in. Join in with the recording:

- some of you play the chords on a chordal instrument;
- others could share out the notes of the chords;
- others mark the beat and add rhythm on percussion instruments;
- others take it in turn to improvise solos above the chord pattern.

You could have five different soloists, improvising a solo for each of the five choruses. Or, in choruses 1 and 5 several players could play in unison the melody at the top of the opposite page (or compose a blues melody of your own which will fit this chord pattern). The piece would then follow this plan:

12-bar chorus:	1	melody
	2	first improvised solo
	3	second improvised solo
	4	third improvised solo
	5	melody

Although this melody is in C major, the note B in bar 2 and the notes E in bar 10 are flattened. In blues and jazz (and in other music influenced by these styles) the 3rd and 7th notes of the major scale are often sung or played below pitch. They are then called **blue notes**.

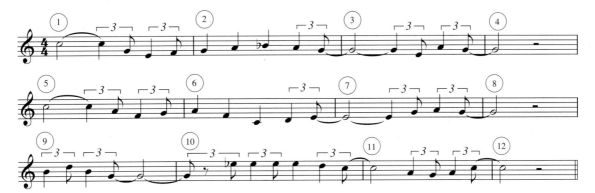

Listening

Play (or listen as someone else plays), several times, this chord pattern or progression:

Then listen to a Russian dance known as 'The Three Ivans' from Tchaikovsky's ballet *The Sleeping Beauty*. First, the chord pattern is played through twice as an introduction. Then this short tune is played sixteen times – though not always in exactly the same way:

Tchaikovsky arranges the sixteen playings of the tune in *pairs*. And for each pair, he uses a different orchestration (combination of timbres or orchestral tone-colours). Sometimes he repeats the original chord pattern, but sometimes he brings in new harmonies.

This is how the piece begins:

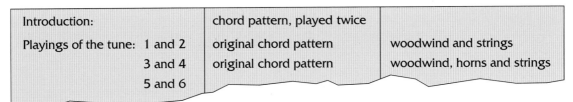

Introduction:	chord pattern, played twice	
Playings of the tune: 1 and 2	original chord pattern	woodwind and strings
3 and 4	original chord pattern	woodwind, horns and strings
5 and 6		

Listen to 'The Three Ivans', and see if you can spot which playings of the tune bring in harmonies which are different from the original chord pattern. (After the tune has been played sixteen times, Tchaikovsky rounds off the dance with a loud and vigorous coda).

Chord Guide

Here are key signatures, main chords and chord-symbols for several major and minor keys. Each major key is paired with its relative minor – the minor key which shares the same key signature.

Play or listen to this harmonized version of the chorus of *My Lord, What a Morning*:

Each pair of chords marked with a bracket forms a **cadence**. Cadences in a piece of music are 'resting-points', marking the ends of phrases or sections. They serve as 'musical punctuation' – musical equivalents of commas, full stops, and in some instances, exclamation marks.

There are four basic types of cadence. They are shown below in the key of **C** major.

1   A **perfect cadence** (or **full close**) consists of chord V (dominant chord) followed by chord I (tonic chord), giving the music a sense of completion.

2   A **plagal cadence** consists of chord IV (subdominant chord) followed by chord I (tonic). It, also, gives a sense of completion – and is sometimes called an '**Amen' cadence** since it is often used to harmonize this word at the end of hymns.

3   An **imperfect cadence** (or **half close**) consists of chord I (tonic) – or perhaps chord IV (subdominant), or chord II (supertonic) – followed by chord V (dominant). The music at the point where this cadence is used sounds incomplete, unfinished (as its name suggests).

4   An **interrupted cadence** (or **surprise cadence**) deceives the listener into expecting a perfect cadence – but this is 'interrupted'. Instead of the dominant chord being followed by the expected tonic, the ear is surprised by another chord instead – very often chord VI (submediant), or perhaps an even more startling chord.

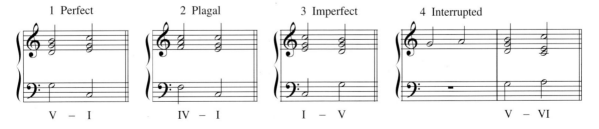

Again, play or listen to the music at the top of this page. Identify each cadence, marked with a bracket.

Arranging and Composing

1   Form a group of three or more musicians. First, two of you sing or play this two-part music:

The key is F major. And the music can be harmonized with four chords:

I (tonic chord)	=	F chord – F A C
V^7 (dominant 7th)	=	C7 – C E G B♭
II^7 (supertonic 7th)	=	Gm7 (G minor seventh) – G B♭ D F
VI^7 (submediant 7th)	=	Dm7 (D minor seventh) – D F A C

Here are possible **spacings** (spacing out of the notes) of these chords:

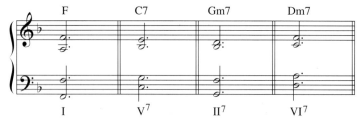

In the two-part music above, an asterisk (∗) indicates a change of chord. (R) means repeat the previous chord.

Now experiment, and fit the four chords at appropriate places in the music. (Chord VI^7, or Dm7, should appear once only.) If you are using the chord facility on an electronic keyboard, check your manual to see how to finger 'minor seventh chords' such as Gm7 or Dm7 (minor chords with the minor 7th added).

Then perform the piece, with one or more other musicians now adding the chords.

Try making the piece longer by composing another eight bars, adding chords to fit. Then, perhaps, repeat bars 9–16, above, to end the piece.

Make a recording of the complete piece, and listen to it.

2   Find a song or instrumental melody which has chord-symbols printed above it (your teacher will help you to choose a suitable one).

First, play the melody through, adding the chords. Then devise ways of using the chords to create a rhythmic and/or flowing accompaniment to suit the mood of the melody (perhaps also adding percussion).

Practise your arrangement of the music. Then make a recording of it, and listen to it. Judge whether there are any ways in which you could improve or refine your arrangement.

3   Work out, and play, each of the three chord progressions on the opposite page. Choose one of them. Decide upon:

⬤ tempo;

⬤ rhythm, and number of beats to a bar.

Then, as you repeat the chord progression several times, improvise a melodic line above the chords.

(a)   In any key, major or minor:

$$\| : \quad I \quad VI \quad IV \quad V^7 \quad : \|$$

(b)   In the key of G minor:

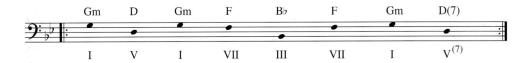

(c)   In the key of C major:

4   Now experiment, and find a chord progression of your own – perhaps an unusual, intriguing one. You might also like to experiment with different combinations of notes (not necessarily triads). Let your ear guide you, and judge whether you like the effect.

When you discover a chord progression that you really like, store it in some way, so that you don't 'lose' it – perhaps by noting it down, or recording it, or programming it into a computer or electronic keyboard (though not all keyboards have this facility).

Play your chord progression (perhaps adding rhythm), and improvise or compose a melodic line which sounds well with your progression. You might go on repeating your progression – or continue your music with a different progression and melodic line.

Linked listening

Other pieces based on repeating chord progressions
(In some of these, the progression may not be repeated absolutely strictly. For variety, harmonies may sometimes be varied.)

Purcell: *Chacony* in G minor, for strings
Corelli: Violin Sonata, Opus 15 No. 12, *La Folia*
Handel: *Sarabande* from Keyboard Suite No. 11 in D minor
Järnefelt: main theme (A) from *Praeludium* (see page 110)
Rawsthorne: second movement, *Chaconne*, from Piano Concerto No. 1
Grace Williams: first movement from *Penillion for Orchestra* – composed in 1955 for the National Youth Orchestra of Wales

Jelly Roll Morton (piano) **and his Red Hot Peppers:** *Dead Man Blues*
Jelly Roll Morton: *Doctor Jazz* (composed by King Oliver) – 8-bar introduction, then a 32-bar structure ('popular song form') in five choruses. Chorus 3 is a vocal, sung by Morton himself.
Louis Armstrong (trumpet) **and his Hot Five:** *West End Blues*
Big Bill Broonzy (vocal and guitar)**:** *Friendless Blues*
Albert Ammons (piano)**:** *Boogie-woogie Stomp* – 12-bar blues structure, in five choruses

CHAPTER 8

Graphic notation

Any way of writing down music on paper, so that it can be stored for future performance, is called **notation**. The sounds may be notated in the form of signs, symbols, shapes, lines, curves, numbers, letters, words, syllables. Some methods of notating sounds on paper are more precise, more accurate in details of pitch and rhythm, than others.

Western music most commonly uses **staff notation**, based on the idea of a five-line stave (or staff) with black and white notes, rests, and other information. You can see an example of Japanese notation on page 97, and of Chinese notation on page 118.

In 20th-century music, **graphic notation** is sometimes used. This may consist of symbols, drawings, shapes, lines, patterns, and so on – visually indicating the composer's intentions to the performer(s). Normally notated notes and traditional signs and symbols may or may not be included. There is almost always a key to explain the graphics, and sometimes also verbal instructions.

Listening

Listen to a riff, on bass guitar. Which of these three graphics best matches the melodic shape and the rhythm of the repeating riff?

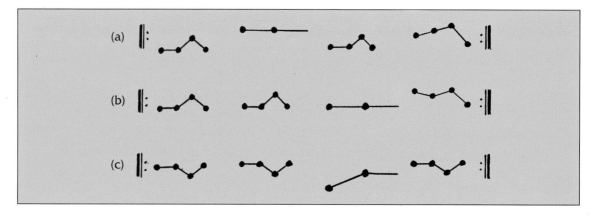

Look at the six boxes of graphics printed opposite. How would you interpret these, turn them into sounds? Colour is used – which may suggest to you the timbres (tone-colours) of contrasting instruments, or perhaps different timbres obtainable from a single instrument.

How, do you think, is *pitch* suggested in the graphics (even though there is no indication of *precise* pitch)?

Are there any indications of *duration* (length) of sounds? And of *silence*?

Are there any suggestions when sounds should be smoothly joined to each other – or disconnected from each other?

The fifth box includes traditional signs for dynamics. But do you think there are any suggestions, in any of the other five examples, for contrasting or changing dynamics?

On your own, or with a partner, investigate each of these examples of graphics. Using voices or suitable instruments, turn the graphics into sounds.

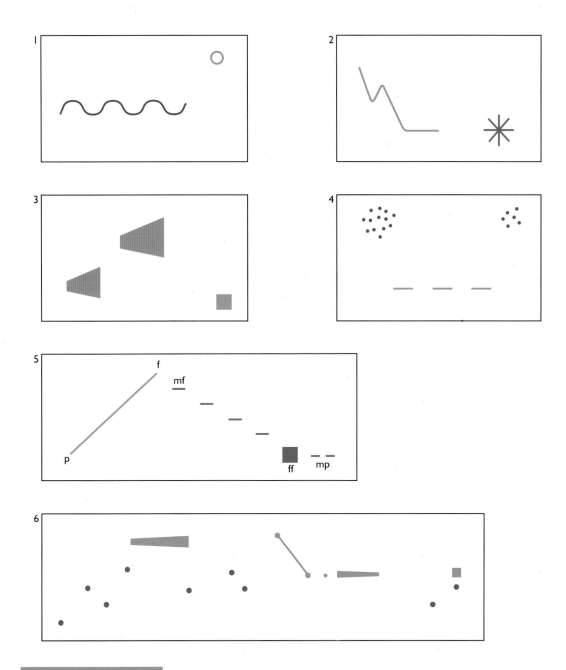

Performing

Perform your interpretations of the graphics to the rest of the class.

As you listen to others performing, compare their ideas with yours.
How similar – or different – are they?

Now create your own graphics for the sounds on the CD. There are three examples, and each is played three times. Use colours, if you like.

Afterwards, compare your graphics with those of other members of your class. How similar – or different – are they?

Performing

Form a group of four musicians, to perform the graphic score below. First, investigate the score. The piece is for four musicians – 1 and 2 each using voice or a melody instrument, 3 playing a chordal instrument, and 4 serving as conductor.

The graphics are drawn on a grid, and each box of the grid lasts for ten seconds. The key, opposite, explains the graphics which are used.

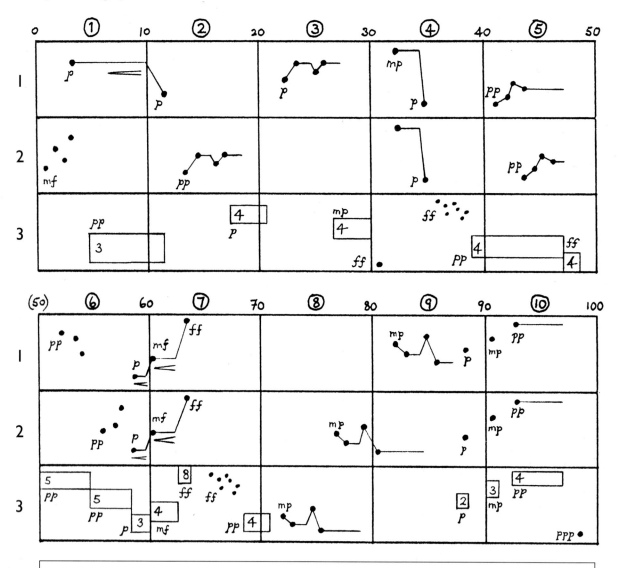

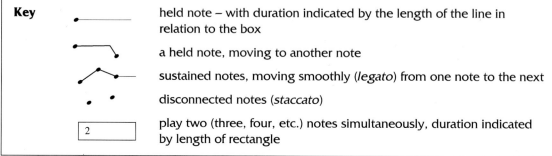

Key		held note – with duration indicated by the length of the line in relation to the box
		a held note, moving to another note
		sustained notes, moving smoothly (*legato*) from one note to the next
		disconnected notes (*staccato*)
	2	play two (three, four, etc.) notes simultaneously, duration indicated by length of rectangle

The height of each box represents the total range of each voice or instrument. The actual pitches are random (performers make their own choices) – but the notes or chords in each box are positioned in such a way as to indicate low, middle or high register of each range. Traditional dynamic signs are used.

In performance, the conductor indicates with a down-beat the point where each ten-second box ends. However, be flexible and musically sensitive in this – take the ten-second timings as being approximate, rather than rigidly precise. Follow the score, and cue performers at points where they must be precisely together in attacking or releasing notes (for example, in boxes 4, 7, 9, 10).

The score includes indications of various contrasts – for example, in pitch, dynamics, durations, texture, the timbres you choose to use. Looking through the score:

- can you detect any *repetition* of musical ideas?
- are there indications of *silence?*

Prepare, and try out, a performance of this graphic score. Practise, experiment, adjust, and polish – perhaps also making a recording of your performance.

Afterwards, give a performance of the piece to the rest of your class. As you listen to the performances of others, follow the score, and compare the interpretations of different groups, including your own. Discuss the similarities and differences between them.

Composing and Performing

Form a group of four musicians. (Keep in mind the possibility that one of the group may need to serve as conductor.) Using instruments and/or voices, create your own sounds, patterns, textures. Invent graphics for them. Make sure that your graphics represent the sounds as clearly and precisely as possible. Discuss and decide:

- how you will show the duration of sounds;
- how you will indicate pitch.

Organize your sounds and patterns into the most effective order, to create a short composition. Discuss and decide:

- tempo;
- dynamics.

Notate your composition in the form of a graphic score. Include, in some way, indications of tempo and dynamics.

Add an explanatory *key* to your score (as shown on the opposite page), clearly explaining your graphics so that performers will understand how to interpret them. (Also add any verbal instructions, if you think these are necessary.)

Perform your graphic score, perhaps making a recording of it.

Now exchange graphic scores with another·group – and prepare and re-create each other's compositions.

Listen to the other group's performance of your piece, and discuss the results. How different were they from what you intended?

CHAPTER 9

Ternary form

Play or sing this Romanian folk-tune:

Now listen to a Romanian folk-dance called *The Girls So Fair*. The music begins with the 16-bar tune you have just performed. But what happens afterwards?

Romanian folk-dance

The piece is made up of the first tune, then a very different tune, and then the first tune again.

A plan, showing how the piece is built up, looks like this:

A¹	B	A²
moderate in speed; major key	faster; minor key; loud and vigorous; brighter timbres	moderate in speed; major key (the same music as at first)

The way in which a piece is shaped and structured is called the **form** of the music. This particular musical form is called **ternary form** (*ternary* meaning 'three-part'). It is built up in three sections of music: A¹ B A². And it is based upon the ideas of **repetition** and **contrast:**

⬤ the third section, A², is a repetition (exact, or perhaps with some changes) of the first section, A¹;

⬤ the middle section, B, makes a contrast.

The most likely way for B to present a contrast to A is to bring in a completely different tune. But musical contrast can also be achieved in several other ways. Here are some of them:

Ways of making musical contrasts

You can bring in a contrast (change) of:

⬤ mood   ⬤ time (or metre)

⬤ key   ⬤ rhythm

⬤ mode (major/minor)   ⬤ pitch (high/low)

⬤ tempo (speed)   ⬤ timbre (or tone-colour)

⬤ dynamics (loud/soft) ⬤ texture (for example, heavy/light, *legato/staccato*)

In a piece of music in ternary form, the repetition of A in the third section brings a feeling of **unity**, and **balance**, to the piece. The contrast of music B adds **variety**.

Composing

First, play this tune on any suitable instrument. Add your own dynamics and expression to the music.

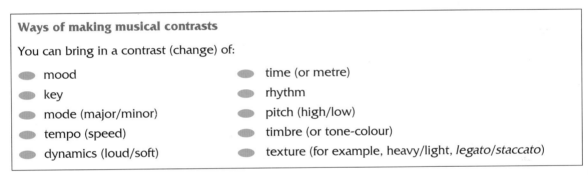

Think of the tune above as being tune A, forming the outer sections of a piece built up in ternary form: A¹ B A².

Compose your own tune for section B. Make sure your tune contrasts with tune A. Use some of the ways of making musical contrasts given in the box above.

When you have composed your tune for section B, make a recording of the complete ternary piece, and then listen to it. Does tune B make a good contrast to tune A?

Listening

Here is another piece structured in ternary form – *Dance of the Flutes* from Tchaikovsky's ballet *The Nutcracker*.

A two-bar introduction leads into the first section, A^1, a light and graceful dance featuring three flutes.

The contrasting middle section, B, is played above a two-note figure, continually repeated in the bass with this rhythmic feature:

First listening

Follow the melody-line score as you listen. Discover:

1   where the middle section (B) begins;

2   where music A returns as A^2.

(violins)

(flutes)

(violins)

pizz.

Second listening

1   Which of these instruments plays a solo at bar 19?

cor anglais   trumpet   cello

2   Which of these words describes the bass, during the middle section?

walking   ostinato   off-beat   drone

3   When music A reappears as A^2, is it exactly the same as at first, or does Tchaikovsky make any
     important changes?

Third listening

1   Mention two important differences between the tune of music A and the tune of music B.

2   Describe any other noticeable contrasts (differences) between music A and music B.

Can you discover repetition and contrasts in this painting called 'Rythme Syncopé, dit Le Serpent Noir'
(Syncopated Rhythm, otherwise known as The Black Serpent) by the French artist, Sonia Delaunay?

Composing

Compose your own piece in ternary form.

1 First, make a tune for the outer sections (A^1 and A^2) of the piece. Either compose your own tune – or use one of these beginnings, and continue it.

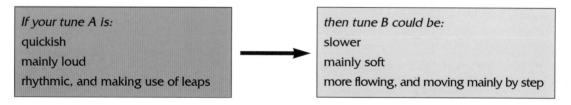

2 Now make a tune for the middle section (B) of your ternary piece. The effectiveness of a ternary piece largely depends on the amount of musical contrast between music A and music B. Play your tune A. Decide how tune B could provide a good contrast. For example:

If your tune A is:	then tune B could be:
quickish	slower
mainly loud	mainly soft
rhythmic, and making use of leaps	more flowing, and moving mainly by step

You could also use any of the ways of making musical contrasts mentioned on page 71.

3 When you have finished the middle section, make a recording of your complete ternary piece, then listen to it.

● Does music B provide an effective contrast to music A?

● Does the ending of the piece sound satisfactory? Or do you think it would be a good idea to add a few more bars after A^2 – making a coda, which will round off the whole piece?

Performing

Perform your ternary piece to the rest of the class. As others perform theirs, listen carefully and note down the ways in which music B contrasts with music A.

Linked listening

1   Listen, two or three times, to one of the ternary pieces in this list.

● Listen for when the middle section, B, begins.

● How does music B contrast with music A?

● When music A returns as A^2, is it exactly the same as at first – or do you hear any important changes?

Bizet: *Les dragons d'Alcala*, Prelude to Act 2 of the opera *Carmen*
Ippolitov-Ivanov: *The Procession of the Sardar* from *Caucasian Sketches*
Prokofiev: *Masks* from the ballet *Romeo and Juliet*
Chopin: Prelude No. 15 in D♭ major, 'Raindrop', in which a repeated note (in sections A^1 and A^2, the note A♭; in section B, the note G♯) represents steady drops of rain
Grieg: Norwegian Dance No. 3 – section B uses the *same* tune as section A, but Grieg still brings in several effective musical contrasts
Carl Orff: *Swaz hie gat umbe – Chume, chum geselle min* from *Carmina burana*
Leroy Anderson: *The Typewriter*
Handel: Recitative *E pur così* and Aria *Piangerò* from the opera *Giulio Cesare* (Julius Caesar)

2   Listen to the opening of George Enescu's *Romanian Rhapsody No. 1* for orchestra. You will hear three varied presentations of the Romanian folk-tune which you performed, printed on page 70. (On the first and third occasions, staves 3 and 4 are repeated.)

Follow the printed tune as you listen. Discover:

● when the staves of the printed tune match the sounds you hear;

● when the sounds are slightly different;

● when the sounds are very different.

Listen also to the way Enescu varies the instrumental timbres in this music.

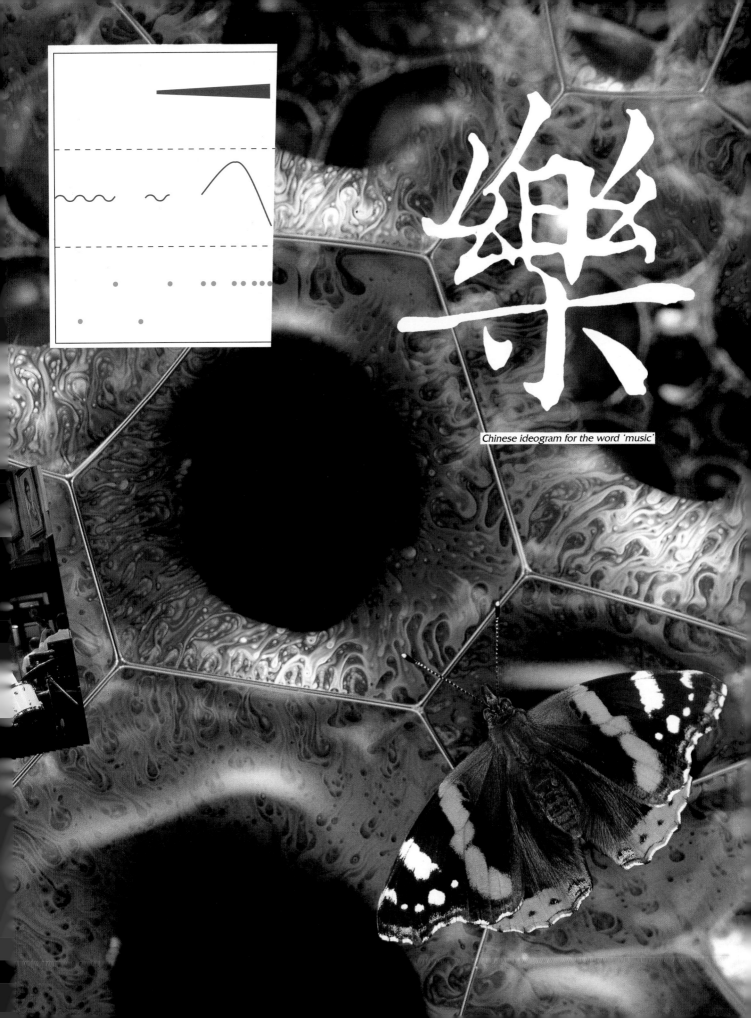

Chinese ideogram for the word 'music'

CHAPTER 10

Using ostinatos

Performing and Listening

Clap or tap each of these rhythmic patterns, to a lively beat:

Now listen to part of a Renaissance dance called *Welscher Tanz*, by an anonymous 16th-century composer. The music is played by a shawm and two sackbuts (see page 215), accompanied by a large drum called a tabor.

Which of the three rhythmic patterns is repeated, over and over, by the tabor player?

Listen to the music again. Clap or tap the repeating rhythmic pattern, along with the tabor player.

Any musical pattern which is continually repeated – either during part of a piece, or throughout an entire piece – is called an **ostinato**.

> An ostinato may be:
>
> - a repeating rhythmic pattern (as in *Welscher Tanz*);
> - a repeating melodic pattern – perhaps a tuneful fragment, or even a complete melody;
> - a repeating pattern of chords (harmonies); or
> - some combination of these patterns.

Listening

For a melodic and rhythmic ostinato, listen to the last movement of Gustav Holst's *St Paul's Suite*. The tune of an old English country dance called the Dargason, eight bars long, is repeated non-stop, building up excitement and tension. All the instruments have a turn at playing it, so that the ostinato appears at different pitch levels – high to low.

1   As the Dargason tune is repeated, does the music keep to the same dynamic level, or does Holst vary the dynamics?

2   Which other well-known English folk-tune is combined with the Dargason, on two occasions during the piece?

3   Which section of the orchestra plays this music?

If you can, listen to the last movement of Holst's Suite No. 2 in F. The music is the same as the last movement of his *St Paul's Suite*, but played by a military band (made up of woodwind, brass, and percussion). Compare the two versions. Which do you prefer, and why?

In Holst's *The Dargason*, a complete tune is used for the ostinato. In the *Carillon* from Bizet's *L'Arlésienne* Suite No. 1, this melodic ostinato of just three notes is played 98 times altogether:

Now listen to *Street Corner Kwela*, which is based on a chordal ostinato. *Kwela*, meaning 'go up and win', is an urban popular music style of southern Africa. In the 1950s, *kwela* was performed on penny whistles by bands of young boys, in the streets of the townships.

Composing

Many art designs – for example, on fabrics, wallpapers, clothing – include repeating patterns. Look at the examples below. Choose some of the repeating patterns, and turn them into ostinatos. Play each one on a suitable instrument, repeating the pattern several times.

Your ostinatos could be:

- rhythmic;
- melodic;
- chordal;
- or any combination of these.

Notate (write down) each of your ostinatos in any suitable way, so that you will be able to recall them accurately.

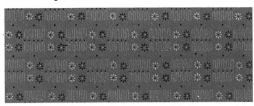

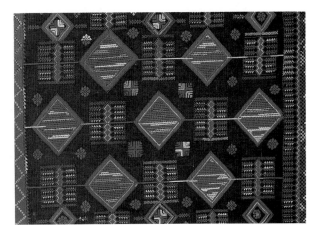

Listening

Much of the music of Africa makes use of ostinatos. Here is a short piece called *Induna Indaba* (Gathering of chiefs). It is played by a xylophone orchestra of the Chopi people of Mozambique. Also included are African flutes and shakers.

In this piece, both rhythmic and melodic ostinatos are used. Listen for the various repeating patterns to join in, one by one, building up an exciting and complex web of sounds.

A section of a xylophone orchestra of the Chopi people of Mozambique, accompanying a mgodo dance.

Composing/Improvising

Form a group of four musicians.

Each one, using vocal sounds or a suitable instrument, makes up an ostinato pattern – to represent a moving part of a large machine. (Think of levers, pistons, cogs, and so on.)

In turn, perform your ostinato pattern to the rest of your group.

Try fitting the four patterns together (you may find that some adjustment is necessary).

Now build up a short piece. The ostinato patterns are going to join in one at a time. Discuss and decide what will be the best order.

Also decide:

⬤ whether the tempo (speed) should remain steadily the same throughout – or whether it should change;

⬤ how your piece will end.

Rehearse your piece.

Performing

Perform your 'machine' piece, twice, to the rest of the class. As each group performs their piece for the second time, members of another group could *become* the machine – acting out movements suggested by the sounds and rhythms, tempo and dynamics, of the ostinatos.

When an ostinato pattern is used in the bass, it is called a **ground bass**, or **basso ostinato** ('obstinately repeating bass'). The ostinato may be short and simple, or it may be a complete melody.

The repeating ostinato in the bass brings *unity* to the piece. Above the ostinato, the melodies and harmonies are continually changing, to give *variety*.

Listening

Listen to part of a vocal piece, with instrumental accompaniment, called *Lamento della ninfa* (The lament of the nymph). It was composed by Monteverdi in 1638. This four-note pattern is persistently repeated as a ground bass:

Above this ground bass, the melodies and harmonies are continually varied. The nymph (solo soprano) laments that her lover has deserted her. Three male voices (two tenors and a bass) add comments, sympathizing with her.

Composing/Improvising

On your own, or with a partner, choose one of these patterns and use it as a ground bass. Make the notes any length you like, but keep to a fairly slow tempo. (Make up a ground bass of your own, if you prefer.)

Above the repeating ground bass, improvise varying melodic patterns, or a long, floating melody.

Afterwards, swap parts (using the same, or a different, ground bass).

Listening

In popular music, particularly jazz, a melodic phrase repeated persistently during all or part of a piece is called a **riff**. A riff is usually two or four bars long. It may change its shape slightly, or move up or down to a different pitch level, to fit with the accompanying harmonies.

Listen, two or three times, to a short illustration of jazz based on a riff, played by Graham Collier Music.

1   Which of these instruments plays the riff?

| trumpet and piano | trombone and guitar | trumpet and trombone |

2   How many times is the riff played?

3   What happens in the gaps *between* the playings of the riff?

Listening

Listen to a song by the rock group, Conquest. The first time the recording is played, follow the structure and words of the song.

Then, as the recording is played again, two or three times, answer the questions on the opposite page.

Chance   (Haggett/Hodges)

Introduction	(Instrumental)

Verse 1
> Embraced in the same neo love scene
> Left forlorn on the edge of the night
> Captive within the spotlights of passion
> Curtain down, just a smile goodbye
> Retracing the worn path to nowhere
> Red roses, shooting stars, loving heart
> Anxious moments at the doors of desire
> Love is dead, love is dead.

Chorus
> Chance
> Look at the two of us evolving
> Silhouettes of romance hide from their eyes
> Chance
> One of the two of us hides emotion
> Me to you behind the scar of a lie.

Interlude 1   (Instrumental)

Verse 2
> From within a five star sleep
> Your Achates steals your heart
> To be proclaimed within a white satin dance
> A tear of love pulls the eyelids apart
> Retracing the confrontations
> Source of anguish perspires in need
> Body motion, hot imagination
> Love is alive under a debris of sleep.

Chorus
> Chance
> Look at the two of us evolving
> Silhouettes of romance hide from their eyes
> Chance
> One of the two of us hides emotion
> Me to you behind the scar of a lie.

Interlude 2   (Instrumental)

Verse 3
> Bathed in this void of emotion
> It's dragging me down
> Drowned in this void of emotion
> It's dragging, dragging, dragging,
> Dragging me down.

Coda   (Instrumental)

[*Conquest*: Jon Haggett – vocals, Simon Cross – guitars, Pete Hodges – bass guitar and keyboards, Stephen Payne – drums]

Introduction   The sounds of solo flute and strings are electronic *samples* of real instruments. Suggest a word to describe the mood of the music up to the point where the drums enter.

Verse 1   Which instruments are prominent in the accompaniment?

Chorus   Electric guitar joins in with the voice. Which of the following is true?

| 1 | the guitarist doubles (plays the same notes as) the vocalist's melody |

| 2 | the guitarist plays a completely different melody |

| 3 | some of the notes are different, some are the same as the vocalist's |

Interlude 1   Again the sampled sounds of solo flute and strings. Name the instruments of the drum kit which are featured in the accompaniment.

Verse 2   How many *different* pitches make up the bass-line of this verse? (The first bass note is C.)

Chorus   The harmony is based on three different chords: D minor, C major, and A minor. The first chord arrives with the first word, 'Chance'. On which other *six* words, or parts of words, do the harmonies *change*?

> Chance
>
> Look at the two of us e-vol-ving
>
> Sil-hou-ettes of ro-mance hide from their eyes
>
> Chance
>
> One of the two of us hides e-mo-tion
>
> Me to you be-hind the scar of a lie.

Interlude 2   The electronic samples, on the left, now suggest the sounds of deeper-pitched woodwinds. Which kind of guitar, on the right, adds a contrasting timbre?

| electric guitar | bass guitar |

| acoustic (Spanish) guitar | Hawaiian (steel) guitar |

Verse 3   Give two ways in which this verse is different from the previous two verses.

Coda   Excitement and tension build up in the coda as the guitarist improvises above a four-note ostinato – a ground bass – played on bass guitar:

1   How many times is this ostinato played before the bass guitarist changes to a new pattern?

2   Is the new pattern repeated until the end of the song – or does the first pattern return?

Members of the Somerset rock group, Conquest

Composing/Improvising

Form a group of four, or more, musicians and build up a piece based on a rhythmic ostinato and a riff.

One musician plays a two-bar rhythmic ostinato in $\frac{4}{4}$ time. (Use the one below, or make up one of your own.) Play it on percussion, or use hand percussion pads on an electronic keyboard. The ostinato should begin the piece, and repeat steadily until the end.

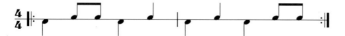

After four bars of the ostinato, the riff joins in, played by one or more musicians. (Use the one printed below, or compose a four-bar riff of your own.) Play the riff once, then rest for four bars, play the riff again, rest for four bars, and so on.

In the gaps between the playings of the riff, two or more other musicians either:

● take turns to improvise four-bar melodic phrases against the continuing ostinato, or

● make up and recite a rap, two lines in each gap.

After one or more playings of the riff, chords could be added to it (perhaps using the chord facility on electronic keyboard).

Eventually, end the piece with the riff, played twice in succession, plus a final crash on percussion.

Linked listening

More pieces which make use of ostinatos

Ravel: *Bolero* – an ostinato snare drum rhythm is repeated throughout the piece in a gradual crescendo

Holst: *Mars* from the suite *The Planets* – a rhythmic ostinato with five beats to a bar

Monteverdi: the closing love duet, *Pur ti miro*, from the opera *L'incoronazione di Poppea* – the first and third sections are structured on a four-note ground bass (the same as ground bass 2 on page 81)

Bach: *Crucifixus* from the B minor Mass – a ground bass descending in semitones (similar to ground bass 3 on page 81)

Purcell: *Dido's Lament* from the opera *Dido and Aeneas* – another ground bass which makes use of descending semitones

Walton: *The Death of Falstaff* – structured on a ground bass ('Musical Forms: Listening Scores')

Chopin: *Berceuse* – a one-bar chordal (harmonic) ostinato, based on alternating tonic and dominant chords

Morton Gould: *Pavane* – in this jazzy piece the ostinato pattern, first heard on bassoon, sometimes changes shape, appears at different pitch levels, sometimes stops then starts up again

Bob Marley: *Could You Be Loved?* (from *Uprising*) – the opening solo melodic-rhythmic pattern is used as a varied ostinato throughout

Mike Oldfield: *Tubular Bells* – especially the opening, and the last 8′ 24″ of side one; also *Tubular Bells II*

In the Mood, played by **Glenn Miller** – a riff-tune, with the riff altering to suit the accompanying harmonies

Michael Jackson's recording of *Thriller* – repeating bass guitar riffs against changing harmonies

Harrison Birtwistle: *Chronometer* – composed entirely from 'everyday sounds': 100 recordings of tickings, strikings and bell mechanisms of clocks – with Big Ben as a background ostinato – computer organized and electronically transformed into a *musique concrète* tape montage

Terry Riley: *In C* (for any number of instruments) – in the musical style known as **minimalism**, in which the composer bases the music on considerable repetition of short melodic/rhythmic/harmonic motifs or fragments, and often includes the idea of 'process' or gradual change taking place within ostinato textures as the musical material gradually moves out of phase with itself. *In C* consists of 53 fragments; players begin independently and play through these fragments, deciding individually how many times to repeat each one. A steady pulsed background is provided throughout by two high Cs played in continuous quavers on a piano.

CHAPTER 11

Some musical devices

Performing

Perform this melody, adding your own dynamics and expression.

In this melody, the opening phrase of three notes is repeated as the second phrase (bars 3 and 4), but in a **decorated** version. The three notes (G, C, A) are included – but other, extra notes are now added in, as **decoration** of the three main notes.

Perform the melody again. In which other bars is there another example of decoration?

Decoration may be used to vary the repetition of a phrase, a melody, or a whole section of music. Often, some of the extra notes which are added in are **ornaments** (see the opposite page).

Listening

Listen to the first part of Chopin's Nocturne No. 2 in E♭. (A *nocturne* is a 'night-piece'.) The opening melody, A¹, is presented again as A² and A³. As you listen, spot which parts of A¹ are decorated when they reappear during A² and A³.

3

Ornaments

These are notes which are extra to the main notes of a melodic line, serving to decorate or embellish it. Ornaments may be indicated by special signs, or they may appear as small-sized notes printed among the main notes.

Here are some commonly used ornaments, with indications as to how they may be performed. However, some ornaments vary according to the tempo of the music and, especially, the period when it was composed.

Trill (or **shake**) – essentially, this consists of the alternation of the main (written) note with the note above it:

Upper mordent (from Italian: 'biting') – the main note, the note above, the main note again:

Lower mordent – the main note, the note below, the main note again:

Appoggiatura (a 'leaning' note) – this usually steals half the value of the main note; often two-thirds if the main note is a dotted note:

Acciaccatura (a 'crushed' note) – crushed in quickly, either on the beat, or just before it:

Turn – consisting essentially of four notes, 'turning' around the main note – the note above, the main note, the note below, the main note again:

Performing

Perform this German folk-melody called *Es ist ein Schnitter* (He is a Reaper):

Now perform bars 1–8 again. And then just bars 5 and 6.

The melodic pattern of bar 5 is repeated in bar 6, at a slightly lower pitch. The immediate repetition of a melodic pattern at a lower or higher pitch is called a **sequence.**

- If the melodic pattern is repeated at a lower pitch, it makes a **falling sequence**;
- if it is repeated at a higher pitch, it makes a **rising sequence.**

Repetition of the pattern need not be absolutely exact (some intervals may be slightly altered), but the general outline of the pattern is kept. Very often, the rhythm is as important as the melody.

The melodic pattern in a sequence may be repeated more than once – the number of repetitions is according to the judgement of the composer. But too many repetitions will cause the music to become predictable.

Sequences can play an important part in music in a modern style, since they give the listener something to 'latch onto'.

Perform *Es ist ein Schnitter* again.

1 In which bars is there another example of sequence?
2 Is it a falling sequence, or a rising sequence?
3 How many bars long is the melodic pattern which is used?
4 How many repetitions are there of the pattern?

Listening

Listen, two or three times, to the Theme from Brahms's *Variations on a Theme by Haydn*. In which bars do sequences occur?

Describe each one – say whether it is a falling sequence or a rising sequence, and how many repetitions there are of the pattern.

Listening

Now listen to the beginning of a piece from *The Musical Offering* by Bach. It is played by flute and violin accompanied by cello and harpsichord. In this music, Bach makes use of a very common musical device called **imitation**. One instrumental (or vocal) part sets off with a musical idea and is immediately 'imitated' by another part copying the same idea – usually at a higher or lower pitch.

The imitation may be **strict** (an exact copy), or it may be **free** (a recognizably similar copy).

Bach's music unfolds at a slow pace. The first musical idea is presented by the violin, and imitated by the flute at a higher pitch. A second idea is presented by the violin in bar 6, imitated at a lower pitch by the flute, and then (much lower) by the cello.

As the recording is played, follow the printed music and listen for imitation.

Listen again to the music by Bach.

1   In which bars are musical ideas presented first by the flute, then imitated by the violin?

2   Are these musical ideas new – or have they been heard earlier in the piece?

Another interesting musical device is **voice-exchange**. Snatches of tune, or whole phrases, are exchanged between voice-parts of equal range. For example, while one voice is singing phrase A followed by phrase B, another voice, at the same time, is singing phrase B followed by phrase A:

Voice-part 1:	phrase A	phrase B	phrase C	phrase D

Voice-part 2:	phrase B	phrase A	phrase D	phrase C

Voice-exchange was a popular musical device with Medieval composers, especially in 13th-century England. It was also sometimes used by Baroque composers – for example, in exchanges between the two violins in a trio sonata.

Listening

Listen to a piece called *Alle, psallite cum luya* by an anonymous 13th-century English composer. At bar 4, the voices exchange tunes – each now sings the tune which the other sang in bars 1–3. And this voice-exchange continues to happen until the last three bars.

Here is a translation of the Latin words:

Alle — praises sing with — *luya,*
Alle — let your voices loudly ring with — *luya,*
Alle — with a full, devoted heart now praise your God with — *luya,*
Alleluya!

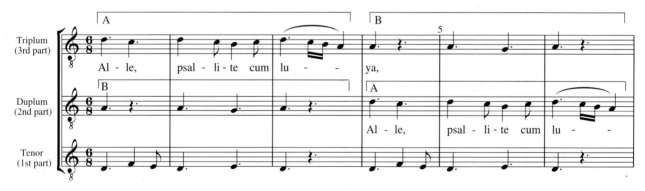

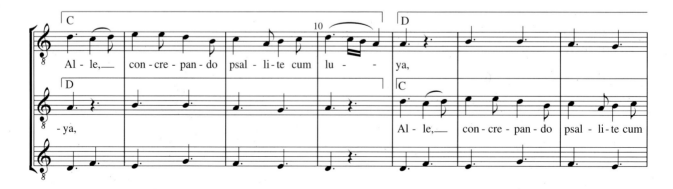

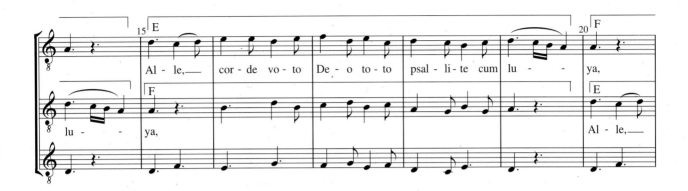

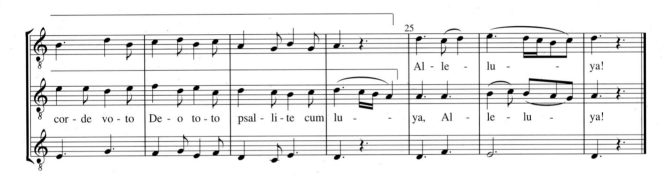

Performing

When you have heard this piece three or four times, try your own performance. Voices form two groups for voice-parts 1 and 2 (if no words appear below a phrase, vocalize to the sound 'Ah' – as at the beginning of the word 'Alleluya'). The tenor part could also be vocalized, and/or played on instruments. The piece could be performed twice through, and perhaps accompanied by rousing rhythmic patterns on percussion (as on the CD). Aim for a bright, joyful and vigorous performance of the music!

Composing

Try one or more of these ideas:

1   Compose or improvise a melody, in any style, in which phrases are first presented in a fairly straightforward way, then re-presented in a *decorated* version.

2   Construct a melody which makes use of *sequence*.

3   Compose some music for two (or more) voices or instruments which features the device of *imitation*.

4   Compose a piece which includes *voice-exchange* between two voices or instruments of equal range.

Whichever of these ideas you try, make a recording of your finished music (if necessary, asking others to help you). Then listen back, and judge its effectiveness.

Performing

Here is one of several versions of the Welsh folk-song, *Watching the Wheat (Bugeilio 'r Gwenith Gwyn)*. Sing or play this melody.

Listening

Now investigate an instrumental arrangement of the folk-song. The arranger, Henry Geehl, structures his piece like this:

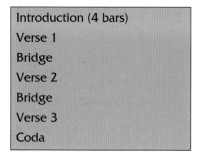

Introduction (4 bars)
Verse 1
Bridge
Verse 2
Bridge
Verse 3
Coda

As you listen, two or three times, to *Watching the Wheat*, discover answers to these questions. (You will find that there are several differences between the printed and recorded versions of the melody.)

Introduction

For which kind of instrumental ensemble is this music arranged?

Verse 1

(a) Which bars of the melody printed above are *decorated* in the recorded version?

(b) In which bars do you hear a falling sequence?

(c) Which bars contain a rising sequence?

Bridge

The arrangement includes percussion (but used very sparingly). Name the percussion instrument which adds a 'highlight' to this bridge.

Verse 2

(a) How are bars 1 and 2 different in the recorded version?

(b) And how are bars 13 and 14 different?

Bridge

Which two percussion instruments are included – and how are they used to add tension and excitement?

Verse 3

(a) Suggest a musical word to describe the part played by the high-sounding instruments during this verse.

(b) In which bars does a triangle stroke add expressive highlights to the music?

Coda

On which musical material is the brief coda based?

Linked listening

Decoration

Bach: *Sarabande* and *Double* (decorated repetition of the *Sarabande*) from English Suite No. 6

Mozart: opening of slow movement of Piano Concerto in B♭ (K450) – each of the two sections of the melody is first presented by the strings, then in a decorated version by the solo piano

Chopin: first part of Mazurka in A minor, Opus 17 No. 4

Verdi: Gilda's aria, *Caro nome*, from the opera *Rigoletto* – varied decorations, almost throughout, of this main musical idea:

Sequences

Traditional Irish jig: *The Irish Washerwoman*

Vivaldi: slow movement of the Violin Concerto called *Winter* from *The Four Seasons*

Mozart: slow movement (main theme) of the Clarinet Concerto

Walton: *Touch Her Soft Lips and Part* from music for the film 'Henry V'

Stravinsky: *Sinfonia* from *Pulcinella*

Antonio Carlos Jobim: *The Girl from Ipanema* – as you listen, distinguish between musical ideas being straightforwardly repeated (at the same pitch) and falling and rising sequences

Lionel Bart: *Where is Love?* from *Oliver*

Imitation

Byrd: *Kyrie* from *Mass for Four Voices*

Wilbye: *Sweet Honey-sucking Bees* – madrigal for five voices

Mozart: last movement of Symphony No. 41 in C ('Jupiter')

Dvořák: Slavonic Dance in C minor, Opus 46 No. 7 – imitation sometimes at two beats distance, sometimes only one beat

Fauré: *Offertoire* (first part) from the Requiem

Bartók: opening (first $1\frac{1}{4}$ minutes) of String Quartet No. 1 – first violin imitated by second violin, then cello imitated by viola

Tippett: opening (first $1\frac{1}{4}$ minutes) of *Fantasia Concertante on a Theme of Corelli* for strings; the spiritual *Nobody Knows* from the oratorio *A Child of Our Time*

Voice-exchange

The first half of *Veris ad imperia* (In the reign of spring), conductus by an anonymous 13th-century composer

The *pes* sung by two bass voices in the 13th-century round *Sumer is icumen in* (described in 'Enjoying Early Music')

Walter Odington: *Ave mater Domini* – three-part rondellus with voice-exchange between all three vocal parts

CHAPTER 12

Mood and character

Listening

Music can immediately conjure up a mood – though listeners may not all agree upon an exact description of that mood.

Listen to three varied extracts of music. In each of them, the composer deliberately intends to present a distinctive mood.

For each extract, choose two of these words which you think best describe the mood of the music.

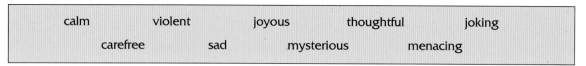

calm	violent	joyous	thoughtful	joking
carefree	sad	mysterious	menacing	

Afterwards, compare your choices with others in your group, and discuss them.

The way in which a composer treats and combines various musical elements gives the music its particular **mood** or **character**. These elements might include:

- rhythm – perhaps gently flowing, or urgent and strongly accented;
- tempo – the speed at which the music moves along;
- dynamics (loud/quiet) – perhaps unchanging, or with gradations of volume over a very wide range;
- timbres – and how they are used;
- melodic lines – their range, and the way they move along in musical time and space;
- harmonies – perhaps mainly concordant, or harshly discordant;
- the type of scale on which the music is based – major, or minor, or perhaps some other kind of scale;
- the use of silence.

Listen to the three extracts again. In each case, which of the musical elements listed above are most noticeable in conjuring up the mood?

Composing

1. Look carefully at the two contrasting pictures on the opposite page. Each has its own mood. For each picture, note down a few words to describe its mood.

2. Choose one of the two pictures, and compose a melody or a short piece which matches the mood you have described.

3. Make a recording of your music, then listen to it. In what ways does it match the mood of the picture you chose?

Listening

Investigate a piece of Japanese *gagaku* music – 'elegant' music of the Imperial Court, played at ceremonies and banquets. A *gagaku* ensemble is made up of wind, plucked string, and percussion instruments:

- *ryūteki* – a transverse bamboo flute, with seven finger-holes
- *hichiriki* – a small double-reed instrument (a shawm)
- *shō* – a mouth organ with seventeen bamboo pipes
- *biwa* – a lute with four or five strings, plucked with a plectrum
- *koto* – a long zither with thirteen strings, each stretched over a movable bridge, and plucked with ivory plectrums worn on the thumb, forefinger, and middle finger of the right hand
- *shōko* – a small gong made of bronze
- *kakko* – a small double-headed barrel drum
- *tsuridaiko* – a large hanging drum, struck with leather-covered beaters

Listen to a version of the most famous *gagaku* composition, called *Etenraku* (which means 'Music coming through from Heaven'). There are two sections of music, A and B, printed below in Western staff notation. Then follows a *tomede* – a coda, or 'finishing off'. In the music below, each instrument is indicated when it is first heard. The *ryūteki* and *hichiriki* add slides, ornaments, and nuances (shadings) of pitch to the basic notes of the main melody.

Follow the printed music as you listen. You will find that there is often a 'stretching' of the time on some beats.

Listen again to *Etenraku*, this time concentrating on the percussion sounds, and the plucked string sounds.

Listen to *Etenraku* once or twice more.

1 Suggest a word (or words) to describe the mood and character of this music.
2 Does the mood change – or remain the same throughout?
3 Which musical elements especially, do you think, create the mood and character of this piece?

Performing

You could try your own group performance of *Etenraku* – with melody instruments (playing just the basic notes, if necessary) supported by sounds on percussion, and perhaps guitar and/or cello.

Part of a Japanese gagaku ensemble of the Imperial Palace, including a biwa *(front left) and nine wind players playing three* ryūteki *(held sideways), three* hichiriki *(held straight in front), and three* shō *(with bamboo pipes pointing upwards)*

On the right, you can see the Japanese *gagaku* notation for the *hichiriki* part of *Etenraku*. As is often the case with the Japanese language, the music is written from top to bottom of the page, and in columns arranged from right to left.

Column 1 gives the title of the composition.

The columns marked 3 give the notation in the form of mnemonics (memory aids) with which the melodic line is sung when it is learnt. No ornaments or nuances are indicated, since these are passed on orally from player to player.

In each column 4 are symbols referring to the *hichiriki*'s finger-holes.

The dots in each column 2 show the percussion sounds on the basic beats – the larger dots representing accented strokes on the *tsuridaiko*, the large hanging drum.

Listening

Now listen to part of a piece called *Svevende Jord* (Floating earth) composed and performed (using multi-tracking) by the Norwegian composer, Tone Hulbaekmo. She begins the piece with synthesizer sounds, soon joined by wooden flute. Later, the music changes in mood and character.

Here is a plan of the music:

0′0″	2′06″
Section 1	**Section 2**
based on an old Norwegian cattle-call	based on an old Norwegian folk-dance

As you listen to *Svevende Jord*, describe the mood conjured up in each section of the music. Which musical elements come across most noticeably to create each of these contrasting moods?

Composing/Improvising

On your own, or with other musicians, compose or improvise a piece which starts out by creating a particular mood. Then during the piece, change the mood. Decide:

- whether the mood will change suddenly, or gradually;

- what musical means you will use to create each of the different moods;

- how your piece will end – perhaps at the close of the second section, or with a return of the opening mood, or in some other way.

Improvising

Musical conversations

1   In twos. Each using voice or a melody instrument, build up a musical conversation in which performer B 'agrees' with performer A. Throughout, B reflects the mood of A with phrases which are in some way similar, yet a *little* different. For example:

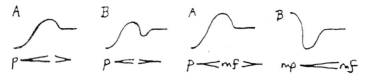

2   In groups of three. Performers A and B build up a musical conversation in which B soon begins to 'disagree' with A and the mood changes. Use pitch, tempo, dynamics and timbre to build up a heated argument. Throughout, performer C – on percussion – reflects, responds to, and highlights the pace, temperature and build-up of the argument between A and B. (How does the argument end?)

Performing

Perform your 'musical argument' to the rest of the class. As you listen to others, decide how effective is:

- the build-up of the heated dialogue between A and B;

- the response and back-up of C.

Listening

Afterwards, if you can, listen to *Match* for two cellos and percussion by the Argentinian composer, Mauricio Kagel. This piece, extremely difficult to play, is a 'musical duel' between the two cellists, with the percussionist acting as umpire. He eventually stops the contest and shakes hands with the cellist who, in his opinion during the performance, has won the duel.

Composing

In films and television, background music often plays an important part in setting, or enhancing, the right mood or atmosphere. The suspense would be less exciting, the eerie bits less frightening, and the sad bits less 'tear-jerking', without the support of effective music in the background.

Form a group of musicians. Think up a short scene from an imaginary film or television play. Briefly write out what happens during the scene.

Then make up some music which will create the right mood or atmosphere and match the timing of the action. Make sure that your music matches any *change* of mood. (If your group is large enough, some of you could mime the action while others perform the supporting music.)

Linked listening

Listen to the beginning of some of these pieces.

- What is the mood or character of the music?
- How is it created?

Copland: *Hoe-down* from *Rodeo*; *Quiet City*
Holst: *Venus* from the suite *The Planets*
Stravinsky: *Sacrificial Dance* from *The Rite of Spring*
Satie: *Gymnopédie* No. 1
Nono: *Coma una ola de fuerza y luz* (Like a wave of force and light)
Shostakovich: Polka from *The Golden Age*
Palestrina: *Sanctus* from *Missa Papae Marcelli*
Bach: Bourrée II from English Suite No. 2, performed by the Swingle Singers
Bach: Overture from Orchestral Suite No. 3 in D
Sibelius: *The Swan of Tuonela*
Schoenberg: *Vorgefühle* (Premonitions) – the first of the *Five Pieces for Orchestra*, Opus 16
Bartók: third movement from *Music for Strings, Percussion and Celesta*
Sousa: March – *Semper Fidelis* for military band
Duke Ellington: *Mood Indigo*; *Black and Tan Fantasy*
American Patrol, played by **Glenn Miller**
Led Zeppelin: *Stairway to Heaven*; *The Rain Song*
Maki Ishii: *Sō-Gū* II – this is a simultaneous performance of his two pieces, *Sō* for orchestra and *Music for Gagaku* (EMI Records, EMD 5508)

Had I the heavens' embroidered cloths,
Enwrought with golden and silver light,
The blue and the dim and the dark cloths
Of night and light and the half-light,
I would spread the cloths under your feet:
But I, being poor, have only my dreams;
I have spread my dreams under your feet;
Tread softly, because you tread on my dreams.

William Butler Yeats

Texture

Listen to three varied extracts of music:

Ligeti: fourth movement from Chamber Concerto for thirteen players

Barber: *Adagio for String Orchestra*, Opus 11

Stravinsky: *Sacrificial Dance* from *The Rite of Spring*

In each one, the composer is aiming to present a particular type or quality of sound. As you listen to each extract, choose the description which you think best matches the type of sound the composer is presenting:

| sustained, smooth, rich, flowing |

| heavy, dense, thick, complicated |

| light, open, thin, yet 'busy' |

In each of these boxes, the words are describing what musicians call the **texture** of the music. It might be:

- heavy or light in sound;
- thick and dense, or thin and sparse;
- smooth (*legato*) and flowing, or detached (*staccato*) and jagged;
- made up of few notes at a time, or many notes at a time.

The type of musical texture will also depend on:

- the number of parts or musical strands – instrumental and/or vocal – and their heaviness or lightness;
- the way they move along in musical time – the tempo, durations and rhythms which are used;
- the spacing between the parts or strands – whether they are closely packed together, or widely spaced apart in pitch;
- their relationship to each other – the way in which they are combined and interrelated.

Listen again to the three extracts of music. Listen for how each composer is creating the texture in the music.

Composing/Improvising

Either on your own (using a keyboard), or as a member of a group of musicians, choose one of the boxes above. Compose or improvise some music whose texture matches the words in the box.

Perform your music to the rest of the class. As you listen to others performing theirs, decide which of the three boxes they chose, and judge how effectively the texture of their music matches the words in the box.

Listening

Importantly, the word **texture** also refers to the particular way in which the various parts, or strands, in the music are put together. Here are descriptions of four basic styles of musical texture.

1   The first, and simplest, style of texture is called **monophonic** ('single sounds'). This musical texture consists of one strand only, a single melodic line, with no supporting harmonies – as in plainsong, most medieval dances and songs, and much folk-music all over the world.

The single melodic line may be performed by a solo instrument or voice, or by several instruments and/or voices in **unison** – all playing or singing the same melody, though not necessarily at the same octave. The melody may be accompanied by percussion instruments or a drone.

As an example of monophonic texture, listen to *Prendés i garde* (Keep a good lookout), a short song by a 13th-century composer called Guillaume d'Amiens. The words are light-hearted. A boy is trying to distract a pretty girl who is doing her best to keep her mind on the cows she is supposed to be looking after.
   Listen for when the melody is performed solo, and when it is performed in unison.
   Listen again, and identify the instruments taking part.

2   A second style of musical texture is called **homophonic** ('like-sounding'). In this texture, the composer focuses the listener's attention on a single melody, with accompanying harmonies – melody (foreground) plus accompaniment (background).

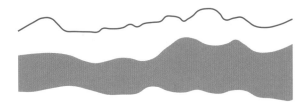

The melody is usually, though not always, at the top of the texture – higher in pitch than the notes of the accompaniment. The other parts in the texture often tend to keep rhythmically in step with each other.

As an example of homophonic texture, listen to the opening of the slow movement of Khatchaturian's Piano Concerto. Two melodies are presented in turn (on bass clarinet, then on piano) against a chordal accompaniment.
   Listen again. Where does Khatchaturian place each melody in the musical texture – at the top, at the bottom, or in the middle of the texture?

3   A third style of musical texture is called **polyphonic** ('many sounds', 'music in more than one part'). Another word used with much the same meaning is **contrapuntal**. A polyphonic or contrapuntal texture consists of two or more melodic lines (strands of melody) weaving along at the same time. The strands are mainly equal in importance.

The way in which this kind of musical texture is woven can be compared with the way in which the threads are organized in a woven fabric.

A polyphonic texture may combine together melodies which are quite different, or it may be woven from a single musical idea taken up by each part in turn, in *imitation.*

Listen to the opening of Contrapunctus 13 from J. S. Bach's *The Art of Fugue.* The polyphonic texture, woven by four woodwind instruments, is based on this musical idea:

The four instruments you will hear, in turn, are:

| alto flute | cor anglais | bassoon 1 | bassoon 2 |

Listen for the musical idea to be presented by the four instruments in turn.

Listen again – still listening for each instrument to enter. But this time (and this is something of a challenge), try also to hear how each instrument, having presented the idea, *continues* to weave its melodic strand in the musical texture.

4   A fourth style of musical texture is called **heterophonic** ('difference of sounds'). This texture is made up of the simultaneous performance of different versions of the same melody. For instance, one voice or instrument performs a melody while, at the same time, another performs a more elaborate, decorated version of it.

Other voices or instruments may join in with yet more versions of the melody, perhaps elaborating it still further, or even simplifying it (picking out just a few important notes).

Heterophonic texture is found in the folk-music of certain European countries, in Turkish music, Japanese *gagaku* music, Indonesian *gamelan* music, and in Arab music. As an example, listen to a folk-tune from Turkey, called *Haunted Mountain.* To a rhythmic accompaniment on drums, three instrumentalists – on *keman* (violin), *kirnata* (single-reed woodwind), and cello – simultaneously play their own versions of the folk-tune, creating a heterophonic texture.

As you listen, see if you can hear differences between the three simultaneous versions of the folk-tune.

A composer need not keep the musical texture exactly the same throughout a piece. For instance, homophonic texture (melody plus accompaniment) may alternate with polyphonic texture (two or more melodic strands weaving along together). A composer may also vary texture in other ways – such as contrasting textures which are thin and light with textures which are more dense and heavy and perhaps richly and intricately decorated.

Other factors which are important in creating a certain type of musical texture include the kind of rhythm used, and the particular choice of timbres and the ways in which they may be blended or sharply contrasted. In fact, texture and timbre are closely linked, and are often given special emphasis in 20th-century music.

Listening

Listen to the first movement of *Venetian Games* (1961) by the Polish composer, Lutosławski. The music is structured in eight sections of different length (one is only two seconds long). Each section begins with a sharp, incisive sound on percussion. Listen for changes in *density* of texture, and other contrasts of texture between sections.

Listen again, and assess the effect of *timbre*, and contrasts of timbre, in this music.

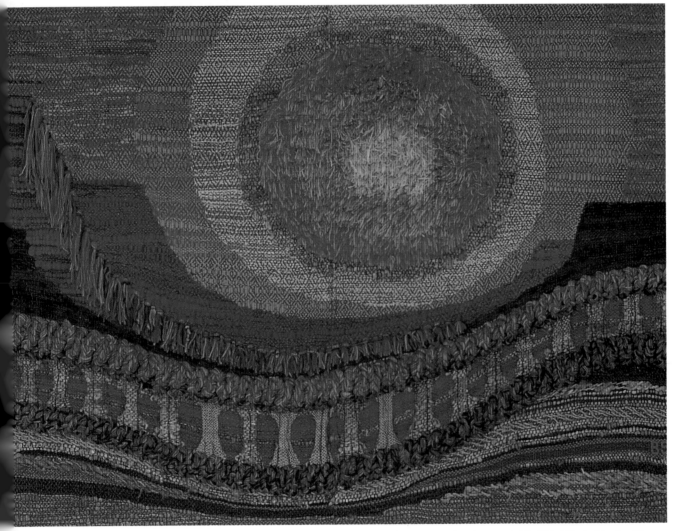

Varied and contrasted textures in a handwoven tapestry called 'Red Centre' by Ben Shearer

Composing

Try one (or more) of these ideas:

1 Create a piece in *monophonic* texture by composing a single melodic line. Give your piece interest and variety by having phrases sometimes performed by a solo instrument or voice, and sometimes by two or more in unison – perhaps varying the combination of instruments and/or voices so that there are changes of timbre. Decide whether to add a simple percussion accompaniment (here and there, or throughout).

2 Compose a piece of music in *homophonic* texture, which focuses attention on a melody, supported by an accompaniment built from chords.

3 Create some music which has a *polyphonic (contrapuntal)* texture – two or more strands of sound weaving along independently. Carefully consider which timbres to use from those available to you.

4 Compose a piece which has a *heterophonic* texture. One instrument or voice performs a straightforward melody. A second performs, at the same time, the same melody but in a more elaborate way, with extra notes and decorations. A third performs a simplified version – picking out only a few important notes, which might be short in value, or sustained (held on).

5 Form a group of musicians, and compose or improvise a piece which is structured in the following way:

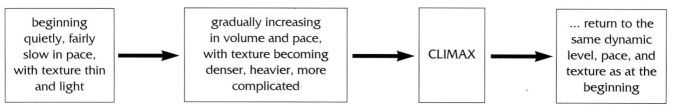

6 First, listen again to the first movement of *Venetian Games* by Lutosławski. Then form a group of musicians. Compose or improvise your own piece built up in sections of music emphasizing contrasts of texture (and perhaps also of timbre). Discuss and decide the various kinds of musical texture you will aim for.

If you are improvising, one member of the group could give a cue to mark the beginning of each new section – or a signal could be given on percussion.

Performing

Whichever of these six ideas you choose, organize a performance of your piece, and make a recording of it. Then listen back. Assess the effectiveness of your music, and judge whether you can improve or refine it in any way.

If you choose idea 6, above – when you have listened to your recording, make a graphic or diagrammatic score of the music, showing the changes and contrasts in musical texture.

Linked listening

Monophonic texture

Examples from plainchant, medieval dances and songs ('Enjoying Early Music' cassette), unaccompanied folk-songs

Bizet: opening of the *Prélude* to *L'Arlésienne*

Verdi: opening of the *Agnus Dei* from the Requiem – two solo voices in unison, then four-part choir and orchestra in unison

Homophonic texture

Handel: the aria *Lascia ch'io pianga* from *Rinaldo*

Haydn: second movement from Trumpet Concerto in E♭

Chopin: *Étude* No. 3 in E major; Prelude No. 4 in E minor

Liszt: *Liebestraum* No. 3 – opening with melody in the middle of the texture

Borodin: opening of the *Notturno* from String Quartet No. 2 in D

Prokofiev: *Troïka* (Sleigh ride) from *Lieutenant Kijé* – after the introduction, the tune is placed at the bottom of the texture

Villa-Lobos: first movement from *Bachianas brasileiras* No. 5 for soprano accompanied by eight cellos

Messiaen: *Quartet for the End of Time*, movements 5 (cello and piano) and 8 (violin and piano)

Polyphonic (contrapuntal) texture

Byrd: *Agnus Dei* from *Mass for Four Voices* – the music is in three sections: the first in two voice-parts, the second in three voice-parts, the third in four voice-parts

Bach: Two-part Inventions, and Fugues from *The Well-Tempered Clavier* – if possible, compare Bach's original versions (for keyboard) with versions/arrangements by the Swingle Singers, Jacques Loussier, and W. Carlos (for Moog synthesizer)

Bartók: first movement from *Music for Strings, Percussion and Celesta*

Stravinsky: second movement from *Symphony of Psalms*

Examples of collective improvisation in early and traditional jazz

Heterophonic texture

Examples from Balinese and Javanese *gamelan* music, Japanese *gagaku* music, Arab music

Varying textures (and timbres) in electronic music

Stockhausen: *Gesang der Jünglinge* (Song of the youths); *Kontakte* (described in 'Enjoying Music' Book 3)

Berio: *Visage*

Mimaroğlu: *Agony*

Ligeti: *Artikulation*

Changing textures

Handel: *Hallelujah Chorus* from *Messiah* – as you listen, identify examples of monophonic, homophonic and polyphonic textures

Malcolm Arnold: No. 1 of *Three Shanties* for wind quintet

Ligeti: *Atmosphères* for orchestra – changes in densities of texture

Compare, and discuss, the textures of two contrasting pop or rock songs. For example, **Genesis:** *Follow You Follow Me* and *Down and Out* (both on the album *And Then There Were Three . . .*); or **Deep Purple:** *Never Before* and *Speed King* (*24 Carat Purple*); or **Bob Marley:** *Redemption Song* and *Coming in from the Cold* (*Uprising*).

CHAPTER 14

Rondo form

Performing

Play or sing this Somerset folk-tune called *Seventeen Come Sunday*:

Listening

Now listen to the music recorded on the CD. It begins with the folk-tune you have just performed. How many times is the tune played during this piece?

Listen to the music again. Between playings of *Seventeen Come Sunday* you hear two other folk-tunes: first *I Sowed the Seeds of Love* and later *I Will Give My Love an Apple*. Each of these presents some kind of *contrast* to the main tune. As you listen, follow the music printed on the opposite page.

The piece is built up in five sections of music. A plan, showing the structure of the music, looks like this:

A^1	B	A^2	C	A^3
the main tune	**a contrast**	**main tune again**	**another contrast**	**main tune, (last time)**
4 beats to a bar, rhythmic, fairly brisk, vigorous	in the major key, more flowing, change of timbres		3 beats to a bar, slower and quieter, change of timbres	

This piece is structured in the musical form known as **rondo form**. In a rondo, the main tune (A) 'comes round' at least three times, with contrasting sections of music heard in between. The contrasting sections are called **episodes**.

In some rondos, there are three or more episodes, and so the main rondo tune comes round four or more times. The plan of the piece then becomes: A^1 B A^2 C A^3 D A^4 (E A^5 . . .).

Sometimes, the main rondo tune is shortened or varied in some way when it returns. A brief passage of music called a **link** may be used to join two sections of music smoothly together. And the last return of the rondo tune may be followed by a **coda** – a few more bars of music to round the piece off in a satisfactory way.

In a piece in rondo form, the repetitions of the main rondo tune (A) bring a feeling of **unity**, and **balance**, to the piece. The contrasts presented by the episodes (B, C . . .) add **variety**.

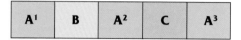

Investigate an orchestral piece called *Praeludium* by Järnefelt, a Swedish composer of Finnish birth. Järnefelt structures the music in rondo form, with two episodes:

A¹	B	A²	C	A³

Here are the three tunes which Järnefelt uses in *Praeludium*:

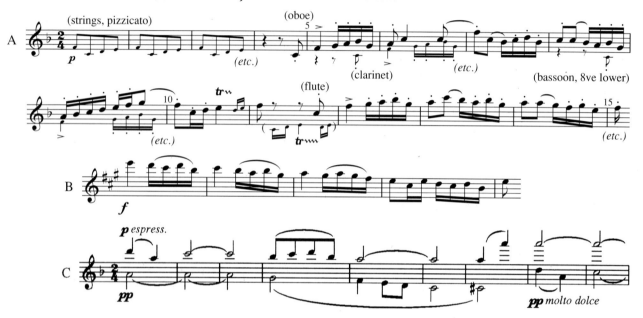

In this rondo, the first time music A returns (as A²) it is very much shortened.

First listening

Listen for the three tunes – A, B, and C – and match what you hear to the diagram of rondo form, printed above.

Second and third listenings

Answer these questions:

1   The piece begins with a musical pattern of four notes, repeated throughout section A¹. What is the name given to this particular musical device?

2   The rondo tune itself is begun by the oboe – soon 'copied' by the clarinet, and then by other instruments. What name is given to this musical device?

3   Section B presents several musical contrasts to section A¹. Mention two of them.

4   Which of these describes the bass-line of section B?

5   Section C begins with solo violin and horn. Which instrument takes up the melody in bar 8?

6   Describe three ways in which the music of section C contrasts with all the music heard before it.

7   Section A³ is exactly the same as section A¹ – and, as at first, the music gradually builds up. Explain how this happens.

8   Järnefelt rounds off the piece with a short coda, nine bars long. Describe the music of this coda.

Composing

On your own, or with three other musicians, compose a rondo.

First, compose your main rondo tune. Try to make a tune which will be easily recognizable each time it returns during the rondo.

Then construct your episodes. There must be at least two episodes, and each should contrast in two or more ways with the rest of the music. (It may help to look at the 'Ways of making musical contrasts' given on page 71).

If you are working in a group of four, two of you could be responsible for composing episode B, while the other two compose episode C.

Decide whether it would be effective:

● to shorten A on one occasion – or make some slight changes to it;

● to add a few more bars after the last return of A – making a coda which will round off the whole piece.

Practise your rondo, and listen carefully as you play. Do the episodes present effective musical contrasts?

Performing

Perform your rondo to the rest of the class. As you listen to others performing theirs, consider:

● Is it easy to tell when music A returns each time?

● Do the episodes (B, C . . .) present effective contrasts? In what ways?

Linked listening

Other pieces in rondo form

Couperin: Gavotte – *Les Moissoneurs* (The harvesters); and Rondeau – *Soeur Monique* (Sister Monica)

Purcell: Rondeau from *The Fairy Queen*; and Rondeau from *Abdelazer* – in this piece (printed complete on the next page) the main rondo tune is the theme on which Benjamin Britten based *The Young Person's Guide to the Orchestra* (Variations and Fugue on a Theme of Purcell)

Bach: Rondeau from Orchestral Suite No. 2 in B minor (discussed in 'Musical Forms' Book 1)

Gluck: *Che farò senza Euridice* ('What is life to me without thee?') from *Orfeo ed Euridice*

Haydn: Finale from Piano Sonata No. 37 in D ('Musical Forms' Book 1); and 'Gypsy' Rondo from Piano Trio No. 25 in G

Mozart: Rondo from Horn Concerto No. 2, K417 (a full score is printed in 'Musical Forms: Listening Scores'); Rondo from Horn Concerto No. 3, K447; last movement from Serenade No. 10 in B♭, K361, for thirteen wind instruments; and Figaro's aria *Non più andrai* from *The Marriage of Figaro* ('Musical Forms' Book 3)

Beethoven: second movement from Piano Sonata No. 8 in C minor – the *Pathétique Sonata* ('Musical Forms' Book 1)

Chopin: Mazurka in A minor, Opus 17 No. 4

Bizet: *Prelude* to *Carmen*

Brahms: third movement of Violin Sonata No. 1 in G major ('Musical Forms' Book 1)

Ravel: *Pavane pour une infante défunte* (Pavan upon the death of a Spanish princess)

Bartók: *Three Rondos on Folk-tunes* (1926–7) for piano

Play or listen to this rondo by Purcell. He composed it as part of the incidental music to a play called *Abdelazer*. Discover:

● how many times the main rondo tune is heard;

● how Purcell structures bars 3–6 of his main tune;

● how many episodes there are, and where each one begins.

CHAPTER 15

Programme music

Listening

Listen to three extracts of music. Each of the three composers is using the orchestra to create a picture in sound. Match the extracts to these descriptions:

| a flock of sheep | a storm at sea | birdsong at sunset |

Listen to the music again, and describe any features in each extract which give 'clues' to the sound-picture the composer is creating.

Music which attempts to conjure up pictures in the mind of the listener is called **programme music**, or is said to be **programmatic**. A piece of programme music may be:

- **narrative** – attempting to 'tell a story in music'; or
- **descriptive** – perhaps describing a scene, sounds of nature, a season of the year.

The 'story-line' or the descriptive idea on which the composer bases the music is called the **programme**.

Improvising

On your own, or with other musicians, improvise some programme music to describe one of the ideas in the box below. Use instruments and/or vocal sounds to create your sound-picture.

> Night ride
> Icicles
> Sunrise
> Wind and waves
> Jungle

Examples of programmatic pieces date back as far as the 14th century. But it was not until the 19th century, when closer links were being made between music and literature and painting, that composers keenly took up the idea of programme music. And, of course, it was in music for the orchestra – which was then swiftly developing and expanding – that they were able to express their ideas most vividly.

A single-movement programmatic piece for orchestra is called a **symphonic poem**, or **tone poem**. The programme on which the music is based may be a legend or folk-tale, a poem, a play, an episode from history, a painting, or a scene from nature.

A good example of a symphonic poem based on a folk-tale is *The Water Goblin*, composed by Dvořák in 1896. To achieve the dramatic and colourful effects he wants to make, Dvořák uses a fairly large orchestra.

Instruments often included in the modern **orchestra** are shown on the opposite page. In an orchestral score showing all the staves of music for the instruments taking part in a composition, the instruments are arranged down the page according to the **four sections** of the orchestra. The order is always:

- **woodwind**
- **brass**
- **percussion**
- **strings**

In his symphonic poem *The Water Goblin*, Dvořák includes these instruments:

Woodwind	*Percussion*
piccolo	kettledrums
2 flutes	tubular bells
2 oboes	triangle
cor anglais	cymbals
2 clarinets	bass drum
bass clarinet	tam-tam
2 bassoons	
Brass	*Strings*
4 horns	first violins
2 trumpets	second violins
3 trombones	violas
tuba	cellos
	double basses

This diagram shows a typical layout of these instruments on the concert platform: strings spread across the front, woodwind in the centre, with brass and percussion behind.

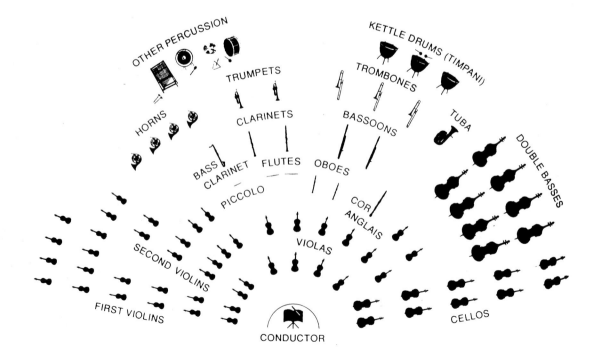

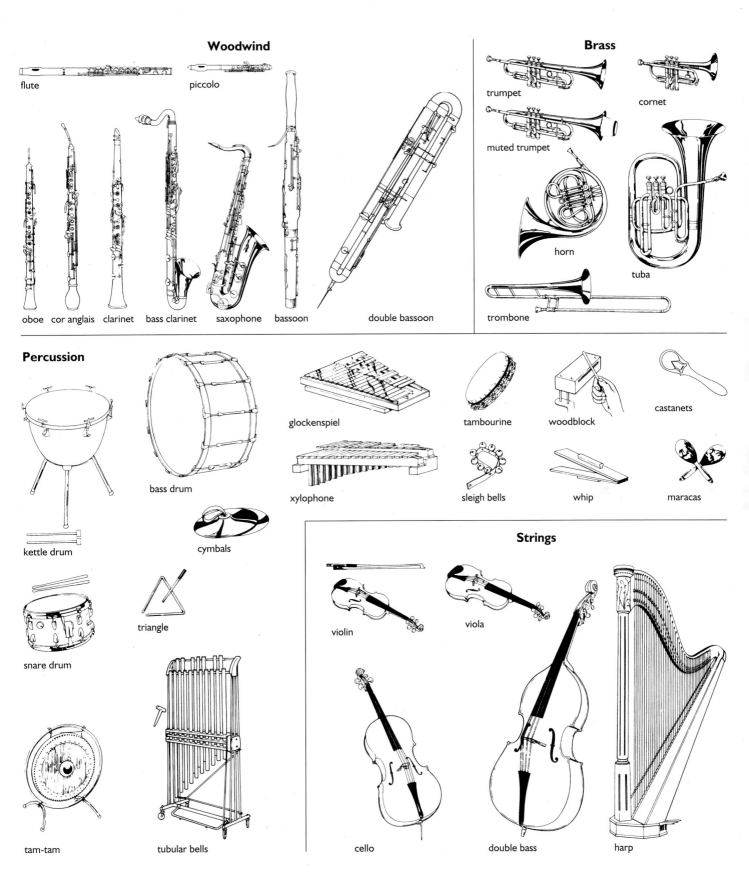

Woodwind

flute

piccolo

oboe cor anglais clarinet bass clarinet saxophone bassoon double bassoon

Brass

trumpet cornet

muted trumpet

horn tuba

trombone

Percussion

kettle drum

bass drum

glockenspiel

xylophone

cymbals

tambourine woodblock castanets

sleigh bells whip maracas

snare drum

triangle

tam-tam

tubular bells

Strings

violin viola

cello double bass harp

Clap or tap this rhythm, several times:

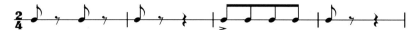

This is the rhythm of the main theme of Dvořák's symphonic poem, *The Water Goblin*:

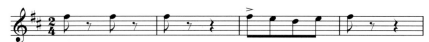

This theme, which represents the water goblin himself, is heard over and over again during the music.

Listening

Listen to six extracts from *The Water Goblin*. The programme on which Dvořák bases this symphonic poem is a Czech folk-tale. In Czech folklore, a water goblin is a malicious, evil being who drowns humans and imprisons their souls under upturned cups in his house, deep in the waters of a lake.

1 The water goblin sits on the branch of a tree, making a coat of green and shoes of red. Tomorrow will be his wedding day.

2 A village girl is warned by her mother not to go down to the lake.

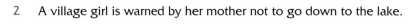

3 But the girl is irresistibly drawn to the lake. The water goblin's theme is heard as he watches with glee as the girl begins to cross the footbridge. It gives way – and the girl sinks down into the depths of the lake. She is now in the power of the water goblin's magic.

4 At the bottom of the lake. The girl has become the water goblin's wife. She sings a sad lullaby to their green-haired child.

Her singing irritates the water goblin. Eventually, he becomes enraged and threatens to turn her into a fish.

5   The girl pleads with the water goblin to be allowed to visit her mother.

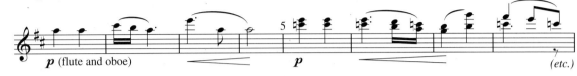

Reluctantly he agrees, warning her that she must return before the evening bells. He will keep the child as a pledge for her return.

6   But the mother refuses to let her daughter go. Twilight falls, and the water goblin leaves the lake.

He makes his way to the cottage, and the evening bells are heard in the distance. The goblin hammers violently on the door (listen for the first three notes of his theme to be hammered out *fortissimo*, three times). When the goblin says their son is crying with hunger, the mother tells him to bring the child to them.

In fury, the goblin obeys. A sudden storm comes up over the lake. Something is heard crashing against the cottage door. The mother opens it – and finds the headless body of the child . . .

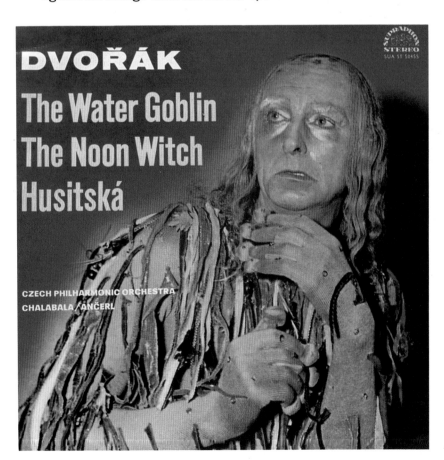

A great deal of the instrumental music of China and Japan consists of programmatic pieces (almost always to do with nature) with descriptive titles such as *Little Boat on the Lake*, *The Plum Branch*, *The Rainbow*, *Spring Haze*, *In an Autumn Garden*, *Fantasy of the Waves*, *Rain Spell*, and *High Mountains, Flowing Streams*.

Listening

Listen to a piece called *Moonlight Night* by the Chinese composer Kay Hua Heng. The music is played on a woodwind instrument and two string instruments (one plucked, one bowed):

● *hsiao* – an end-blown bamboo flute

● *cheng* – a zither, with usually sixteen metal strings, stretched over movable bridges and plucked with the fingernails of the right hand;

● *erh-hu* – a two-string bowed instrument with a mellow (even haunting) timbre.

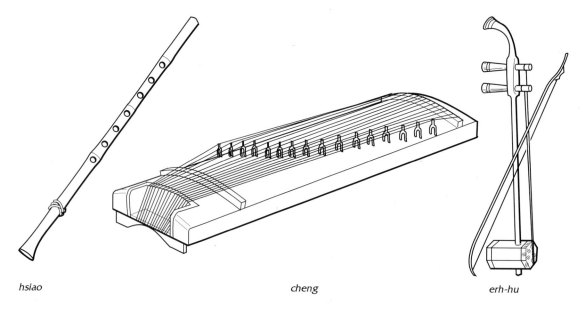

hsiao   cheng   erh-hu

Listen again to *Moonlight Night*. In what ways, do you think, does Kay Hua Heng's music match the title of her piece?

Chinese music uses various kinds of notation – ways of writing down music. That on the opposite page is the *kung ch'e* (pitched notation) system, which was used for notating music for the *cheng* from the 13th century to the early 20th century.

Kung ch'e notation consists of ten characters, or ideograms. Each stands for a syllable that represents a note. This is a system of *movable* pitch (like tonic sol-fa, where doh can be set at any chosen pitch). Here are the Chinese characters and syllables, with *ho* set here at the C below middle C:

The music printed below is part of a piece called *Chiang-hu-hsui* (River and lake waters). Most Chinese music, like the Chinese language, is written from top to bottom of the page, and in columns arranged from right to left.

Columns 1 and 2 give the title and number of the piece.

Column 3, each time, shows symbols for the *cheng* player's right hand, which plucks the strings.

Column 4 gives the pitch symbols.

Column 5 shows symbols for the left hand, which sometimes raises the pitch of a string by finger pressure upon it.

The vertical lines, alongside the pitch symbols, give the rhythm:

- single line – quaver (♪)
- double line – semiquaver (♫)
- no line shown – crotchet (♩)

Now try this...

Discover for yourself what the opening of this piece sounds like.

1   Look at the Chinese pitch symbols in the first column 4 (the first column 4 from the *right*) showing the opening notes of the piece. Write down the *rhythm* of these notes, in Western notation – quavers, semiquavers, crotchets.

2   Now match the Chinese pitch symbols of these opening notes with the characters at the bottom of page 118 – and add *pitch* to the rhythm you have notated.

3   Finally, sing or play the opening notes of *Chiang-hu-hsui*, as you have notated them.

Composing

On your own, or with others, compose a piece of programme music.

It could be *narrative*, 'telling a story in music' (as Dvořák's *The Water Goblin*) – in which case, first briefly note down the events which you imagine will take place in your story.

Or your piece could be *descriptive* – in which case, you could compose music to one of the titles mentioned on page 118, or think up one of your own, or try the following suggestion.

Suggestion: a programmatic piece called *Winter Landscape*

- *Imagine* what kind of landscape it might be, and what is in view.
- *Choose* which instruments, of those available to you, could provide the most suitable sounds.
- *Experiment* and discover effective instrumental (or vocal) sounds, pitches, tone-qualities, note-patterns.
- *Decide* whether the scene remains the same throughout – or whether there should be any changes (for example: sky changes, a snowstorm), and how your music could illustrate this.
- *Consider* which musical elements and devices will be useful in structuring your music and expressing the mood(s) you wish to create – for example: tempo, dynamics, textures, repetitions, contrasts, perhaps drones and/or ostinatos.

Compose your piece. When you have finished it, write down your music (if you like, in the form of a graphic score). Afterwards, make a recording of your piece, and then listen to it. How well, do you think, does your music match the programme you chose?

Chinese handscroll, 'Clear Weather in the Valley', by an anonymous 13th-century artist

Linked listening

Other Chinese or Japanese descriptive pieces
Rameau: *La poule* (The hen) for harpsichord
Vivaldi: *The Four Seasons* (four programmatic violin concertos)
Haydn: Introduction ('Representation of Chaos') to *The Creation*
Beethoven: Symphony No. 6 in F – the *Pastoral Symphony* (described in 'Musical Forms' Book 2)
Berlioz: *Symphonie fantastique*
Liszt: *Les préludes**
Smetana: *Vltava*†
Saint-Saëns: *Danse macabre*†
Borodin: *In the Steppes of Central Asia**
Balakirev: *Tamara* – a legend about a beautiful vampire queen
Musorgsky: *Night on the Bare Mountain*†; *Pictures at an Exhibition**
Tchaikovsky: *Romeo and Juliet* ('Enjoying Music' Book 3)
Rimsky-Korsakov: *Sheherazade*
Debussy: *La mer* (The sea); *Nocturnes*; *Images* for orchestra – and *Images* for piano
Delius: *On Hearing the First Cuckoo in Spring*† (melody-line score in 'Musical Forms: Listening
  Scores'); *Summer Night on the River**
Richard Strauss: *Don Juan**; *Till Eulenspiegel* ('Enjoying Music' Book 3)
Dukas: *The Sorcerer's Apprentice* ('Enjoying Music' Book 3)
Sibelius: *Finlandia*†; *The Swan of Tuonela*†; *En saga**; *Tapiola* (Tapio is the Finnish god of forests);
  Night Ride and Sunrise
Vaughan Williams: *Sinfonia antartica* (Antarctic symphony)
Schoenberg: *Verklärte Nacht* (Transfigured night) for string sextet
Ravel: *La vallée des cloches* (Valley of the bells) from *Miroirs* for piano – and also in the orchestral
  arrangement by Grainger
Respighi: *The Fountains of Rome*; *The Pines of Rome* ('Enjoying Music' Book 3)
Harty: *With the Wild Geese* – based on two poems telling of Irish soldiers who died fighting for the
  French at Fontenoy: (1) the camp at night, before the battle; (2) after the battle: at early dawn, the
  ghosts of the dead soldiers – in the form of wild geese – are seen returning to their native land
Bax: *Tintagel**; *The Garden of Fand*
Villa-Lobos: *The Little Train of the Caipira*† from *Bachianas brasileiras* No. 2 (*caipira* means 'peasant')
Honegger: *Pacific 231* – the journey of a giant locomotive
Gershwin: *An American in Paris*
Grace Williams: *Sea Sketches* – 1 High wind; 2 Sailing song; 3 Channel sirens; 4 (Scherzo) Breakers;
  5 Calm sea in summer
William Mathias: *Helios*, Opus 76 – Helios was the sun god of Greek mythology; the music also
  expresses 'the luminous transparency of the Greek landscape', with hints of Greek dances
Messiaen: *Oiseaux exotiques* (Exotic birds) for piano and orchestra (described in 'Enjoying Modern
  Music')
Britten: *Four Sea Interludes*† from the opera *Peter Grimes*
Reich: *Different Trains* for string quartet and pre-recorded sounds
Toru Takemitsu (20th-century Japanese composer): *Rain Tree Sketch* for piano – the rain tree is so
  named because its thousands of tiny leaves continue to let fall raindrops collected from last night's
  shower until well after midday; *riverrun* for piano and orchestra – 'a lush evocation of a river, and
  its surrounding landscape, by night'

*Described in detail in 'Musical Forms' Book 1. †Described in 'Enjoying Music' Book 1.

'We walked in the meadows along the River, and heard the distant singing from the Church across the River. The mist had not entirely left the river bed, and the colours, the running water, the banks and elm trees were something that one would always remember.'

'Shell Bay', created by a Year 11 art and design student

CHAPTER 16

Timbre (2) – new sounds, new colours

Timbre – tone-quality, or tone-*colour* – can be one of the most expressive elements in music. For centuries, composers have enjoyed using contrasts in timbre, both instrumental and vocal. And never more so than during the 20th century. In fact, in some pieces, timbre has been given more importance than melody, rhythm and harmony.

Some composers have experimented with new sounds and effects from familiar instruments (often involving new playing techniques), varied percussive sounds, muted brass effects, and instruments playing at the extremes of their ranges – often forcefully, even harshly.

Instruments may be fitted with contact microphones so that their sounds are amplified. And any sounds may be modified or transformed by means of electronics.

Below, and on the next three pages, are details of some of these new sounds, new colours, new techniques. Some of them are 'mechanical noises' rather than musical notes. A few of the sounds included have been in use for some time – but in their quest for ever-increasing contrasts of timbre, 20th-century composers have used them with more emphasis and much greater frequency.

Strings

muting (*con sordino*, 'with the mute' – see page 26)
various kinds of vibrato – slow, normal, fast
col legno ('with the wood') – bow the strings with the wood of the bow, instead of the horse-hair; *col legno battuto* – beat the strings with the wood of the bow
glissando – 'sliding', from one pitch to another some distance away
pizzicato with immediate glissando
snap pizzicato – a strong pizzicato so that the string slaps the fingerboard
harmonics – high-pitched sounds, with a soft and flute-like timbre, produced by lightly touching a string at a certain point
bowed *tremolo* – rapid repetitions of a note by making swift up-and-down movements of the bow, producing an agitated, dramatic effect
sul ponticello ('on the bridge') – bowing the string(s) very close to the bridge, producing a rather eerie tone-quality (especially when combined with bowed *tremolo*)
bowing the strings between the bridge and the tailpiece
bowing actually *on* the tailpiece
tapping on the body of the instrument, with the bow or fingertips
the use of excessive bow pressure

Listening

Listen to an extract from Penderecki's *Threnody: To the Victims of Hiroshima* for 52 strings, composed in 1960. This piece was written in memory of those killed or injured as a result of the atomic bomb exploded over Hiroshima fifteen years earlier. Penderecki includes most of the sounds and techniques listed above.

Woodwind

flutter-tonguing – while blowing, the player rolls the letter 'r'

pitch-bending

glissando

percussive key-clicking, with or without producing tone

muting – by inserting a piece of cloth or a cork or felt plug into the bell

breathy tone

singing while playing – different effects can be achieved by singing in unison with the instrument, or an octave higher or lower, or at some other interval

blowing on the reed alone

multiphonics – the sounding, on a single instrument, of two or more notes at once (produced by special fingerings and lip usages)

Listening

Of all the woodwind instruments, experimental composers have mostly favoured the flute, for its wide range of dynamics, tone-colour, and articulation. Listen to part of Luciano Berio's *Sequenza I* for solo flute, composed in 1958. Sounds and techniques you will hear include: flutter-tonguing, key-clicking, and multiphonics.

Brass

flutter-tonguing

pitch-bending

valve rattling without blowing

use of various kinds of mute

blowing without producing tone; breathy sounds

singing, speaking, whispering, shouting into an instrument

blowing on the detached mouthpiece

multiphonics

Listening

Listen to the opening of the third movement, *Interlude*, from Leonard Salzedo's Divertimento for three trumpets and three trombones. Trumpet 3 and trombones 1 and 2, all with cup mutes, play chordal phrases. Against these, there is a dialogue between trumpets 1 and 2 with harmon (wow-wow) mutes, and bass trombone with straight mute.

Brass mutes

plunger   harmon   cup   straight
or wow-wow

For more examples of brass techniques, listen to an extract from Berio's *Sequenza V* (1966) for solo trombone. Sounds and techniques include: opening and closing plunger mute, vocal sounds (including singing into the instrument, usually while playing), flutter-tonguing, breathy sounds, and rattling the mute inside the bell of the trombone. Sometimes the trombone imitates the vocal sounds, and sometimes the vocal sounds imitate the sound of the instrument.

Percussion

new ways of striking or sounding instruments
new positions or areas of striking
use of unusual striking agents
a vast expansion in numbers and types of instruments, some of them from 'exotic' sources – for
    example:

- Africa – many different types of drum, such as the darabukka, and log and slit drums;

- Latin America – bongos, cabaca, claves, conga drums, güiro, maracas, reco-reco, timbales;

- the Far East – bells, wood and glass chimes, various types of cymbal, sets of gongs and
  tam-tams of different sizes, temple blocks and wood blocks;

also – the invention of entirely new instruments.

Listening

Listen to part of John Cage's *Second Construction*, composed in 1940. This is for four percussionists
playing fourteen instruments – including tam-tam, sleigh bells, 'string piano' (see opposite), Indian
rattle, Japanese temple gong, and a 'water gong' (the player, having struck the gong, manoeuvres it
in and out of a tub of water). *Second Construction* presents a wide range of colourful timbres, catchy
rhythms, and varied musical textures.

The piano

There have been two main ways of exploring new timbres and effects from the piano – either by
treating it as a 'prepared' piano, or as a 'string piano'.

The 'prepared' piano
This was an idea invented in 1938 by John Cage. In many of his compositions involving the piano,
the instrument must be 'prepared' before the music can be performed. Nuts, bolts and screws, and
pieces of rubber and plastic, are fixed between, under, and over certain strings in the piano. Cage
always gives precise details about which strings are to be prepared, which objects are to be used,
and how far away from the dampers the objects should be fixed.

There are two main results of Cage's preparations. The timbres of the prepared strings are affected
according to the different kinds of material which are used – producing richly varied sonorities which
may suggest the sounds of Eastern bells, gongs, and drums. Also, wedging the materials between
the strings produces a tightening effect, which raises the pitch.

A further important effect is that, after being prepared, the separate strings of a note may not reach
the *same* tension – the result being two, or even three, sounds of quite different pitch played by a
single key.

Listening

Listen to an extract from Interlude 2 from Cage's *Sonatas and Interludes* for prepared piano,
composed during 1946–8.

The 'string piano'
This is the normal grand piano, with the music desk removed, and with the player(s) using the hands directly upon the strings of the instrument – the sustaining (right) pedal down. Sounds and techniques (many of them also possible on an upright piano) include:

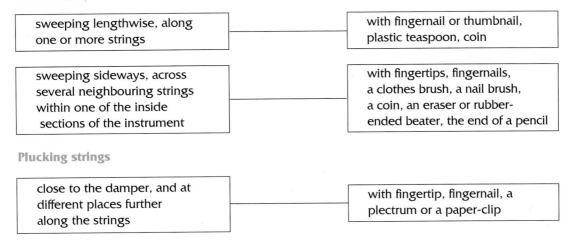

Glissandos

sweeping lengthwise, along one or more strings	with fingernail or thumbnail, plastic teaspoon, coin
sweeping sideways, across several neighbouring strings within one of the inside sections of the instrument	with fingertips, fingernails, a clothes brush, a nail brush, a coin, an eraser or rubber-ended beater, the end of a pencil

Plucking strings

close to the damper, and at different places further along the strings	with fingertip, fingernail, a plectrum or a paper-clip

Tapping or drumming on strings

with fingertips, fingernails, bunched fingertips, knuckles, clenched fist, rubber-ended beaters, drummer's wire brush, pencils, teaspoons, thimbles on fingertips

Muting

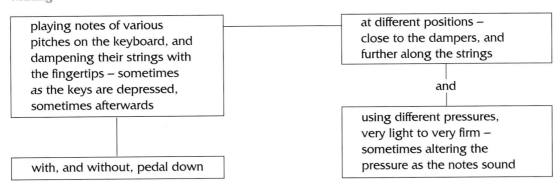

playing notes of various pitches on the keyboard, and dampening their strings with the fingertips – sometimes *as* the keys are depressed, sometimes afterwards	at different positions – close to the dampers, and further along the strings
	and
	using different pressures, very light to very firm – sometimes altering the pressure as the notes sound
with, and without, pedal down	

2.32

s t e n i n g

Listening

Listen to a short piece for 'string piano' by Vince Cross called *Night-Spell*. The opening sounds include: a glissando, sweeping lengthwise along strings with the finger nails; dampened, and undampened, strings plucked with a guitar plectrum; strings hit with the flat of the hand; another glissando; strings lightly beaten with a drummer's wire brush.

Then listen for other sounds and techniques, described above.

On the next page are notations for some of these instrumental sounds and techniques. Not all of them, however, have gained worldwide acceptance – some composers prefer to invent their own symbols.

String instruments

♯ or ♯   tremolo – rapid up-and-down movements with the bow

♪   strong pizzicato, so that the string slaps the fingerboard

⌣   pizzicato glissando – upwards

⌐   pizzicato glissando – downwards

⊤   bow on the strings between bridge and tailpiece

⍬   arpeggio on strings between bridge and tailpiece

⊢   play with bow actually on the tailpiece

Wind instruments

♦   blow without producing any instrumental tone

♯ or ♯   flutter-tongue (roll letter 'r' while blowing)

key-clicking or valve rattling, without tone

key-clicking, with pitched note

breathy sound

✛ and ○   (brass) closed and open positions of mute or other bell stopping

Piano (playing inside, on the strings)

⁺♩   pizzicato

⌣   pizzicato with fingernail

⊕   damp (stifle) vibrating string(s) with fingertip or hand

✛   dampen (mute) string with fingertip

sweep fingernail along length of string

glissando over the strings (with fingertip, with fingernail, or with some other agent)

Composing and Performing

Try one of these three composing ideas. Whichever you choose, take great care, *at all times*, not to damage an instrument in any way.

Whichever of these three ideas you try, give your finished piece a title which suits its mood and character. Organize a performance of your piece and make a recording of it. Afterwards, listen back, and assess the effectiveness of your music.

Also, try notating a score for your piece (or part of it). Use any of the notations opposite which are suitable for the sounds you create – and/or invent others of your own. Add an explanatory key to your score, clearly explaining the notational symbols you have used. If necessary, also add any verbal instructions.

1   On your own, or with a partner, compose some music for 'string piano' – creating sounds by playing directly on the strings of the piano. Explore some of the sounds and techniques mentioned on page 127 – and also, perhaps, create some of your own.

   Experiment, trying:

   ● different registers in the piano's range – bass, middle, treble;
   ● different places along the strings – near to the dampers, and further away.

   Compare the differences in timbre and dynamics, according to:

   ● what 'agent' you use – for example, fingertips, fingernails, perhaps some other agent;
   ● how much force or pressure you use.

   When you have experimented with various sounds and techniques, select the ones you find most interesting. Then organize them into an effective order, to create a composition.

   Consider: contrasts of timbres, varied dynamics, repetition of sounds or patterns, durations of sounds, mood and atmosphere – and, perhaps, some use of silence (which may need the sustaining pedal to be raised, then lowered again).

2   On your own, or with others, compose a piece for 'prepared' piano. Decide which strings you will prepare – it would be best to restrict yourself to a few only (preparing a piano can take some time). Also decide which materials you will use. For example:

   ● erasers (india rubbers) wedged between the strings of some keys;
   ● screws or nails hanging loosely between strings;
   ● paper-clips hanging from strings;
   ● strips of rubber (perhaps cut from thick elastic bands) threaded through strings;
   ● nuts and bolts – large enough to fit firmly into place, but not so large that the strings are pushed sideways.

   Experiment by trying the various materials in different places along the strings, and judging the effectiveness of the results.

   Your piece for prepared piano could consist of sounds from prepared strings only, or a mixture of sounds making use of both prepared strings and normal strings.

3 Compose a piece for a solo instrument, or for two or more instruments, which mixes sounds and timbres which are 'normal' with other more unusual timbre effects. You could use some of those mentioned in this chapter – and perhaps also discover/create others of your own. It would be a good idea, though, to have in mind the player(s) who will perform your finished composition, and to make sure they are able to achieve all the sounds and effects that you want to include.

In creating your piece, consider:

- contrasts – in timbre, dynamics, and pitch;
- repetition – of certain sounds, musical ideas and patterns;
- changes – in mood, and pace (the speed of change in musical events).

Linked listening

Webern: the first of *Five Movements for Strings*, Opus 5 – colouristic string effects

Elisabeth Lutyens: opening of String Quartet No. 6 – colouristic string effects and expressive use of glissandos

Xenakis: *Syrmos* for 18 strings – *col legno* effects, and glissandos at different speeds (upwards, downwards, sometimes both simultaneously, sometimes parallel, sometimes col legno); *ST/4* for string quartet – glissandos, pizzicato glissando, *col legno*, tapping on instrument, tremolo *sul ponticello*, tremolo glissandos

George Crumb: *Black Angels* for electric string quartet (especially the first part, *Departure*, which includes 'Threnody I: Night of the electric insects', 'Sounds of bones and flutes', 'Lost bells', 'Devil-music', and 'Danse macabre') – the performers must also play other instruments such as gongs and maracas and also add vocal sounds of various kinds

Berio: *Sequenza VII* for solo oboe (against the note B sounding as a background drone throughout)

Xenakis: *Akrata* for sixteen wind instruments

Birtwistle: *Verses for Ensembles* for brass quintet, two woodwind quintets, and two percussion ensembles

Henze: Symphony No. 6 for two orchestras (especially the last five minutes or so) – many unusual timbre effects and techniques from a wide range of instruments, including piano, vibraphone, guitar with contact microphone, electric organ, marimba, violin with contact microphone, and varied percussion

Ligeti: *Atmosphères* for large orchestra, including 'string piano' – two performers sweeping across the strings with various objects

Varèse: *Ionisation* for thirteen percussion players playing 42 instruments plus two sirens (described in 'Enjoying Modern Music')

Stockhausen: *Zyklus* for solo percussionist

James Macmillan: *Veni, Veni, Emmanuel*, 'Concerto for Evelyn' (the percussionist, Evelyn Glennie) – this work, composed in 1992, is based upon the 15th-century advent hymn 'Veni, Veni, Emmanuel' and exploits a great variety of percussion instruments

Cage: other pieces from *Sonatas and Interludes*; Concerto for Prepared Piano and Chamber Orchestra; *Amores* – two solos for prepared piano, framing two trios for percussion

Cowell: pieces for 'string piano', such as *The Banshee, Aeolian Harp, Sinister Resonances*

George Crumb: *Makrokosmos* Books I and II – each consisting of twelve pieces for amplified piano, played both 'normally' (from the keys) and as a 'string piano' (directly on the strings)

Penderecki: the second of *Three Miniatures* for violin and piano – the pianist depresses the sustaining pedal, but plays no notes; instead, loud violin notes excite the piano strings to vibrate in sympathy (Try a similar idea yourself?)

Stockhausen: *Mixtur*, for five orchestral groups and live electronics – sine-wave generators and ring modulators (described in 'Enjoying Modern Music'); *Mantra*, for two pianists (each also playing wood block and a set of antique cymbals) and live electronics – two ring modulators

Tim Souster: *The Transistor Radio of St Narcissus*, for flugelhorn, pre-recorded tape, and live electronics using digital transposition and digital delay

André Previn: third movement from Concerto for Guitar and Orchestra plus electric guitar, electric bass guitar and drum kit

Glenn Miller's recording of *Tuxedo Junction* – trombone players opening and closing plunger mutes

Duke Ellington: *Black and Tan Fantasy* (see page 58) – muted brass effects such as plunger mute and 'growl' tone; also, *The Mooche*

The Jimi Hendrix Experience: *Voodoo Chile* – guitar fuzz-tone, distortion and wah-wah effects

Songs by **Madonna** with computer backing – e.g. *Justify My Love* and *La Isla Bonita*

A Year 11 art student's 'bark study', created from hand-made paper and pulp, polyvinyl acetate, dyes, pastel and paint

CHAPTER 17

Words and music

Read this poem by the Irish poet, Moira O'Neill. Sea wrack is seaweed, growing where it becomes exposed by the tide.

Sea Wrack

The wrack was dark an' shiny where it floated in the sea,
There was no one in the brown boat but only him an' me;
Him to cut the sea wrack, me to mind the boat,
An' not a word between us the hours we were afloat.
  The wet wrack,
  The sea wrack,
  The wrack was hard to cut.

We laid it on the grey rocks to wither in the sun,
An' what should call my lad then, to sail from Cushendun?
With a low moon, a full tide, a swell upon the deep,
Him to sail the old boat, me to fall asleep.
  The dry wrack,
  The sea wrack,
  The wrack was dead so soon.

There's a fire low upon the rocks to burn the wrack to kelp,
There's a boat gone down upon the Moyle, an' sorra* one to help!
Him beneath the salt sea, me upon the shore,
By sunlight or moonlight we'll lift the wrack no more.
  The dark wrack,
  The sea wrack,
  The wrack may drift ashore.

- What is the overall mood of this poem?
- What story does it tell?
- If you were to set these words to music to make a song, what tempo would you choose – slow, moderate, or fast?
- How would you treat the dynamics? For example, are there any particular places where you would make your music very quiet, or very loud, or use a crescendo?
- At which lines, do you think, does the climax of the poem occur?

Listening

'Sea Wrack' has been set to music as a song for solo voice and piano by the Irish composer and conductor, Sir Hamilton Harty. Listen to the song – and compare Harty's ideas with your own. Do you agree with the tempo, mood, and dynamics of the music? (In this recording, *Sea Wrack* is sung by a mezzo-soprano – see the chart of voices on the opposite page.)

(* 'no one around to help')

Listen to *Sea Wrack* again.

1   At which line in the poem does the style of the accompaniment first change?

2   Which two lines does Harty take to be the climax of the poem? (Do you agree?)

3   What happens in the music at this point?

Types of voices

This chart gives the names which are used to describe both the range and the timbre (tone-quality) of different types of voices. For each voice, the average range is given. (Music for tenor voice is generally written in the treble clef, one octave higher than the actual sounds.)

Women's voices

soprano   mezzo-soprano   alto, or contralto

Men's voices

countertenor,   tenor   baritone   bass
male alto

Boys' and girls' voices

treble   alto

Choirs

A choir (or chorus) is a group of singers in which there are several performers per part.

A choir of 'mixed' voices includes sopranos, altos (contraltos), tenors, and basses – S. A. T. B. for short.

A female choir includes two group of sopranos and one or two groups of altos.

A male choir may consist of men's voices only, or of boys' and men's voices – trebles, altos, tenors, and basses.

Solo voices can be combined to sing:
a duet (for two voices),
a trio (three),
a quartet (four),
a quintet (five),
a sextet (six).

When setting words to music, composers often use an interesting musical device called **word-painting**. This means selecting certain words in the text and 'painting' or illustrating them in the music, in ways which vividly bring out their special meaning. The effect of word-painting may be heard in the instrumental accompaniment as well as (or instead of) the vocal part of the music.

Listening

Listen to *Midnight's Bell* from Britten's *Nocturne*. Britten sets this poem by Thomas Middleton for tenor voice, solo horn, and string orchestra. In this song there are many examples of word-painting, in both the voice part and the horn part. Alongside the lines of the poem, below, are the ways in which the horn-player (Barry Tuckwell in this recording) must vary his sounds to suggest midnight's bell, dog, nightingale, owl, raven, cricket, mouse, and cat.

Tenor voice	**Solo horn**
Midnight's bell goes ting, ting, ting, ting, ting,	(normal, open tone)
Then dogs do howl, and not a bird does sing	
But the nightingale, and she cries twit, twit, twit, twit, twit;	muted
Owls then on every bough do sit;	open
Ravens croak on chimneys' tops;	stopped, *sforzando*
The cricket in the chamber hops;	stopped, + flutter-tonguing
The nibbling mouse is not asleep,	
But he goes peep, peep, peep, peep, peep, peep,	muted, *pp*
And the cats cry mew, mew, mew, mew,	nasal
And still the cats cry mew, mew, mew, mew, mew, mew.	

(*Muted* – the player inserts a pear-shaped or cone-shaped mute into the bell of the horn. *Stopped* – the player inserts the right hand deep into the bell. *Flutter-tonguing* – while blowing, the player rolls the letter 'r'.)

Composing

Make your own setting of words to music. Here are some guidelines to follow.

- First, choose a text from those given on pages 136 and 137.
- Read the words *aloud*, so that you can appreciate the sounds – and especially the rhythms and accents – of the words.
- Write the words out. Decide which words and syllables are accented, and mark them in some way. For example:

   The sóunds of músic flóating on the mídnight aír,

● Think of rhythms and rhythmic patterns which will match the natural rhythms and accents of the words you have chosen, and also the mood. Accented syllables should coincide with accented notes. Unaccented syllables should occur on weaker beats, or between beats.

● Now add pitch to your rhythm to create a melodic line. Your melody should match the mood of the words. Think especially of contour – the curve, or rise-and-fall, of your melody. But always keep the range of the singer's voice in mind.

   You may find now that there are places where you want to adjust or change your rhythm. And there may be instances where you feel that it would be more effective to set a certain word or syllable to several notes, instead of just one.

   Look for really important words which you could treat in some special way – perhaps opportunities for *word-painting*.

   Also consider using melodic repetition, varied repetition, and sequence. Words, phrases, or whole lines can be repeated.

● Write out your melody – with the notes (and any rests) well spaced out. Then write the words, in a straight line, below the notes. Take care to write each syllable *exactly* below the note to which it belongs.

   Put hyphens between syllables of the same word (as at (a) in the music below).

   If you give more than one note to a syllable, write the syllable under the first note, and join all the notes belonging to it with a curved line (as at (b) below).

   If a single-syllable word has more than one note, draw a low line continuing as far as the end of the last note (as at (c) below), and join the notes with a curved line.

● Add expression markings to your music. Write all these *above* the stave so that they are not confused with the text.

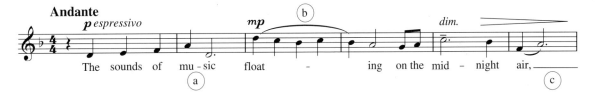

● You may think it good to add an instrumental accompaniment or backing. If so, consider whether it would be effective to have an introduction, a coda, and perhaps an instrumental interlude.

Performing

When you have finished your song, perform it – if necessary, asking others to help you. Make a recording, and afterwards listen to it, and discuss it.

Spring, the sweet spring, is the year's pleasant king;
Then blooms each thing, then maids dance in a ring,
Cold doth not sting, the pretty birds do sing:
Cuckoo, jug-jug, pu-we, to-whitta-woo!

'Spring' by Thomas Nash

Darkness lies before me now,
Black evil waits its turn.
We shall not let it conquer us –
Use the power, make it burn!

Dragon's breath and goblin's glare
Pursue me through the night.
Escape the evil Sorcerer –
Blind him with the shield of light!

Glen Tavener

How sweet the moonlight sleeps upon this bank!
Here will we sit, and let the sounds of music
Creep in our ears: soft stillness and the night
Become the touches of sweet harmony.

'The Merchant of Venice', Act V Scene 1,
by Shakespeare

My heart rests near the cool fountain.
(Bind it with your threads,
spider of oblivion.)

My awakened heart tells of its loves.
(Spider of silence,
weave your mystery.)

'Dream', by Federico García Lorca

You will hear the beat of a horse's feet
And the swish of a skirt in the dew,
Steadily cantering through
The misty solitudes,
As though they perfectly knew
The old lost road through the woods...
But there is no road through the woods.

'The Way through the Woods', by Kipling

Don't the moon look lonesome shinin' through the trees?
Oh, don't the moon look lonesome shinin' through the trees?
Don't yo' house look lonesome when your baby packs up to leave?

Traditional

The sun has gone down, and the sky it looks red,
And down on my pillow where I lay my head
I lift up my eyes for to see those stars shine,
And the thought of my true love still runs in my mind.

Folk, traditional

Ben Battle was a soldier bold,
And used to war's alarms:
But a cannon-ball took off his legs,
So he laid down his arms!

'Faithless Nelly Gray', by Thomas Hood

About, about, in reel and rout
The death-fires danced at night;
The water, like a witch's oils,
Burnt green, and blue and white.

'The Rime of the Ancient Mariner', by Coleridge

Now the great winds shoreward blow;
Now the salt tides seaward flow;
Now the wild white horses play,
Champ and chafe and toss in the spray.

'The Forsaken Merman', by Matthew Arnold

'Twas brillig, and the slithy toves
Did gyre and gimble in the wabe;
All mimsy were the borogoves,
And the mome raths outgrabe.

'Through the Looking-Glass', by Lewis Carroll

Awake! for Morning in the Bowl of Night
Has flung the Stone that puts the Stars to Flight
And lo! the Hunter of the East has caught
The Sultan's Turret in a Noose of Light...

And when Thyself with shining Foot shall pass
Among the Guests Star-scattered on the Grass,
And in thy joyous Errand reach the Spot
Where I made one – turn down an empty Glass.

'The Rubáiyát of Omar Khayyám', translated by FitzGerald

Listening

Investigate a song called *White* by the rock group, Conquest. First, read through the words of the song (printed below). Which of the words are in some way connected with water?

White   (Cross/Haggett/Hodges)

Introduction   X   (Instrumental)

Verse 1   X   Rain in my heart, tired waters collect,
Spill from my eyes the streams of regret,
The rivers of life flow through my veins,
My tortured body, my careless pain.

Chorus   Y   White horses of the sea,
White horses carry me,
Cascading visions I see,
The fountains of life have betrayed me.

Verse 2   X   The shouts of emotion that no one can hear,
The poisoned orchid has flowered with fear,
A journey so long it may never end,
The wild white waters I've come to defend.

Chorus   Y   White horses of the sea *(etc.)*

Interlude   Z   (Instrumental)

Chorus   Y   White horses of the sea *(etc.)*

Coda   Z   (Instrumental)

[John Haggett – vocals, Simon Cross – guitars, Pete Hodges – bass guitar and keyboards, Russell Heal – keyboards, Simon Sharman – drums]

The music of *White* is based upon the repetition of short chord progressions. Play each of these:

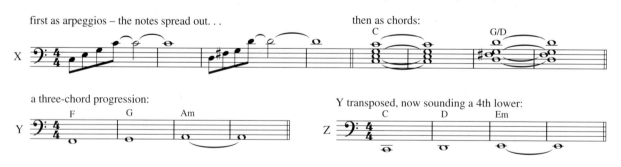

Listen to the song, first following the structure and the words. Then listen once or twice more, answering these questions:

1   Do you think that the words and music in this song match each other in mood? (Give a reason for your answer.)

2   How many times is the three-chord progression, Y, played during the chorus?

3   In the interlude, which of the following does the guitarist play?

arpeggios   chords   a melody in notes moving by step

A great many songs are composed by setting music to words written beforehand.

In other songs, the music is composed first, and then the words written to match.

White was a group composition, in which 'the words and music were written hand in hand'.

First, the words were written for verse 1, and then the chord progression decided – which, in turn, suggested the tune.

Next, the chorus music (chord progression + tune) was composed, and then the words were added – keeping in mind the inclusion of 'water images'.

Then the structure was finalized. Words were written for a second verse, and it was decided that there should be an instrumental introduction, interlude, and coda (the coda, in fact, was mainly improvised, over the chord progression).

Composing

On your own, or joining with others, compose a song, in any style, for which you write both the music *and* the words. You could write the words first, or compose the music first, or compose words and music 'hand in hand'.

Linked listening

Other, varied examples of word-setting

Elizabethan madrigals, including examples of word-painting – such as *All Creatures Now Are Merry-minded* by Bennet, *As Vesta Was from Latmos Hill Descending* by Weelkes, *Sweet Suffolk Owl* by Vautor

Purcell: recitative – *Thy Hand, Belinda*, and *Dido's Lament** from the opera *Dido and Aeneas*

Schubert: *The Erlking*, and *Death and the Maiden* (both included in 'Musical Forms: Listening Scores')

Vaughan Williams: *Serenade to Music* – setting lines from Act V Scene 1 of Shakespeare's play 'The Merchant of Venice' (beginning 'How sweet the moonlight sleeps upon this bank') for sixteen solo voices and orchestra

Constant Lambert: *The Rio Grande*, for piano, mixed chorus and orchestra (with large percussion section)

Tippett: *A Child of Our Time* (Part 1*), for soprano, alto, tenor and bass soloists, chorus and orchestra (Tippett sets his own words)

Britten: *Now the Great Bear and the Pleiades** from Act 1 of the opera *Peter Grimes*; *Spring Symphony* – which includes a setting of Nash's poem 'Spring'; *Winter Words* – setting poems by Thomas Hardy

Berio: *Cries of London*; and *Circles* – setting poems by e. e. cummings for soprano, harp, and two percussionists

Judith Weir: *Scotch Minstrelsy*, songs for tenor and piano

The Moody Blues: *Minstrel's Song* and *Melancholy Man* from the album *A Question of Balance*

The Beatles: *Lucy in the Sky with Diamonds* and *She's Leaving Home* from *Sgt Pepper's Lonely Hearts Club Band*

Genesis: *The Lady Lies* and *Follow You Follow Me* from *...And Then There Were Three...*

Led Zeppelin: *The Rain Song* and *Stairway to Heaven*

Records of folk, blues, reggae

* Described in 'Musical Forms' Book 3

CHAPTER 18

Making comparisons

Performing

Play or sing, several times, this Russian folk-tune called *Down in Yonder Field Stands a Birch Tree:*

1   How many phrases make up this tune?
2   How many bars are there in each phrase?
3   Is the tune in the major, or in the minor?

Listening

When you are really familiar with the folk-tune, listen to two extracts of music. Each is based on the tune, played three times:

> Balakirev: *Overture on Three Russian Themes*, composed in 1858;
> Tchaikovsky: Finale of Symphony No. 4 in F minor, composed in 1877.

Compare each extract with the original folk-tune, printed above.

1   Which of the two extracts most closely matches the original tune?
2   How is the other extract different? For instance, consider:

   - notes/pitches;
   - rhythm and phrases.

Listen to the two extracts again, and compare them.

3   To which instruments does each composer give the tune each time it is played?
4   Comment on any use of percussion instruments.
5   Which of the two extracts do you prefer? Why?

In 1874, another Russian composer, Musorgsky, composed a set of descriptive piano pieces called *Pictures at an Exhibition*. Each of the ten pieces describes a picture from an exhibition of paintings, drawings and sketches by a Russian artist called Victor Hartmann.

At various times, these piano pieces by Musorgsky have been orchestrated (arranged for full orchestra) by other musicians. The most famous version is by the French composer, Ravel. Another version is by the pianist and conductor, Vladimir Ashkenazy – born in Russia, but now of Icelandic nationality.

The music on the opposite page is the beginning of the second 'picture', *The Old Castle*, in Musorgsky's original version for piano. A troubadour sings outside a medieval castle on a warm summer night. There are two main musical ideas, marked X and Y on the music.

[Original key: G♯ minor]

Listening

First, play (or listen as someone else plays) Musorgsky's original version for piano. Suggest a word, or words, to describe the mood or atmosphere of this music.

Now listen, two or three times, to two orchestrations of this music:

first by Ravel;
then by Ashkenazy.

(Ravel, in his version, puts in an extra bar between bars 18 and 19.)

1   Each of these two orchestrators carefully chooses his timbres (instrumental tone-colours) for the two musical ideas, X and Y. Which of the following instruments does each orchestrator choose for X, and which for Y?

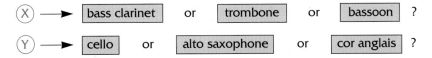

2   What kind of instruments does each orchestrator choose to play the accompaniment, or background, each time that Y is being played?

3   Which orchestrated version – Ravel's or Ashkenazy's – do you prefer? Why?

4   If you were orchestrating this piano music by Musorgsky, which instruments would you choose to play X and Y?

Listening

Now another comparison – two different settings of the same text. The two extracts you will hear are from

Verdi's *Requiem*;
Britten's *War Requiem*.

Each extract presents a picture of the terrifying Day of Judgement. Here are the Latin words, and their English meaning:

> Dies irae, dies illa,
> Solvet saeclum in favilla,
> Teste David cum Sibylla.
>
> Quantus tremor est futurus,
> Quando judex est venturus,
> Cuncta stricte discussurus!

> Day of wrath, that day when
> the ages shall dissolve in ashes,
> as David and the Sibyl foretell.
>
> What trembling there will be
> when the Judge shall appear
> to judge all things truly!

1   Listen to the extracts in turn, three or four times. As you compare the two extracts, note down any main differences between them – and also any similarities. For example, consider:

> use of voices   main instruments used   dynamics
>
> beat/pulse, rhythm   any other interesting features

2   Which of these two settings of the text do you think is the most effective? Give reasons for your choice.

Composing

1   Compose a melodic line, and make a recording of it played on two different instruments in turn (if necessary, asking others to help you). Then listen to the recording. On which of the two instruments does your melodic line sound most effective?

2   Select two lines of text (or write your own) and make two different settings of them. Organize a recording of the two settings. Then listen back, and compare them. Which best matches the mood of the text?

3   Make your own arrangement of the Russian folk-tune printed on page 140. Have the tune played at least three times – each time, in some way different. For instance: played on different instruments, with different kinds of accompaniment or backing – perhaps:

- a drone;
- an ostinato;
- using simple percussion;
- more complicated percussion;
- chords.

Performing

Perform your arrangement of the Russian folk-tune to the rest of your class (if necessary, asking others to help you).

As you listen to others, compare their arrangement with your own.

Linked listening

Make other musical comparisons, using some of the ideas suggested below. In each case, as you listen, note down the main differences between the two versions – and also any similarities. Which version do you prefer? Why?

- Two performances of the same piece – e.g. a movement from a Beethoven symphony, conducted by Toscanini and by Claudio Abbado; two recordings of a 20th-century piece, one of them conducted by the composer.

- Two performances of an aria from an opera – e.g. *La donna è mobile* from Verdi's opera *Rigoletto*, sung by Luciano Pavarotti and by Placido Domingo; *Un bel di* (One fine day) from Puccini's opera *Madama Butterfly*, sung by Kiri te Kanawa and by Montserrat Caballé.

- Two interpretations of a *Lied* (song) by Schubert – e.g. *The Erlking*, sung by Dietrich Fischer-Dieskau and by Sarah Walker or Brigitte Fassbaender.

- Two arrangements of the same folk-song – e.g. *Scarborough Fair, O Waly, Waly*.

- Two versions of the same jazz title – e.g. *St Louis Blues*, recorded by The Dixie Stompers (1927) and by Louis Armstrong (1929); *Stompin' at the Savoy*, recorded by Benny Goodman (see page 28) and by Charlie Christian (1941); *One O'Clock Jump*, recorded by Count Basie (1937) and by Sidney Bechet (1940).

- Two recordings of the same piece by the same jazz ensemble – e.g. recordings by Duke Ellington of his 'signature tune' *East St Louis Toodle-oo* (several in 1927–8, and others later).

- Two performances ('live', and studio) of a song by a rock group – e.g. *Child in Time* by Deep Purple ('live' on *24 Carat Purple*, or *Made in Japan*; studio on *Deep Purple in Rock*, or *Deepest Purple*).

- Two interpretations of a song by Lennon and McCartney – e.g. *Yesterday, A Hard Day's Night, The Fool on the Hill*.

- Compare an arrangement or orchestration of a piece with the original – e.g. Liszt's arrangement for piano (as No. 5 of his 'Paganini Studies') of Paganini's Caprice No. 9, *La chasse*, for solo violin; Ravel's orchestration of his own piano piece *Alborada del gracioso* (The jester's morning song from *Miroirs* (Mirrors); Percy Grainger's orchestration, including bells and gamelan-like percussion, of Ravel's piano piece *La vallée des cloches* (Valley of the bells) also from *Miroirs*.

- Also compare different recordings of a piece, recorded on different instruments – e.g. a dance from a Baroque orchestral suite, played on 'period' instruments and on 'modern' instruments; some of the 'Goldberg' Variations by Bach, played on harpsichord (e.g. Wanda Landowska or Scott Ross) and on piano (e.g. Glenn Gould or Daniel Barenboim); Elgar's *Pomp and Circumstance* March No. 1 performed in the original version for full orchestra, and in arrangements for brass band and for military band; Schoenberg's Theme and Variations – Opus 43a for symphonic band, Opus 43b arranged for orchestra.

Street Music

Bright day shall turn to night, my love,
And the rocks shall melt with the sun,
And the fire will freeze and be no more,
And the raging sea will burn.

(Anon)

Happily may I walk.
Happily, with abundant showers,
 may I walk.
Happily, with abundant flowers,
 may I walk.
Happily on the trail of pollen,
 may I walk

Happily may I walk.
May it be beautiful before me.
May it be beautiful behind me.
May it be beautiful below me.
May it be beautiful all around me
In beauty it is finished.

Navajo (North American Indian)
'Night Chant'

The Chinese and Japanese ideograms for the word 'sounds'

CHAPTER 19

Rhythm (2)

Listening

Listen to two extracts from the last movement of Mozart's Serenade No. 12 in C minor, K388. Mozart scores this serenade ('evening music') for an ensemble of eight wind instruments: two horns, two oboes, two clarinets, and two bassoons. The last movement is structured as a theme and eight variations.

First listen to the theme, which is in **binary form** – the music is built up in two sections, A and B, with each section repeated. The theme is played by the oboes and bassoons only. The time signature $\frac{2}{4}$ indicates that there are two crotchet beats to each bar.

THEME

The second extract is Variation 2, played by the first oboe, clarinets and bassoons. In this variation, Mozart alters the theme so that it now fits into $\frac{6}{8}$ time, like this:

VARIATION 2

Mozart's theme is in **simple time**. Time (or metre) refers to the number of beats to a bar, and their value. In simple time, each beat is a simple, plain note (that is, not a dotted note) which is divisible into *halves*. The theme is in $\frac{2}{4}$ time (simple duple time). There are two crotchet beats to each bar, and each beat may be divided into two quavers:

Listen to the theme again. As the music is played, softly tap or clap the beat – and at the same time, think or quietly say '**1** and **2** and **1** and **2** and . . .':

tap or clap: 1   2   1   2

$\frac{2}{4}$

think or say: 1 & 2 &   1 & 2 &   (and so on. . .)

The music of Variation 2 is in **compound time**. In compound time, each beat is a *dotted* note, which is divisible into *thirds*. In this case, the time signature is $\frac{6}{8}$ (compound duple time). There are two dotted crotchet beats to each bar, and each beat may be divided into three quavers:

$\frac{6}{8}$ ♩. ♩. | = | ♪♪♪ ♪♪♪ |

    1   2   1 & a 2 & a

Listen to Variation 2 again. Softly tap or clap the beat – and at the same time, think or quietly say '**1** and a **2** and a **1** and a **2** and a . . .':

tap or clap: 1   2   1   2

$\frac{6}{8}$

think or say: 1 & a   2 & a   1 & a   2 & a   (and so on. . .)

Performing

Play or sing this old French dance-song called *L'autre jour en voulant danser* (The other day as I was dancing).

What is unusual about the way this melody ends?

Composing

Clap or tap these rhythms in $\frac{6}{8}$ time:

(1) $\frac{6}{8}$

(2) $\frac{6}{8}$

The melody of *L'autre jour en voulant danser* is in $\frac{2}{4}$ time (simple duple time). Compose a variation on the melody which transforms it into $\frac{6}{8}$ time (compound duple time). In your $\frac{6}{8}$ version sometimes use the ♪♪♪ rhythm – but you may find that occasionally using ♪ 𝄽 ♪ enhances the lilting $\frac{6}{8}$ dance-rhythm.

Here is a chart showing most time signatures, giving the number of beats to each bar (central column) and the note-value of each beat.

Simple time			Number of beats to each bar	Compound time		
Note-value of each beat				*Note-value of each beat*		
𝅗𝅥	♩	♪		𝅗𝅥.	♩.	♪.
2/2 or 𝄵	2/4	2/8	**2** (duple)	6/4	6/8	6/16
3/2	3/4	3/8	**3** (triple)	9/4	9/8	9/16
4/2	4/4 or 𝄴	4/8	**4** (quadruple)	12/4	12/8	12/16

Listening

Listen to some of these pieces in compound time. As the music is played, count the beat, and listen for how the beat divides into three. Music in compound time often has a swaying or lilting rhythm if the tempo is slow or moderate, and often a skipping or jigging rhythm if the tempo is swift.

6/8
Elvis Presley: *Can't Help Falling in Love*
Irish jig: *The Irish Washerwoman*

9/8
Wagner: *The Ride of the Valkyries*
Bridge: *Sir Roger de Coverley*, Christmas dance, for strings

12/8
Steiner: Title-music from the film 'A Summer Place'
Bach: Brandenburg Concerto No. 3, last movement

Composing

Compose a melody or a short piece in compound time – for example, in 6/8 time, or 9/8 time. When you have finished, write down your music, and include markings for tempo, dynamics and expression.

Make a recording of your music. Afterwards, listen to it, and assess the rhythmic and expressive effects of your music.

Listening

Listen now to Variation 3 from the last movement of Mozart's Serenade No. 12 in C minor. The music is in 2/4 time (simple duple time), and the melody is played by the second oboe, doubled an octave lower by the first bassoon:

VARIATION 3

In this variation, Mozart uses **syncopation**. This is a rhythmic effect in which the composer deliberately alters or disturbs the expected pattern of accents. Here, Mozart gives the accompanying instruments staccato notes which always fall on the beat – but, except in two of the sixteen bars, the notes of the melody occur *off* the beat.

Listen to Variation 3 again. Softly tap the beat, and you should find that only two melody notes actually coincide with your tapping. All the others are delayed one quaver after the beat.

Here are some ways of creating syncopation. (Sometimes, two or more of these ways are combined.)

1   By placing an accented note or chord on a weak beat. For instance: in $\frac{3}{4}$ time, on beat 2; in $\frac{4}{4}$ time, on beat 2 or beat 4.
Example: Scherzo from Symphony No. 4 in D minor by Schumann.

2   By placing an accented note or chord *between* beats (*off* the beat, or on a subdivision of the beat).
Example: *Dance of the Cygnets* from *Swan Lake* by Tchaikovsky.

3   By placing a rest on a strong beat – especially the first beat of a bar.
Example: *Waltz* from *Masquerade Suite* by Khatchaturian. First, a twelve-bar introduction, strongly establishing the waltz rhythm. Then:

4   By tying (holding on) over a strong beat.
Example: *Maple Leaf Rag* by Scott Joplin. This is a typical piano **rag** – a syncopated tune in the right hand rides above a steady beat in the left hand. (See the music printed on the next page.)

Listening

Listen, two or three times, to the beginning of the third movement of Tchaikovsky's Piano Concerto No. 1 in B♭ minor, following the music printed below. Tchaikovsky bases his main theme on the syncopated rhythm of a Ukrainian folk-dance.

Which of the ways of creating syncopation described on page 149 are included in this music?

Allegro con fuoco

Composing

Compose some music which includes syncopation. Use one or more of the ways of creating syncopation described on page 149.

  Perform your music, and make a recording of it.

The chart on page 148 shows time signatures with 2, 3, and 4 beats to a bar. Music can be composed in more than four beats to a bar – but each bar is then made up of some combination of two and three. For example, $\frac{5}{4}$ or $\frac{5}{8}$ time (quintuple metre) may be counted as 2 + 3, or as 3 + 2, depending upon where the secondary accent falls:

$$\|: \quad \underline{1} \quad 2 \quad \underline{3} \quad 4 \quad 5 \quad :\| \qquad \text{or} \qquad \|: \quad \underline{1} \quad 2 \quad 3 \quad \underline{4} \quad 5 \quad :\|$$

And $\frac{7}{4}$ or $\frac{7}{8}$ time may be counted as 3 + 2 + 2, or as 2 + 2 + 3:

$$\|: \underline{1} \quad 2 \quad 3 \quad \underline{4} \quad 5 \quad \underline{6} \quad 7 :\| \qquad \text{or} \qquad \|: \underline{1} \quad 2 \quad \underline{3} \quad 4 \quad \underline{5} \quad 6 \quad 7 :\|$$

Steadily count each of the above repeating rhythms. Clap on each beat which is accented. Times (metres) such as these, made up of a mixture of groups of two and three, are often described as **irregular**.

Listening

Listen to three pieces of music from three different countries.

1   A folk-dance from Romania, called *Dangle Dance*. The music is in $\frac{5}{8}$ time and is accented like this:

$$\frac{5}{8} \|: \quad \text{♩} \quad \text{♩} \quad \text{♩} \quad \text{♪} \quad ↷ \quad :\|$$
    <u>1</u>   2   3   <u>4</u>   5

   After a while, another quaver is added to each bar – changing the metre to $\frac{3}{4}$. See if you can spot when this happens.

2   A popular Greek folk-tune called *Glare pu petas?* (Where are you flying to, seagull?). The main instrument you will hear is a *bouzouki* – a long-necked lute with metal strings plucked with a plectrum. This music is in $\frac{7}{8}$ time and is accented like this:

$$\frac{7}{8} \|: \quad \text{♩} \quad \text{♩} \quad \text{♩} \quad \text{♩} \quad \text{♩} \quad \text{♩} \quad :\|$$
    <u>1</u>   2   3   <u>4</u>   5   <u>6</u>   7

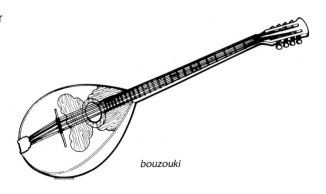

As you listen, count the beats – and, after the three-bar introduction (played by the solo *bouzouki*), also clap the beats which are accented. (You will find that the plucked bass notes coincide with your claps.)

bouzouki

3   Here is a challenge! This piece is *South of the Border Dance*, from Bulgaria. The music is in $\frac{11}{8}$ time (eleven quavers to each bar).

   (a)   Before listening, clap the rhythm below, repeating it steadily without pause, at a moderate tempo. Each bar in this $\frac{11}{8}$ rhythm divides into three parts.

      1 2 1   2   **1** 2 3   **1** 2 1   2

   When you can clap this fluently, perform it at a faster tempo.

   (b)   Now listen to *South of the Border Dance*. The tempo is probably faster than you expect! But see if you can recognize the $\frac{11}{8}$ rhythm you have been clapping. Notice how the '1 2 3' in the second part of each bar gives a lift to the music, and causes it to bounce onto the third part.

   (c)   After a while, the music changes to a simpler time or metre. Which of these time signatures matches what you hear?

      $\frac{2}{4}$ $\frac{3}{4}$ $\frac{4}{4}$ $\frac{5}{4}$

   (d)   Spot when the $\frac{11}{8}$ rhythm returns.

   (e)   Afterwards, listen to the music again – and work out dance steps and movements to match the rhythms, and mood, of this dance.

Composing and Performing

Compose some music in an irregular time or metre – such as 5 beats to a bar, or 7 beats to a bar. Write down your music. Then perform it, and record it.

Another interesting and often exciting rhythmic effect is called **polyrhythm**. Two or more different (and sometimes complex) rhythms or metres are heard going along at the same time, creating a 'rhythmic counterpoint'. Sometimes, the rhythms vigorously conflict, and pull against each other.

Listening

Listen to some drum music from the Polynesian island of Tahiti. Three players are involved: 1 and 2 play *tō'ere* – slit drums (see the photo, opposite); 3 plays a *tariparau* – a double-headed barrel drum.
   Read through the following plan of the music. Then follow it as you listen, two or three times, to the recording.

1	Player 1, alone, plays a rhythmic pattern.
2	Player 2 joins in with the same pattern.
3	As Player 3 joins in, all three play different, contrasting patterns, building up a complex texture of rhythmic counterpoint – a *polyrhythmic* texture.
4	A brief pause (silence).
5	Player 1 sets off again, with another rhythmic pattern.
6	Player 2 joins in with the same pattern.
7	Player 3 joins in and all play contrasting rhythmic patterns, again building up a polyrhythmic texture.
8	The music ends abruptly – on the recording you will hear a voice giving the cue (signal) to end.

tō'ere *(slit drum), Tahiti*

Now try this...

Form a group of three musicians, each with a percussion instrument.

1   Create a piece of polyrhythmic music which follows the plan (printed at the bottom of page 152) of the Tahitian drum music.

You may like to try, straight off, an on-the-spot improvisation – if so, record your music from the start.

Or you could experiment and work out some rhythmic patterns first, and then try out the piece (recording it as you do so).

In either case, make sure your individual rhythms contrast – perhaps even strongly conflict against each other – and also make use of *syncopation*. Also decide how one of you will give the cue for the brief pause (at stage 4 on the plan), and the abrupt, clean end of the piece.

2   Try another version of the piece (recording it as before) – but this time, swap parts. You could try each of the three parts in a different time or metre. For example: player 1 in $\frac{3}{4}$ time, player 2 in $\frac{4}{4}$ time, and player 3 in $\frac{5}{4}$ time. The downbeats (strong first beat of each bar) will rarely coincide – and this makes for the most exciting and truly polyrhythmic effect.

3   Afterwards, listen to your recordings and compare them.

Listening

Investigate a jazz piece called *Struttin' with Some Barbecue*, recorded in 1927 by Louis Armstrong's Hot Five. This jazz ensemble is made up of three melody instruments, and a rhythm section (banjo and piano).

Struttin' with Some Barbecue includes several interesting examples of syncopation. The piece is based on a repeating chord pattern, which is 32 bars long, and in two sections – A and B:

1 A♭ ——————————	2	3	4	5 ————————→	6 A♭⁷	7 F⁷ ————	8 ————————→
9 B♭m⁷	10 E♭⁷ Edim	11 Fm ———	12	13 ————→ B♭⁷ —————	14	15 ————→ E♭⁷	16 ————————→

17 A♭ ——————————	18	19	20 ————————→	21 ————→ A♭⁷	22 ————→	23 D♭ ———	24 ————————→
25 D♭	26 D♭m	27 A♭	28 F⁷	29 B♭m	30 E♭⁷	31 A♭	32 A♭ (E♭⁷)

Each playing of this chord pattern is called a **chorus**. A chorus may feature improvisation by one or more solo players, or collective improvisation by the whole ensemble. Sometimes there is a short **break** – a single player improvises without any accompaniment.

Here is an outline plan of *Struttin' with Some Barbecue*:

Introduction:	12 bars, with Armstrong leading
Chorus 1:	ensemble, in collective improvisation, but with Armstrong still to the fore; this chorus ends with a two-bar break
Chorus 2:	bars 1–16 (A) – solo, ending with a two-bar break;
	bars 17–32 (B) – solo, ending with a two-bar break (throughout B, banjo strums each beat, piano plays a chord on each off-beat)
Chorus 3:	solo – with banjo and piano playing on off-beats only; they drop out for the syncopated bars 31–32, which are repeated
Chorus 4:	bars 1–16 – collective improvisation, ending with a two-bar break
	bars 17–24 – collective improvisation
	bars 25–32 – without rhythm section
Coda:	short

1   Listen to *Struttin' with Some Barbecue*, following the plan above, and listening for syncopation.

2   Listen again. In choruses 2 and 3, clap softly on beats 1 and 3 *only* of the $\frac{4}{4}$ metre. In chorus 3 you should find that banjo and piano only coincide with your claps at bars 15 and 31. (In spite of Armstrong's clear articulation in this brilliant improvisation, you may find the persistent syncopation of the accompaniment disorientating – and imagine that the bar-lines have shifted!)

3   Listen once or twice more, answering these questions:
   (a)   Which instrument plays the break at the end of chorus 1?
   (b)   Identify the three instruments which, in turn, play the solo improvisations in chorus 2 (A, then B) and chorus 3.
   (c)   Describe the music of the short coda.

Linked listening

Syncopation

Byrd: *Though Amaryllis Dance in Green* (madrigal for five voices)

Mozart: Symphony No. 38 in D ('Prague') – opening of last movement

Dvořák: Symphony No. 7 in D minor – Scherzo (in $\frac{6}{4}$ time)

Lalo: *Symphonie espagnole* – opening of last movement

Arditi: song, *Il bacio* (The kiss)

Stravinsky: *The Infernal Dance of King Kastchei* from *The Firebird*

Copland: *Buckaroo Holiday* from *Rodeo*

Gershwin: *I Got Plenty o' Nuttin'* from *Porgy and Bess*; *I Got Rhythm*; *Fascinating Rhythm*

Antonio Carlos Jobim: *The Girl from Ipanema*

The Beatles: *Eleanor Rigby*

Bernstein: *The Dance at the Gym* (*Blues, Mambo, Maria Cha Cha, Jump*) from *West Side Story*

Moncayo: *Huapango* – based on Mexican dance rhythms and tunes

Other examples from jazz, blues, ragtime, reggae (reggae features accents on beats 2 and 4, occasional rests on beats 1 and 3)

Irregular times or metres

Tchaikovsky: *Pathétique* Symphony, second movement ($\frac{5}{4}$ time)

Holst: *Mars* ($\frac{5}{4}$ time) from the suite *The Planets*

Samuel Barber: Piano Concerto, last movement (in $\frac{5}{8}$ throughout)

Bartók: No. 2 (in $\frac{7}{8}$ time) and No. 3 (in $\frac{5}{8}$ time) of *Six Dances in Bulgarian Rhythm* from *Mikrokosmos* Book 6

Falla: *Pantomime* ($\frac{7}{8}$) from *El amor brujo*

Revueltas: *Sensemaya* (beginning in $\frac{7}{8}$ time)

Britten: the round *Old Joe Has Gone Fishing* ($\frac{7}{4}$ time) from Act 1 of *Peter Grimes* ('Musical Forms' Book 3)

Bernstein: Psalm 100, 'Make a Joyful Noise...' ($\frac{7}{4}$) from *Chichester Psalms*

Elizabeth Maconchy: String Quartet No. 5, last movement – this begins in $\frac{7}{8}$ time, and changes to $\frac{5}{8}$ for the pizzicato section at 1' 15"; the final bars are in $\frac{7}{4}$ time

Polyrhythm

Examples from African polyrhythmic drumming and dances, and examples from modern jazz

Stravinsky: *Procession of the Sage* from *The Rite of Spring* – bass drum, kettledrums, güiro and tam-tam each play a different rhythm from that of the tuba ostinato; also, the second bransle, *Bransle Gay* from *Agon* – ostinato on castanets continuously in $\frac{3}{8}$ time while other instruments vary between $\frac{3}{8}$, $\frac{5}{16}$ and $\frac{7}{16}$

Ives: *Putnam's Camp* from *Three Places in New England* – at around 2' 35" (letter H in the score) a quiet march on woodwind and strings, then brass and percussion and piano join in with a different march at a faster pace, so that three bars of the first march equal four bars of the second; at around 4' 42" (letter O) a trumpet plays *The British Grenadiers* in $\frac{4}{4}$, while percussion plays in $\frac{2}{4}$ and $\frac{3}{4}$ and the rest of the orchestra plays in $\frac{3}{8}$

CHAPTER 20

Chords and clusters

Play this series of intervals:

Each of these intervals has its own distinctive character, or 'flavour'. In some of them, the two sounds agree with each other, and produce a **consonance**. In others, the two sounds disagree, or clash, and produce a **dissonance**.

Play the intervals again. Which of them are most *dissonant* – produce the most striking clash?

Now play this series of chords, ranging from consonant to more dissonant:

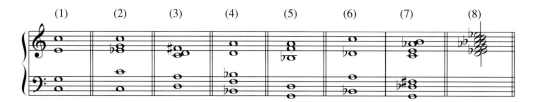

The first two chords are **concords**. In each chord, all the notes agree. Technically, all the other chords are **discords**. Each contains four or more notes of different letter-names, and certain notes disagree, or clash. This creates restlessness or tension, to a greater or lesser degree.

Chords (1) and (2), above, are built from the triads of C major and C minor. Each is named according to the kind of 3rd it contains. Both contain a perfect 5th.

Stacking another 3rd on top of a triad creates a seventh chord – so called because the added note makes an interval of a 7th above the root. It might be a minor 7th, or a major 7th. A minor 7th is a tone less than an octave; a major 7th is a semitone less than an octave.

Chords (3) and (4) in the series above are seventh chords. Which has a major seventh, and which has a minor seventh?

Other, more complicated chords, with a fuller sound, can be created by stacking on yet more 3rds:

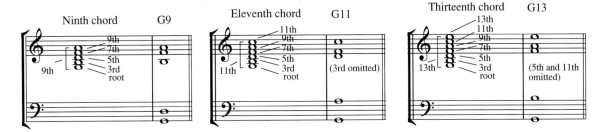

The mood and flavour of these chords can be changed by raising or lowering certain notes (but not the root) by a semitone. This means bringing in *chromatic* notes – notes from outside the key – and the chord becomes a **chromatic chord**. Play these versions of a ninth chord on G. Compare the difference in mood and flavour – and the amount of dissonance. Can you devise any more versions of the chord?

Play (or listen as someone else plays) the beginning of Grieg's piano piece, *In My Native Country*. Grieg uses several seventh chords, and also ninth chords and thirteenth chords. Four of these have been marked above the music. See if you can find (hear) others.

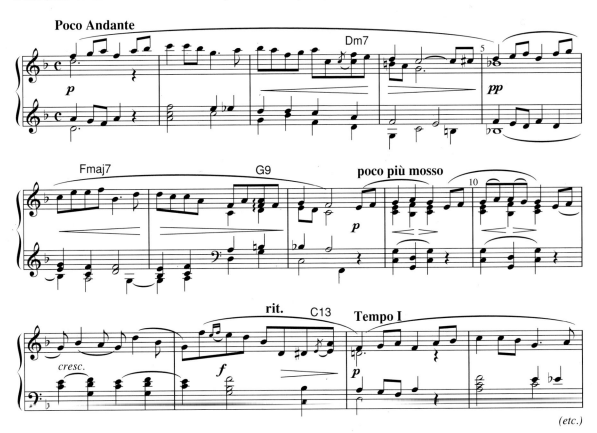

(etc.)

Performing

Below are two possible chord schemes, harmonizing the American folk-tune *Black is the Colour of My True Love's Hair*. The first version uses only triads. The second includes seventh chords and one ninth chord.

On your own, or with one or more other musicians, play each version. Which of them do you prefer, and why?

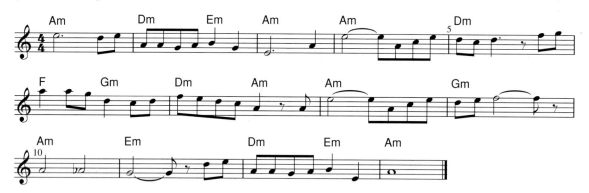

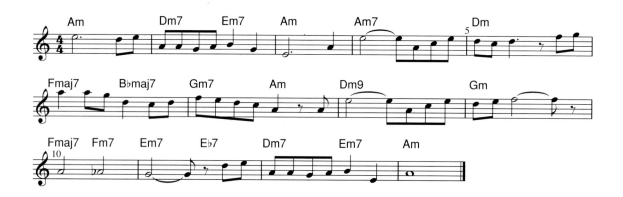

Arranging

Here is a German folk-tune called *Ein Jäger aus Kurpfalz* (A hunter from Kurpfalz). It can be harmonized with six chords: F, B♭, C, D minor, G minor, A minor. Add these at appropriate places (a few suggestions are given). Use some seventh chords – and there are two more opportunities for a G minor ninth chord (one not too far from the end).

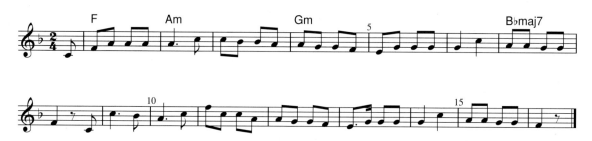

The last chord in the series printed on page 156 is a **note-cluster**, or **cluster chord**. This is made up of several neighbouring notes, closely bunched together. Whereas all the other chords mentioned so far are built from major and minor 3rds, note-clusters are built from major and/or minor 2nds.

The number of notes can range from just a few (say three or four) to a great many. Note-clusters are particularly effective in music for keyboard. Depending upon the number of notes included, they may be played with the fingers, or the fist, or the flat of the hand, or the forearm, or with some object such as a length of wood or a cardboard cylinder. (In Lutosławski's orchestral work called *Venetian Games*, the two piano duettists must each use two cardboard cylinders of such a length that, between them, they press down every note on the keyboard.)

Note-clusters may be notated by writing out the notes in full (as on page 156), or in a variety of other ways. Here are some examples:

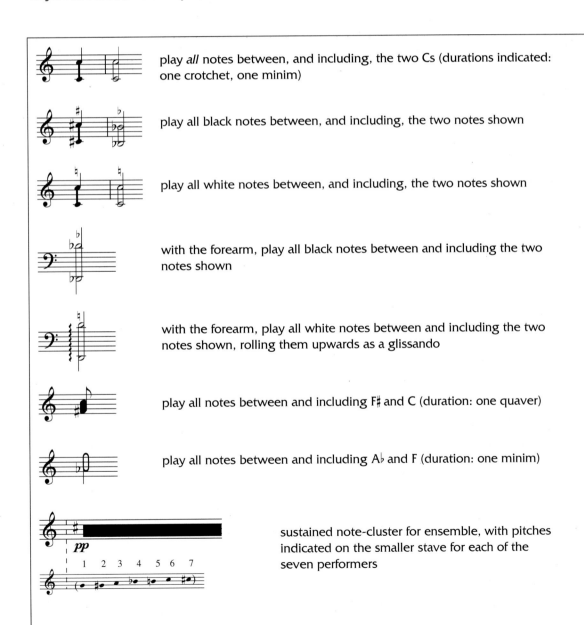

play *all* notes between, and including, the two Cs (durations indicated: one crotchet, one minim)

play all black notes between, and including, the two notes shown

play all white notes between, and including, the two notes shown

with the forearm, play all black notes between and including the two notes shown

with the forearm, play all white notes between and including the two notes shown, rolling them upwards as a glissando

play all notes between and including F♯ and C (duration: one quaver)

play all notes between and including A♭ and F (duration: one minim)

sustained note-cluster for ensemble, with pitches indicated on the smaller stave for each of the seven performers

Listening

Investigate a piece by Jim Northfield called *Accusations* for acoustic and electronic keyboards. The music includes various kinds of note-cluster.

Here is a score of the beginning of the piece. Follow it, as you listen.

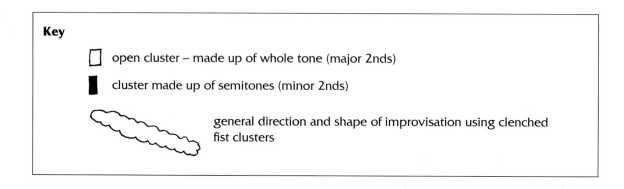

Key

⬜ open cluster – made up of whole tone (major 2nds)

⬛ cluster made up of semitones (minor 2nds)

general direction and shape of improvisation using clenched fist clusters

Composing

1 Compose a melodic line. Then using, for example, guitar or keyboard, experiment, and add chords to it. Aim to bring in some seventh chords, and perhaps an occasional ninth chord.

2 On your own, or with others, create a composition which makes a feature of note-clusters. Use entirely your own ideas, or make use of any of the suggestions below. In either case, consider using contrasts of:

● dynamics;

● pitch;

● texture or density (few notes, many notes);

● and also, perhaps, timbres.

Your note-clusters could be sustained (the notes held on); or short, staccato and jabbing. Or perhaps both, to provide contrasts, like this example:

A note-cluster might be built up in stages, expanding or thickening as it is sounding, perhaps with players starting together on a unison and gradually spreading outwards, or with players coming in one at a time – perhaps with increasing dynamics:

Similarly, a note-cluster might contract, or thin out – with the sounds closing inwards to a unison, or with players gradually dropping out to leave one player only.

Also, consider sliding a note-cluster up, or down, in pitch. For example:

Decide whether you want to create your music entirely out of note-clusters of various kinds, or to combine them with other musical events – such as melodic lines, rhythmic figures.

Performing

When you have completed your composition featuring note-clusters, organize a performance of it, and record it. Afterwards, listen back, and assess the effectiveness of your music. Judge whether you can improve or refine it in any way.

Linked listening

Seventh, ninth, eleventh and thirteenth chords

Bruckner: first movement from Symphony No. 7 in E – a climax (at around $4\frac{1}{4}$ minutes) is structured by building up a thirteenth chord, F♯ A♯ C♯ E G♯ B D♯

Debussy: *Hommage à Rameau* from *Images* Book 1 – contrasting textures, beginning unison, then rich harmonies including seventh, ninth, and thirteenth chords

Satie: *Sarabande* No. 1 – many seventh and ninth chords (in bars 1–8, only one triad)

Jerome Kern: *All the Things You Are* – chords with minor 7th, major 7th, and ninth chords and eleventh chords (this piece has often been used as a basis for jazz improvisation)

John Coltrane (jazz saxophonist and composer): *Naima* – seventh, ninth and thirteenth chords expressively used to create a mood (Coltrane is quoted as saying: 'I am obsessed with chords.')

Led Zeppelin: *The Rain Song* – in G major, and with the frequent, haunting progression of a ninth chord on A♭ (A♭ C E♭ G♭ B♭) sliding down to a ninth chord on G (G B D F A), always followed by a spread G minor ninth chord (G B♭ D F A)

Note-clusters

Cowell: *Exultation* – alternate passages for left and right forearms playing two-octave note-clusters; *Advertisement* – small note-clusters played with the fists; *Tiger* – note-clusters sometimes played with the flat of the hand, sometimes the forearms, sometimes the fists

Bartók: *Melody in the Mist* from *Mikrokosmos* Book 4 – the mist is suggested by four-note clusters

Lutosławski: *Jeux Vénitiens* (Venetian games), movements 2 and 4 (described in 'Enjoying Modern Music')

Penderecki: *Threnody: To the Victims of Hiroshima* for 52 strings – note-clusters sustained, and expanding and/or contracting (recorded example: 2.26)

Ligeti: *Volumina* for organ; *Lux aeterna* for 16 voices; *Atmosphères* for orchestra

Xenakis: *Evryali* for piano (the title can mean 'vast, tempestuous sea' or 'beautiful Medusa with her hair of writhing snakes')

CHAPTER 21

Music as background to words

Several composers have written pieces where the music provides an accompaniment or background to words which are spoken, rather than sung. The words may be:

- recited in strict rhythm, keeping precise musical time; or
- spoken 'in free time', and with the natural rhythms of speech.

The music (which may be instrumental and/or vocal) may alternate with sections of the spoken text, perhaps with some overlapping. Or there may be a more continuous musical background – in which case, music and words must be very carefully synchronized. Usually, the music closely follows and reflects the mood and meaning of the text.

Read this poem, written by Edith Sitwell in 1921.

Tango

When Don Pasquito arrived at the seaside
Where the donkey's hide tide brayed, he
Saw the bandito Joe in a black cape
Whose slack shape waved like the sea—
Thetis wrote a treatise noting wheat is silver like the sea;
The lovely cheat is sweet as foam; Erotis notices that she
Will
Steal
The
Wheat-King's luggage, like Babel
Before the League of Nations grew—
So Joe put the luggage and the label
In the pocket of Flo the kangaroo.
Through trees like rich hotels that bode
Of dreamless ease fled she,
Carrying the load and goading the road
Through the marine scene to the sea.
'Don Pasquito, the road is eloping
With your luggage, though heavy and large;
You must follow and leave your moping
Bride to my guidance and charge!'

When Don Pasquito returned from the road's end,
Where vanilla-coloured ladies ride
From Sevilla, his mantilla'd bride and young friend
Were forgetting their mentor and guide.
For the lady and her friend from Le Touquet
In the very shady trees upon the sand
Were plucking a white satin bouquet
Of foam, while the sand's brassy band
Blared in the wind. Don Pasquito
Hid where the leaves drip with sweet . . .
But a word stung him like a mosquito
For what they hear, they repeat!

Listening

'Tango' is one of 21 poems included in William Walton's *Façade* – 'an Entertainment with poems by Edith Sitwell, for speaking voice and six instrumentalists'. Walton composed accompanying music to express the mood, character and rhythms of each poem.

When *Façade* was first performed, in 1923, many listeners were puzzled by the poems, thinking that they made no sense at all. But Edith Sitwell explained that they are abstract poems, patterns in sound – concerned with the *sound* of words rather their meaning, and aiming for intriguing effects of rhyme and rhythm.

Read 'Tango' again. Then follow the words as you listen to the recording from *Façade* (Walton changes the title to *Tango-Pasodoble*).

Now listen to a rather different piece – *The Incantation of the Witch of Endor* from *King David* by the Swiss composer, Honegger.

Saul, fearing an attack from the Philistine army, goes in disguise to the Witch of Endor. He tells her to summon up the spirit of the dead Samuel 'out of the earth' so that he can ask for his advice.

The words are spoken in French. First read the translation, below. Then follow the words as you listen to the recording.

The Witch of Endor:
Om. Om. By the fire, and by water,
by spoken word, and puff of wind,
even by sight and by sound,
snap the root which binds you fast,
smash the seal which holds the urn.
Appear.   Appear.

Om. Om. I call you, and command:
leave the night-black pit of Sheol,
go into the temple of nine doors.
Appear.   Appear.   Appear!

Give your blood!
Smell of blood, scent of life!
I tear you from the earth!
Appear!   Appear!

The fire burns – the fire below.
It enters me, transfixes me
to the marrow – mysterious fire.
Agni, Agni, like red-hot iron.
Rise, rise, appear – **Aaah!**
You have tricked me! You are Saul!

The Ghost of Samuel: *Why have you disturbed me,*
called me from my grave?

Listen again to these two pieces, by Walton and by Honegger, following the words. Then listen again – but this time, concentrate on the musical accompaniment or background.

Listen especially:

● for ways in which the music reflects the mood of the words;

● for changes in tempo, in dynamics, and in timbre.

Listen once more to *Tango-Pasodoble* by Walton, and *The Incantation of the Witch of Endor* by Honegger. As you listen to each, note down which of the following items match the piece you are hearing. (An item may match one piece only, or both – or neither.)

> (a)   the composer allows the speaker to use the natural rhythms of speech, pacing the text according to mood and meaning
>
> (b)   the composer gives precise rhythms to the words, so that the speaker must keep strict musical time
>
> (c)   there are sudden changes of tempo
>
> (d)   an accelerando is used, to build to the climax
>
> (e)   snare drum and cymbals are used in the accompaniment
>
> (f)   certain points in the text are highlighted by flickering, high notes on a harp
>
> (g)   alto saxophone and castanets are used to give mood and 'colour'
>
> (h)   the climax is marked by a crash on tam-tam (gong)
>
> (i)   the texture of the music remains the same throughout
>
> (j)   the music forms a continuous background
>
> (k)   at times, words are spoken with no music in the background

Which of these two pieces do you prefer? Why?

Later, Walton arranged eleven pieces from Façade *for orchestra, and some of these were eventually made into a ballet. Here, Sherilyn Kennedy and Joseph Cipolla dance the* Tango-Pasodoble

Composing

Form a group (if possible, a fairly large one) and compose some music to provide a background to spoken words. Two texts are printed on the next three pages. You could choose one of these, or find other words which you think are more suitable – or write some of your own.

The words of **'Island Catastrophe'** originated in the work of a group of fifteen-year-olds, all of whom were studying both music and drama.

In Part 1, the Islanders describe their environment and their way of life. And in Part 2, the catastrophe occurs. (Originally, this was to be a typhoon; later, it was decided that it should be the sudden eruption of a volcano, killing one of the community.)

All members of the group, once they had become very familiar with the words, discussed what music would be suitable. A cue-sheet was written, with ideas such as:

- three chords, alternating, peaceful and serene – later, a folk-like melody sung gently above them
- a soft repeating ostinato begins
- a drone, low and resonant...
- a mysterious combination of sounds, quickly growing louder
- an explosion of percussive sounds
- vicious discords, note-clusters, *staccato*, in irregular rhythms
- a muffled drum-beat, repeated rhythmically...

At certain points, the speakers also acted – for example, the 'daily tasks', and when the catastrophe occurred.

Groups A, B and C (see the text opposite) could be single voices if you are too few in number to make groups.

'The Daniel Jazz' (1920) is an early example of a genre which came to be known as 'jazz poetry'. Vachel Lindsay intended poems such as this one to be spoken aloud, very rhythmically.

If you choose this piece, discuss and decide whether all the words should be spoken by solo (single) voices – or whether some of them should be spoken by several voices.

Whichever words you select (or choose to write):

- decide *when* the music should be heard (now and then, *during* the speaking, enhancing and illustrating the spoken words? or *between* lines or sections of the text? or more or less continually throughout?)
- choose suitable instruments and timbres (the background music could be instrumental, or vocal, or both);
- consider whether it would be effective, at certain points, to include any miming, action, movement, dance;
- make your music reflect the mood (and any changes of mood) and also the pace and dynamics of the spoken words;
- at any times when speech and music occur simultaneously, be careful that the music does not drown the voices.

Island Catastrophe

Part 1	**All**	Here, where the sun pours its life-giving warmth,
		Where the wind bends the sapling, the surf beats the shore;
		Here, where the rain, according to season,
		Quickens the earth and gives life to the seed –
		Here ... is our home.
		Our lives are conditioned by natural forces:
		The sun's revolution, the rhythm of seasons,
		The ceaseless tread of the tide ...
	One voice	Here, with the first fresh breeze of the morning,
		Our daily tasks begin:
	Group A	Weaving bright cloths that our bodies be masked
		From the fierce, harsh glare of the sun;
	Group B	Mending our nets, again to be filled
		With the silver store of the sea;
	Group C	Planting and sowing the rich, brown earth
		That we may harvest its fruits.

   *   *   *   *   *   *   *   *   *

Part 2   *[The Catastrophe]*

   *   *   *   *   *   *   *   *   *

Part 3	**Group A**	Chaos ...
	Group B	Destruction ...
	Group C	Utter negation ...
	Group B	Nothing ...
	Group A	Nothing ...
	Group C	Nothing remains ...
	All	Nothing remains, for Nature is cruel.
	One voice	And Man?
	All	Man must endure!
	All	This is the natural course of the universe:
		Birth must be followed by Death.
	Girls	What then can we hope for?
	Boys	What shall we live for?
	One voice	When loss, like an open sore, festers in the memory
		And shrouds the heart in grief?
	All	Once more must we strive to regain what is lost,
		For the sun shall still offer its life-giving warmth,
		The rain shall still fall, according to season,
		To quicken the earth and give life to the seed.
		Man shall survive the fierce onslaughts of Nature
		For after dark Winter ... comes Spring.
		Man shall survive!

The Daniel Jazz, by Vachel Lindsay

Darius the Mede was a king and a wonder.
His eye was proud, and his voice was thunder.
He kept bad lions in a monstrous den.
He fed up the lions on Christian men.

Daniel was the chief hired man of the land.
He stirred up the jazz in the palace band.
He whitewashed the cellar. He shovelled in the coal.
And Daniel kept a-praying: 'Lord save my soul.'
Daniel kept a-praying: 'Lord save my soul.'
Daniel kept a-praying: 'Lord save my soul.'

Daniel was the butler, swagger and swell.
He ran up the stairs. He answered the bell.
And *he* would let in whoever came a-calling –
Saints so holy, scamps so appalling.
'Old man Ahab leaves his card.
Elisha and the bears are a-waiting in the yard.
Here comes Pharoah and his snakes a-calling.
Here come Cain and his wife a-calling.
Shadrach, Meshach and Abednego for tea.
Here comes Jonah and the whale – and the *Sea!*
Here comes St Peter and his fishing pole.
Here comes Judas and his silver a-calling.
Here comes old Beelzebub a-calling.'
And Daniel kept a-praying: 'Lord save my soul.'
Daniel kept a-praying: 'Lord save my soul.'
Daniel kept a-praying: 'Lord save my soul.'

His sweetheart and his mother were Christian and meek.
They washed and ironed for Darius every week.
On Thursday he met them at the door –
Paid them as usual, but acted sore.
He said: 'Your Daniel's a dead little pigeon.
He's a good hard worker, but he talks religion.'
And he showed them Daniel in the lions' cage.
Daniel standing quietly, the lions in a rage.

His good old mother cried: 'Lord save him.'
And Daniel's tender sweetheart cried: 'Lord save him.'
And she was a golden lily in the dew.
And she was as sweet as an apple on the tree.
And she was as fine as a melon in the cornfield,
Gliding and lovely as a ship on the sea,
Gliding and lovely as a ship on the sea.
And she prayed to the Lord: 'Send Gabriel. Send Gabriel.'

King Darius said to the lions:
'Bite Daniel. Bite Daniel.
Bite him. Bite him. Bite him!'

Thus roared the lions:
'We want Daniel, Daniel, Daniel.
We want Daniel, Daniel, Daniel.'

And Daniel did not frown. Daniel did not cry.
He kept on looking at the sky.
And the Lord said to Gabriel:
'Go chain the lions down.
Go chain the lions down.
Go chain the lions down.'

And Gabriel chained the lions,
And Gabriel chained the lions,
And Gabriel chained the lions.
And Daniel got out of the den,
And Daniel got out of the den,
And Daniel got out of the den.
And Darius said: 'You're a Christian child.'
Darius said: 'You're a Christian child.'
Darius said: 'You're a Christian child.'
And gave him his job again,
And gave him his job again,
And gave him his job again.

Performing

When you have organized your piece, practise it. You may find it best for speakers and musicians to try things over, and polish them up, separately at first – and then join together later.

When you are satisfied, make a recording of the whole thing. Then listen to it, and discuss it. (If at all possible – especially if your piece includes any miming, action, movement, dance – make a video recording of it.)

Linked listening

More examples of music as background to words

Beethoven: Act 2 Scene 1, the grave-digging scene, from the opera *Fidelio*

Weber: The Incantation Scene in the Wolf's Glen (end of Act 2) of *Der Freischütz* ('Musical Forms' Book 3)

Debussy: *Chansons de Bilitis* (1900–1; completed by Boulez, 1954), 'music to accompany readings of poems' for speaker, two flutes, two harps, and celesta

Schoenberg: *A Survivor from Warsaw* for narrator, male chorus (in unison) and orchestra

Stravinsky: *Babel; Persephone; The Soldier's Tale* – in the full version (e.g. in the recording featuring Ian McKellen as the Narrator, Vanessa Redgrave as the Devil, and Sting as the Soldier)

Honegger: scenes from *Jeanne d'Arc au bûcher* (Joan of Arc at the stake) – recorded in English translation

Copland: *Lincoln Portrait* for narrator and orchestra – there is a recording with Katharine Hepburn as narrator; another with Henry Fonda

Walton: other pieces from *Façade*

Mátyás Seiber: *Three Fragments from 'A Portrait of the Artist as a Young Man'* (words by James Joyce) for speaker, mixed chorus, and orchestra – try especially the second Fragment

Records of rapping, current and past

Michael Jackson's recording of *Thriller* – at the end, words (described as 'rap') spoken by Vincent Price (of horror movie fame)

Scene – a desert heath

<u>Thunder and lightning. Enter three witches.</u>

1st Witch:	When shall we three meet again?
	In thunder, lightning, or in rain?
2nd Witch:	When the hurlyburly's done,
	When the battle's lost and won.
3rd Witch:	That will be ere the set of sun.
1st Witch:	Where the place?
2nd Witch:	Upon the heath.
3rd Witch:	There to meet with Macbeth.
1st Witch:	I come, Graymalkin.
2nd Witch:	Paddock calls.
3rd Witch:	Anon.
All three:	Fair is foul, and foul is fair:
	Hover through the fog and filthy air.

<u>(The Witches vanish.)</u>

CHAPTER 22

Tension – and release

One of the most exciting, and often dramatic, effects in music is a gradual building up of tension. This is usually achieved by a *combination* of musical elements and devices. Here are some of them:

Ways of building up tension and excitement

crescendo – the music gradually increases in loudness, intensity and power

accelerando – getting faster

a rising in pitch

an increase in dissonance

a thickening of sound and texture – more notes, more instruments, increasing activity

rhythmic urgency

strident (if not harsh) timbres – e.g. muted brass; instruments or voices, *fortissimo*, at the highest extreme of their range

repetitions of a rhythmic and/or melodic idea

a roll on drum or cymbal or tam-tam; agitated *tremolo* strings

the use of a pedal point (see page 222)

Listening

Here is a diagrammatic score of part of Samuel Barber's *Adagio for String Orchestra*. It shows the main melodic lines and, later, block chords.

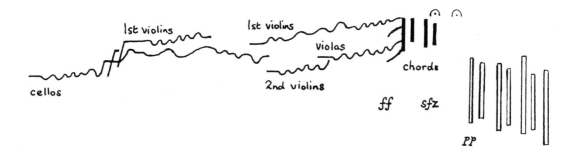

Barber marks the beginning of this extract 'with increasing intensity'. As the music gradually grows louder, it also moves higher in pitch. The tension builds, and the climax is reached with four *fortissimo* chords. Much of the intensity of this climax is due to the fact that all the instruments – particularly the violas and cellos – are playing very loudly in the highest part of their range.

Listen to the extract, following the diagrammatic score.

Tension may be built up over a fairly short period of time – or it may take considerably longer.

There are various ways in which a composer may release, or relax, the tension which has been built up. Some of these are given in the box below. In some cases, though, tension and excitement build up towards the end of a piece or movement, and the release may come only in the final chord(s), or in the silence after the music ends.

Ways in which tension may be released or relaxed

diminuendo – getting softer

rallentando – getting slower

a sinking in pitch, or immediate drop in pitch

less dissonance, or total consonance

a thinning out of sound and texture – fewer notes, fewer instruments, less activity

a smoothing of the rhythm; lengthening of note-values

mellow, softer timbres

resolution of pedal point – e.g. from dominant to tonic

a sudden dramatic pause (silence) – followed by quieter music, often at a lower pitch

at the climax, sustained sounds which die away – or, fragmented sounds (the music 'disintegrates')

Listen again to the extract from *Adagio for String Orchestra*. In which ways does Barber release the tension after the climax?

Listen, two or three times, to another two extracts of music. In each case:

- how does the composer build up tension in the music?
- how is the tension released?

1   First the short, dramatic opening of the piece called *Montagues and Capulets*, from the Second Suite which Prokofiev arranged from his ballet, *Romeo and Juliet*.

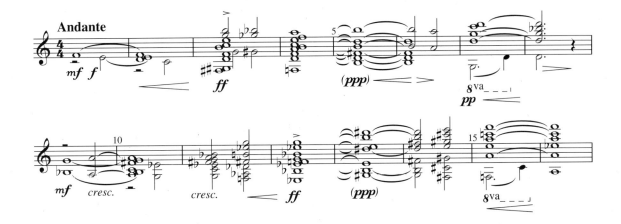

Listening

2   'The scene with the chiming clock' from Musorgsky's opera, *Boris Godunov*. This takes place in the Tsar's apartments in the Kremlin. Having arranged the murder of Prince Dmitri, the rightful heir to the throne, Boris Godunov has become Tsar of Russia. But feelings of guilt and fear are drawing him to the edge of madness.

Twice in this extract, Musorgsky builds up a sinister tension in the music – each time followed by a swift release. Listen for the ticking of the chiming clock, and for it to strike the hour. Then Boris imagines that the ghost of Dmitri, dripping with blood, is menacingly approaching him . . .

Composing

Imagine a scene from a film or play in which tension is built up to a powerful climax, and then released. On your own, or with other musicians, compose or improvise some background music to accompany the scene.

First, briefly write down what happens during the scene. Then decide how you will build up the tension in the music, and then release it. Use some of the ways mentioned in the boxes on pages 172 and 173 – and perhaps also discover other ways of your own.

Performing

When you have completed your music, and practised it, organize a performance.

As you listen to others performing their music, identify the ways which are being used:

● to build up the tension in the music;
● to release the tension.

The Bulgarian bass singer,
Boris Christoff, in the rôle of
Boris Godunov

Linked listening

As you listen to some of these pieces, decide *how* the composer is building up tension and excitement in the music.

Beethoven: fourth movement, 'Storm', from Symphony No. 6 (*Pastoral*)

Weber: The Incantation Scene, in the Wolf's Glen, from *Der Freischütz* (described in 'Musical Forms' Book 3)

Wagner: from the final scene of *Das Rheingold* – Donner summons up a storm (beginning of the extract in 'Musical Forms' Book 3)

Bizet: *Farandole* from *L'Arlésienne* ('Enjoying Music' Book 1)

Saint-Saëns: *Danse macabre* – the last two minutes or so ('Enjoying Music' Book 1)

Tchaikovsky: *Scène*, from the Suite from *Swan Lake*

Dvořák: *The Water Goblin* – extract 3 on page 116 of this book, and extracts 5 and 6 on page 117

Grieg: *In the Hall of the Mountain King* from *Peer Gynt*

Puccini: the final scene from *Tosca* ('Musical forms' Book 3)

Dukas: *The Sorcerer's Apprentice* – the last three-and-a-half minutes ('Enjoying Music' Book 3)

Nielsen: Symphony No. 5, the last quarter of the first movement – the composer instructs the snare drum player to improvise freely 'as if at all costs to stop the progress of the music'

Rachmaninov: Variation 18 from *Rhapsody on a Theme of Paganini*; slow movement from Symphony No. 2 – beginning to build at around 6′, climax at around 7′ 20″, and release

Holst: *Mars* (the final two minutes or so) from *The Planets*

Ives: *The Housatonic at Stockbridge* (the last half of the piece) from *Three Places in New England*

Ravel: *Boléro* – a building up of tension and excitement over a period of about eighteen minutes ('Enjoying Music' Book 2)

Respighi: *The Pines of the Appian Way* from *The Pines of Rome* ('Enjoying Music' Book 3)

Honegger: *The Incantation of the Witch of Endor* from *King David* (see page 164)

Shostakovich: first movement of Symphony No. 7 ('Leningrad') – beginning with the march tune ('Enjoying Music' Book 2, page 57, points 6 to 9)

Britten: Fugue from *The Young Person's Guide to the Orchestra* ('Enjoying Music' Book 3)

Webern: Numbers 1, 2 and 4 of *Six Pieces for Orchestra*, Opus 6; 2 and 5 of *Five Pieces for Orchestra*, Opus 10 ('Enjoying Modern Music')

Berg: third movement of Violin Concerto ('Enjoying Modern Music') – especially the last two minutes or so (Berg marks the climax *Höhepunkt*, 'high-point')

Penderecki: Stabat Mater – from around three-and-a-half minutes to the end ('Enjoying Modern Music', page 61, sections 4 to 6)

Russian folk-song: *Kalinka* (as sung by the Red Army Choir)

Deep Purple: *Child in Time*

Queen: *Bohemian Rhapsody*

Mike Oldfield: *Tubular Bells* – the last 8′ 24″ of side one

More musical devices

Play or sing, several times, this eight-note motive:

Listening

Bach uses this motive, or brief musical idea, to structure the first of his Fifteen Two-part Inventions for keyboard. Listen to this piece, following the music. (Bach intended it to be played on the harpsichord; in the recording on the CD, however, it is played on the piano.)

When Bach published his Two-part Inventions, he explained that his aim was 'to teach clear playing' and also 'good inventions' (good compositional ideas). Investigate the motive he uses to structure this first Invention. It begins with notes rising by step, then two falling 3rds, and then a leap upwards (which varies):

In the first two bars of the piece, this motive appears four times, alternately in the treble (right hand) and the bass (left hand) as shown by the first four brackets.

Then in bars 3 and 4, Bach turns the motive 'upside down'. Notes rising in the original version (above) now fall – and vice versa:

This musical device, of turning the contour of a melody upside down, is called **inversion.** The inversion may be exact – for example, a rising major 2nd becomes a falling major 2nd, a falling minor 3rd becomes a rising minor 3rd. Or it may be inexact – some intervals are altered, to achieve a desired musical effect.

Listen to the recording again. Spot other appearances of the motive – both in its original version, and in inversion. You will need to concentrate your listening on both parts, treble *and* bass, in this two-part contrapuntal texture. (There are, in fact, very few bars in which the motive is not heard.)

If possible, compare this performance of Bach's Invention No. 1 in C with one or more other versions. For instance:

- played on a harpsichord;
- sung by the Swingle Singers (on the album *Jazz Sebastian Bach*);
- performed by Jacques Loussier (on *Play Bach No. 3*).

Another interesting musical device is called **retrograde**, meaning 'going backwards'. This means taking a melody (or a phrase, or a whole section of music) and performing it backwards – beginning with the final note and ending with the first.

If the forwards version of the music is immediately followed by the backwards (retrograde) version, the result is a musical palindrome. The same idea can also occur in numbers and words:

2002   801,108   19.8.91   POP   MINIM   REVIVER   AOXOMOXOA*

(* title of The Grateful Dead's third album, 1969)

Performing

Perform this 'forwards-and-backwards' melody. At which point does the retrograde begin?

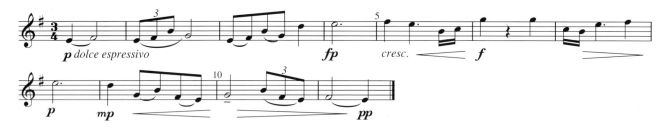

Not only the melodic line, but the entire musical texture may be presented in retrograde – as in the music opposite, by Haydn. He composed it as the third movement of his Symphony No. 47 in G (1772). A year later, he made this piano arrangement of it, and included it in his Piano Sonata in A (Hoboken No. 26; Landon No. 41).

The music is structured in **minuet and trio form**. In this musical form, the overall shape is ternary. But each section, the minuet and the trio, is in fact a complete binary or ternary design in itself:

A¹: Minuet	B: Trio (a contrast)	A²: Minuet (without repeats)
‖: a :‖: b(a) :‖	‖: c :‖: d(c) :‖	‖ a ‖ b(a) ‖

Investigate the music, opposite, of this Minuet and Trio by Haydn. Once the first part of the Minuet has been played twice, it is then played note for note backwards – in retrograde – to become the second part. And exactly the same thing happens in the Trio.

Imagine you are walking across this bridge. Having passed the mid-point, all its features now recur in reverse order (retrograde). The water reflects the bridge upside down (in inversion).

Play, or listen as someone else plays, this piano version of the piece.

Then listen to the recording on the cassette of Haydn's original orchestral version – in which you will hear slight differences.

Menuetto da capo

Which pairs of wind instruments are featured in the Trio? (They help the ear to recognize the music being played in reverse.)

A melodic line, or an entire musical texture, may be presented in **retrograde inversion** – backwards *and* upside down at the same time.

Performing

Play this simple melody. Then, in order to play it immediately in retrograde inversion, turn the page upside down!

Now join up with a partner, and perform this short two-part piece:

This short piece is an example of **canon** (from Greek, meaning 'rule'). A canon essentially relies upon the musical device called *imitation*. One vocal or instrumental part leads off with a melody. Then, shortly afterwards, a second part begins to perform the same melody. And so the 'rule' in a canon is that the second part imitates, note for note, the melody being given out by the leading part.

The imitating part may follow at a distance of half a bar, one bar, two bars, or at any other distance, according to the composer's choice. Other parts may also enter, in turn, with the same melody.

The second part may imitate the melody at the same pitch as the first (this is called *canon at the unison*). Or it may be an octave higher or lower (*canon at the octave*), a 4th higher or lower (*canon at the fourth*), a 5th higher or lower (*canon at the fifth*), or at any other interval – again according to the composer's choice.

You can find out about other kinds of canon on page 182.

Perform the canon again. Notice that, in the second part, the ending of the tune is adjusted so that both parts end up at the same time.

1   At what distance in time does the second part imitate the first in this canon?

2   Is the imitation at the unison, at the octave, at the 4th, or at the 5th?

Listening

Now listen, two or three times, to the opening of the last movement of César Franck's Violin Sonata in A – a famous example of canon.

This is a canon at the octave – the piano leads in playing a long, lyrical melody, imitated by the violin one octave higher (see the music, opposite).

When the printed music ends, continue listening. A little later, the canon returns.

1   Which instrument leads, and which instrument imitates?

2   At what distance in time does the second instrument imitate the first?

More musical devices

Other varieties of canon

(a) **canon by inversion** (or **contrary motion**): in this type of canon, the imitating part presents the melody in inversion (turned upside down).

(b) **retrograde canon**: the imitating part gives out the melody backwards – beginning with the final note and ending with the first. This is also called a **crab canon** (even though crabs move sideways rather than backwards!).

(c) **mirror canon** – this has two meanings: (1) a crab canon, or (2) a canon in which the imitating part presents the melody in retrograde (backwards) *and* in inversion (upside down) at the same time.

(d) **accompanied canon**: a canon accompanied by one or more other parts which do not share in imitating the melody.

(e) **infinite canon** or **perpetual canon**: in this kind of canon, as each part reaches the end of the melody it goes back to the beginning and starts all over again – until everyone agrees to stop. A **round** (such as *Frère Jacques*) is a simple type of infinite canon at the unison.

(f) **canon by augmentation**: the imitating part gives out the melody in longer note-values (usually twice as long).

(g) **canon by diminution**: the imitating part gives out the melody in shorter note-values (usually half as long).

(h) **double canon:** in this kind of canon, *two* melodies are given out at the same time by two parts, and imitated by another two parts – two canons, on two different melodies, going on at once.

Inversion, retrograde, retrograde inversion, and canon are important elements in 20th-century twelve-note serial music (see page 226).

Composing

Try one or more of these ideas. Whichever you choose, you will probably find that you need to experiment. At all times, use your ears. Listen carefully to the sounds you are creating, and judge their musical effectiveness – if necessary, altering, adjusting, and refining.

1   Compose a melodic line in which some fragments or phrases are repeated in inversion. The inversions could be exact – or inexact (but still recognizable as 'upside-down reflections').

2   Construct a melodic line which, when it reaches a certain point, retraces its steps in retrograde – note for note backwards.

3   Create a composition, for one or more performers, called *Reflections*. Build up your music by repeating some musical ideas in inversion, some in retrograde, and perhaps some in retrograde inversion (each of these devices being a kind of 'musical reflection').

4   (a)   Form a group of three musicians, each with a different percussion instrument. First play, together, this palindromic rhythm pattern:

Now perform the rhythm pattern in canon – as a 'rhythmic round'.
Players enter one by one, at one bar's distance, and then continue to repeat the pattern.

- Crisply emphasize the accents – but balance the overall dynamics;
- don't rush the semiquaver groups;
- decide when – and how – to end the piece.

(b)   Make a stereo recording of the piece, with the three performers placed left, centre and right, in relation to the microphones. Then listen back, and discuss the balance of dynamics, and the precision and articulation of the rhythm.

(c)   Now invent your own rhythm canon for three performers, based on a palindromic pattern.

5   (a)   With a partner – each of you using a keyboard – play this melody, which is the leading part in a short two-part canon:

Now add the imitating part to complete the canon. Experiment, and discover *when* the imitating part should begin (two bars after the leading part? perhaps after only one bar?), and on what *pitch* the imitating part should begin, to create what you think is the best effect. For example, try:

- at the unison (the same pitch as the leading part);
- an octave below;
- a 4th below, like this:

- a semitone below, like this:

(b)   Compose your own two-part canon, in any style you choose.

Performing

Whichever of these composing ideas you try, when you are satisfied with your music, organize a performance of it.

As you listen to others performing theirs, see if you can recognize when musical ideas are being presented in inversion, in retrograde, and in canon.

Which, do you think, is the most difficult for the ear to recognize – inversion, retrograde, or canon?

Linked listening

Examples of retrograde – musical palindromes

Guillaume de Machaut (14th century): *Ma fin est mon commencement* (My end is my beginning), rondeau, three voices – the upper part is the middle part's music backwards (in retrograde); the lower part is a palindrome: having reached mid-point in the music, the notes are then performed in reverse

Berg: second movement from Chamber Concerto for piano, violin, and thirteen wind instruments – retrograde begins at bar 361 (also, in the first movement, variation 2 is a retrograde version of the theme, 3 is inversion, and 4 is retrograde inversion)

Webern: second movement from Symphony, Opus 21 – theme and seven variations, each an eleven-bar-long palindrome (variations 1, 6 and 7 also involve canon)

Nono: *Incontri* for 24 instruments – the second half is the first half in strict retrograde

Examples of canon

Anon: *Sumer is icumen in*, circa 1240 (described in 'Enjoying Early Music')

Josquin des Prez: Fanfare, *Vive le Roy!* ('Enjoying Early Music'); *Agnus Dei III* from *Missa L'homme armé sexti toni* – the tenor's line is based on the 15th-century popular song 'The armed man', which the bass sings backwards at the same time, forming a retrograde canon; above, other canons are sung by two sopranos and two altos

Tallis: Canon ('Glory to Thee, My God, This Night')

Pachelbel: Canon – played by three violins in two-bar sections (in slowish $\frac{4}{4}$ time) above a two-bar ostinato bass

Bach: Chorale prelude *In dulci jubilo*, a double canon (in 'Musical Forms: Listening Scores'); *Sarabande* from Orchestral Suite No. 2 – accompanied canon at the fifth ('Musical Forms' Book 1); *Canones diversi* (differing canons) from *The Musical Offering* (No. 1, retrograde canon; No. 2, canon at the unison with an accompanying bass-line; No. 3, canon by inversion accompanied by a higher melodic line)

Mozart: Minuet and Trio from Serenade No. 12 in C minor (K388) – the Trio is a double canon by inversion, for oboe II and oboe I, and bassoon I and bassoon II

Beethoven: *Mir ist so wunderbar*, quartet, from *Fidelio* – the voices enter in the order: soprano I, soprano II, bass, tenor

Schumann: Canon in B minor, Opus 56 No. 5

Borodin: third movement, *Notturno*, from String Quartet No. 2 in D – the opening melody is later played in canon by cello and first violin, and then by first violin and second violin

Bizet: opening of the *Farandole* from *L'Arlésienne* Suite No. 2

Mahler: opening of third movement of Symphony No. 1 – canon based on *Frère Jacques* transformed into the minor

Schoenberg: *Am Scheideweg* (The parting of the ways), Opus 28 No. 1 – canon for mixed voices

Bartók: canons from *Mikrokosmos* – Book 1, pieces 28, 30, 31, 36; Book 2, piece 60

Stravinsky: *In Memoriam Dylan Thomas* for tenor, string quartet, and quartet of trombones

Webern: Five Canons, Opus 16, for soprano, clarinet and bass clarinet

Britten: *Old Joe Has Gone Fishing* from Act I of *Peter Grimes* (described in 'Musical Forms' Book 3); *This Little Babe* from *A Ceremony of Carols* for treble voices and harp – verse 1 is in unison, verse 2 is a two-part canon, verse 3 is a three-part canon

CHAPTER 24

Variations

Play these two versions of the beginning of a well-known tune 'in disguise'. Can you recognize and identify the original tune?

In this first version, the pitch of each note is exactly as in the original tune – but the *rhythm* is altered, and the *metre* has been changed from $\frac{3}{4}$ to $\frac{4}{4}$.

In this second version, the original tune is *decorated* by adding extra notes.
Here is a third version. How has the tune been changed this time?

Building up a whole composition by repeating a tune several times, but each time *varying* it (altering, or disguising it) in different ways, is known as **variation form**, or **theme and variations**. This is one of the oldest musical forms.

The theme itself may be in binary form or ternary form, and it is first presented in a fairly straightforward way. Here are some of the many ways in which a theme may be varied.

You can:

- change the rhythm of the theme, and/or the metre (the number of beats to a bar);
- change the tempo (speed);
- decorate the theme by adding extra notes and ornaments;
- change the harmonies;
- change the mode – from major key to minor key, or vice versa;
- add a counter-melody – a new tune, above or below the theme;
- take away some of the notes in the theme, keeping just the most important ones;
- turn the theme, or part of it, upside down (called inversion);
- 'hide' the theme by putting it down into the bass, or into an inner part of the musical texture;
- treat the theme, or part of it, by imitation, fugato or canon;
- make a noticeable change of timbre;
- omit the theme – but keep the harmony and/or the rhythm, so that there is a strong reminder of the theme.

Variations on a theme? Centre and top right are two of three paintings – 'Pope I', and 'Pope II' – by Francis Bacon based on an earlier portrait, 'Pope Innocent X' (on the left), by the 17th-century Spanish painter, Velasquez. Bacon's paintings in turn inspired Mark-Anthony Turnage to compose his orchestral work which he called Three Screaming Popes *(1989).*

Composing

Think of another well-known tune. Then, keeping the pitches of all the notes exactly the same, disguise the tune by altering the rhythm.

Perform your disguised tune to someone else. Can they identify the original tune?

Listening

Now investigate how Tchaikovsky writes some variations on a theme. The music is from the last movement of his Orchestral Suite No. 3 in G major.

Theme Tchaikovsky's theme is in ternary form (A¹ B A²), and is rather like a Russian folk-song. It is played quietly by the string section of the orchestra:

Listen to the theme two or three times, to fix it in your mind.

Variation 1 The theme is heard in the bass of the musical texture played by strings pizzicato. Woodwinds add a flowing counter-melody above the theme.

Variation 2 A change to a quicker tempo – and violins play a swift, decorated version of the theme:

Variation 3 A noticeable change of timbre – this variation is for flutes, clarinets and bassoons only. Flute plays the A sections of the theme; clarinet (in its low register) plays the B section.

Variation 4 A change to a minor key (B minor):

At bar 9 of this variation, violins bring in a new tune (but beginning with the same rhythm as bars 9 and 10 of the theme):

The pitches at the beginning of the new tune remind Tchaikovsky of the *Dies irae* (Day of wrath) – a plainchant from the *Mass for the Dead* – which is soon solemnly brought in by trombones and tuba:

Variation 5   A change of metre (to ¾ time) for a *fugato* – the same scrap of tune (the first few notes of the theme) is introduced by different groups of instruments, one after another:

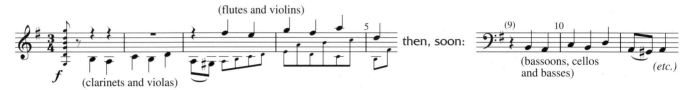

Later, listen for a fragment (from the beginning of section B) repeated at different pitches.

Variation 6   Another change of metre, as the theme is transformed into a whirling dance played by clarinets, bassoons, violas and cellos, accompanied by exciting stamping chords from the rest of the orchestra – now including snare drum.

Variation 7   Woodwind only – playing a version of the theme with the rhythms completely smoothed out, suggesting a Russian chant.

Variation 8   Against tremolo strings, a slow, very expressive and Russian-sounding version of the theme is sung by cor anglais, with its distinctive timbre.

Composing

Play or sing this English folk-tune, called *The Green Grass*

On your own, or with others, build up a set of variations on this folk-tune. You could base your variations on the whole tune, or on bars 1–8 only (as far as the first double bar).

Try any of the ways of making variations listed on page 185 – and perhaps discover other ways of your own. Write down your variations in any suitable way which will make sure you remember them.

Play your Theme and Variations. Are the variations arranged in the most effective order?

Perform your Theme and Variations to the rest of the class. As you listen to others performing theirs, decide how the theme is being varied in each of the variations.

Linked listening

More compositions in variation form

Giles Farnaby: *Loth to Depart*

Haydn: second movement from the 'Surprise' Symphony, No. 94 in G (described in 'Musical Forms' Book 2)

Mozart: Variations on *Ah, vous dirai-je, maman*, for piano; fourth movement from the Clarinet Quintet

Beethoven: fourth movement from the Septet in E♭ (a melody-line score is printed in 'Musical Forms: Listening Scores')

Schubert: fourth movement from the Octet (described in 'Musical Forms' Book 2)

Brahms: *Variations on a Theme by Haydn*

Bizet: *Prélude* to *L'Arlésienne*

Janáček: fourth movement from the *Sinfonietta* ('Enjoying Modern Music')

Dohnányi: *Variations on a Nursery Tune* (*Ah, vous dirai-je, maman*)

Britten: *A Boy was Born* (choral variations)

Britten: *The Young Person's Guide to the Orchestra* (Variations and Fugue on a Theme of Purcell)

Ives: *Variations on 'America'* for organ

Stravinsky: second movement from the Octet for flute, clarinet, two bassoons, two trumpets, and tenor and bass trombones (theme, five variations and a coda, with the first variation repeated after variations 2 and 4)

Schoenberg: *Variations for Orchestra*, Opus 32 – composed in serial, or twelve-note, technique (Theme and Variations 1–3 in 'Enjoying Modern Music'); *Variations* in G minor for symphonic band, Opus 43a

Jazz pieces which are improvised variations on a melody and/or a repeating chord scheme – e.g. **Benny Goodman:** *Stompin' at the Savoy* (see page 28); **Louis Armstrong:** *Struttin' with Some Barbecue* (see page 154); **Jelly Roll Morton:** *Dead Man Blues*; **Bix Beiderbecke:** *At the Jazz Band Ball*

Here is a tune which has appealed to several composers as a theme on which to write a set of variations. It was composed by Paganini, the famous 19th-century virtuoso violinist, who himself wrote a set of variations on the tune.

Get to know this tune. Then choose two of the following works, and listen to the theme and the first few variations in each set.

Compare the ways in which the composers present, and vary, the theme.

Paganini: *Caprice No. 24*, for unaccompanied violin

Brahms: *Variations on a Theme by Paganini*, for piano

Rachmaninov: *Rhapsody on a Theme of Paganini* (a short introduction, then the first variation is heard *before* the theme)

Lutosławski: *Variations on a Theme by Paganini*, for two pianos

Lloyd Webber: *Variations*

CHAPTER 25

Chromatic, whole-tone, and modal

On the keyboard, the step from any note to its nearest neighbour is a **semitone** (half a tone):

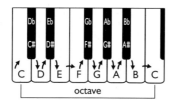

A major scale is a mixture of tones and semitones (shown as S and T, below) which are arranged according to a strict pattern. (*Scale* is from a Latin word meaning a ladder, staircase, or flight of steps.) In any major scale there are steps of a semitone between notes 3 and 4 (mediant to subdominant), and 7 and 8 (leading-note to tonic).

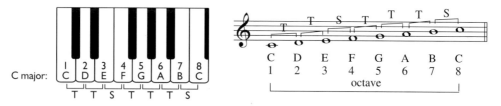

Performing

Sing or play this folk-song from Chile, called *The Tortilla Seller*. In which key is this music? At which points in this melody do steps of a semitone occur?

(*Tortillas* are maize-flour pancakes; *tostaditas* are toasted tortillas.)

The **chromatic scale** moves entirely by semitones – dividing the octave into twelve equal steps of one semitone each. This scale is a 'ladder' whose steps are all the same distance apart. (A chromatic scale can start from any note.)

Chromatic is from a Greek word meaning 'coloured'. If we take the scale of C major, we find that it includes seven notes of different letter-names. As far as the key of C major is concerned, these seven notes are **diatonic** – they belong to the key. The other five notes in the octave are **chromatic** – they lie outside the key of C major. These chromatic notes may be brought in to add 'colour' and expressiveness to the melody, or the harmonies, or both.

There are rules about the notation of chromatic notes – whether pitches should be written as F♯ or G♭, D♭ or C♯, and so on. However, composers usually (but not always) write whatever is most convenient – using sharps when the music moves upwards and flats when it moves downwards, avoiding accidentals whenever possible. For example:

Listening

Listen to the opening eight bars of the slow movement of Mozart's 'Prague' Symphony (No. 38 in D; composed in 1786). The key of this movement is G major, and within the first three-and-a-half bars, Mozart includes all twelve notes of the chromatic scale in the melody line. The accompaniment, however, is completely diatonic – it includes only the notes belonging to the key of G major.

The first phrase (bars 1–4) is repeated. When bar 2 reappears as bar 6, Mozart adds chromatic decorations to the melody. All this floats above the note G (the tonic) held on in the bass. This musical device, when a note is sustained or continuously repeated, against changing harmonies, is called a *pedal*, or *pedal point*. In this case, since the note sustained is the tonic, it is called a tonic pedal.

1   Which is the first chromatic note to appear in the melody line?

2   Half-way through bar 3, a chromatic scale begins on C♯. How many steps of a semitone are there before there is a step of a whole tone?

Now play or listen to these bars from George Gershwin's *Rhapsody in Blue*, composed in 1924. The key signature (of B♭ major) indicates that the notes B and E are to be played as flats unless shown otherwise.

1   Would you say that Gershwin's harmonies are chromatic – or diatonic?

2   How many of the twelve notes of the chromatic scale does Gershwin include in the melody line?

3   Which notes of the chromatic scale are missing from the melody line? Are these included in the accompaniment?

Composing

Compose a melody which includes chromatic notes and phrases. Base your melody in a key which has a simple key signature. First, experiment by improvising. Then shape and polish your melody.

   Write down your chromatic melody, and add markings for tempo, dynamics and expression. Perform your melody.

The **whole-tone scale** contains no semitones. This scale is built entirely from notes which are a whole tone apart – therefore dividing the octave into six equal steps of one whole tone each. Only two whole-tone scales are possible. Play each of these:

In music based on the whole-tone scale, pitches may appear (for convenience in notation) in different guises. For example, A♯ may sometimes be written as B♭, G♯ may be written as A♭, and so on.

   Melodies can be structured from the whole-tone scale, as can accompanying harmonies. However:

●   since the whole-tone scale does not contain the interval of a perfect 5th (nor a perfect 4th) no common chord, such as C-E-G or D-F♯-A, can be built from its pitches;

●   similarly, no perfect cadence or plagal cadence is possible;

●   and as the whole-tone scale contains no semitones, there can be no effect of leading-note to tonic, to offer a definite 'resting place'.

Among the composers who have sometimes used the whole-tone scale in their music are the Russian composer Glinka, Liszt, Vaughan Williams and, particularly, Debussy.

Listening

Listen to an extract from Debussy's second piano Prelude: *Voiles*, composed in 1909. Debussy's title may be translated as 'sails', or as 'veils'. Follow the music printed opposite, and continue listening when the printed music ends.

Listen to this music once or twice more, and answer these questions:

1 Throughout, the note B♭ is continually repeated, sometimes held on, in the bass. What name is given to this musical device?

2 Describe the mood presented by this music, which is entirely based on the whole-tone scale.

3 Which of the two whole-tone scales, opposite, does Debussy use?

4 How many notes of the whole-tone scale are included:
   (a) in the melody of bars 1 and 2?
   (b) in the chords played by the left hand in bar 15?

5 *Voiles* may mean 'sails' or 'veils'. Which of these do you think Debussy intended? Give a reason for your answer.

Composing

Try one of these ideas:

1   Compose or improvise a melody based on one of the whole-tone scales on page 194. Consider including a sequence or two in your melody. Decide which note seems best for your melody to end on.

   When you have completed your melody, you could try adding a simple accompaniment consisting of harmonies built from the whole-tone scale.

2   Compose a piece, in the whole-tone scale, for two instruments. Try using mainly the interval of a 3rd, as Debussy does at the beginning of *Voiles*. Sometimes use movement by step, but sometimes use leaps.

3   Compose a short canon, using the whole-tone scale, for keyboard or for two instruments.

Whichever of these ideas you try, make a recording of your finished whole-tone piece (if necessary, asking others to help you). Then listen back, and assess the mood and expressive effect of the music.

Performing

Sing or play this Dorset version of a folk-song called *The Unquiet Grave*:

Cold blows the wind to my true love, and gently drops the rain, I never had but one sweetheart, and in green-wood she lies slain.

This melody is not in any *key*, major or minor. It is based on one of the old church **modes** – the medieval system of scales on which European music was based until around 1600.

   You can play a mode on a keyboard by starting on a white note (for example, D), then playing upwards step by step but keeping to white notes only. Below are the four modes which were used most often. Each has its own distinctive pattern of tones and semitones (marked S, below). It is mainly the particular order of tones and semitones which gives a mode its own special 'flavour' – its mood and character. The note on which each mode begins and ends is called the **final** (the 'home-note', or tonic). A mode can be transposed to another pitch, but its distinctive pattern of tones and semitones must be kept.

Play each of these four main modes. Notice where the semitones occur, and listen for the special 'flavour' of each mode.

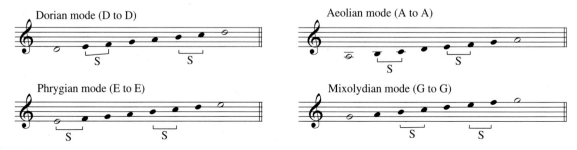

In which of these four modes:

(a)   is there an interval of a minor 3rd between notes 1 and 3?
(b   is there an interval of a major 3rd between notes 1 and 3?
(c)   is the step between notes 7 and 8 a whole tone?

Now sing or play again the folk-tune *The Unquiet Grave*. In which mode is the melody written?

Here are two more folk-tunes – each in a different mode. Sing or play them, and identify the two modes. Describe the *mood* of each tune.

The Sprig of Thyme

Green Bushes (English dance-song, probably 14th-century)

> ### Listening

If possible, listen to the following music:

1   The central section of the *Intermezzo* from Vaughan Williams's *English Folk-song Suite* (for military band; also arranged for orchestra). Vaughan Williams's version of the tune of *Green Bushes* is a tone lower, and does not include the third note of the scale. This allows him to harmonize the tune first in the Dorian mode, with a minor tonic chord, and then in the Mixolydian mode with a major tonic chord.

2   Percy Grainger: *Green Bushes*, folk-music setting for instrumental ensemble. Grainger's version of the melody (also a tone lower) more closely matches the one printed above – but there are still some differences at times.

3   The opening of *Five Variants of 'Dives and Lazarus'* for strings and harp by Vaughan Williams. What similarities do you hear between Vaughan Williams's version of this folk-song (in the Aeolian mode) and the Dorset version of *The Unquiet Grave*?

Much of the **flamenco** music of Spain has the flavour of the Phrygian mode – though sometimes the third note of the scale is sharpened:

Play the descending form of the Phrygian mode – music A, below. There is a definite Spanish flavour – especially the lowest three pitches, and if harmonized as in music B. The particularly plaintive mood and character of the Phrygian mode is mainly due to the fact that one of its two semitones occurs immediately above the most important note – the *final*, or note 1.

Flamenco is dance and dance-music of Spanish gypsy origin, mainly from Andalusia in southern Spain. Typically, it includes song and dance and solo guitar music. The flamenco style of guitar playing is rather more dramatic than the classical style. Almost all the music is improvised, above a number of basic chord patterns. To begin a performance, guitarists always play a *tiento* – an introduction or prelude – to set the proper mood.

Listening

Here is a tiento called *Amor gitano* (Gypsy love), based on the Phrygian mode transposed onto C♯. First play these characteristic melodic motives included in *Amor gitano*. (On the left they are based on E; and on the right, as you will hear them in the recording, transposed onto C♯.)

Listen for these motives as the recording is played.

Composing

Play each of the four main modes (page 196). Play each one ascending, then descending. Choose the one whose flavour, mood or character appeals to you the most. Then compose or improvise a melody or a short piece in your chosen mode.

Consider whether it would be a good idea to transpose your mode. If so, make sure the two semitones occur in the right places. You can, in fact, transpose any mode up a 4th (or down a 5th), and simply have a B♭ as a signature – as Medieval and Renaissance composers often did.

Your modal melody or piece could be unaccompanied, or you could set it above or against:

● a drone;

● an ostinato (or more than one ostinato);

● any other kind of accompaniment which is in keeping with the style and mood of your melodic line.

Performing

Perform your modal melody or piece to the rest of the class (asking others to help you if necessary). As others perform theirs, listen for the modal flavour of the music – especially the whole-tone step between the 7th note and the *final*. Does the mode have a 'majorish' quality to it (Mixolydian), or a 'minorish' quality (Dorian, Aeolian, Phrygian)? Is there a step of a semitone between the *final* and the note immediately above (Phrygian)? Can you identify the mode being used?

Composing

Now try one of these ideas:

1　Make an arrangement or setting of one of the folk-tunes on pages 196 and 197 (or use another modal folk-tune which appeals to you). It is quite possible to harmonize the tunes with just three or four chords. For example, in the case of *The Unquiet Grave*: A minor, D minor, and C major. But you may like to be a little more adventurous.

2　Choose a modal folk-tune, and compose or improvise a set of variations on it.

Flamenco being performed in a Spanish taberna

Listening

Investigate a song called *Gemini* by the rock group Conquest. The first time the recording is played, follow the structure and the words of the song, printed below.

Gemini (Cross/Haggett/Hodges)

Introduction	*(Instruments)*
Verse 1	*Left out in the cold*
	Nothing left to hold
	A victim of your love
	Stranded here alone
	Voices echo in my soul
	Dealer pulls the final card
	From the bottom of the pack
	She dealt my fate
	Cheating on this lonely fool
	Like the joker from the court
	Deception I was taught
	By a lover who twisted the rules.
Bridge	*(Instruments and voices)*
Chorus 1	*Gemini lover*
	Take the tears from my eyes
	Oh let me see
	Untie my soul
	Let me go
	Oh let me run free, so free.
Verse 2	*Flying through a sky of gold*
	On a voyage of seven silver tears
	A wish I make on timeless wings
	To change my barren years.
Bridge	*(Instruments and voices)*
Chorus 2	*Gemini lover* (etc.)
Interlude	*(Instruments)*
Verse 3	*Card that lies before me now*
	Is destiny of life
	Challenged by the evil sword
	Cherished by the holy knife.
Bridge	*(Instruments and voices)*
Chorus 3	*(Instruments only)*
Coda	*(Instruments)*

[John Haggett – vocals, Simon Cross – guitars, Pete Hodges – bass guitar and keyboards, Russell Heal – keyboards, Simon Sharman – drums]

Gemini makes a feature of the basic musical elements of repetition and contrast. Much of the music has a modal flavour, which fits well with several of the images presented in the lyrics.

Listen to *Gemini* two or three times more, discovering answers to the question on this page and the next:

Introduction

- The piece opens with deep, rich, resonant sounds on synthesizer and bass guitar.
  Which of these patterns matches the rhythm which soon emerges above?

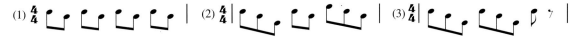

Verse 1

- Here is the vocal line of the beginning of verse 1:

What gives these phrases a *modal* flavour?

- The verse begins over a note held on in the bass. What musical device is this? At which words in the lyrics does the bass begin to move?

Chorus 1

- A change of mood and character. Which instruments now join in for the first time?
- Electric guitar, with distortion pedal, plays an ostinato. Which of these matches the syncopated rhythm of this ostinato?

Verse 2

- Mention two musical features in the accompaniment to this verse.

Chorus 2

- Describe how the chorus each time presents a contrast in mood and character to the music of the verses. For example, comment on: pace, dynamics, rhythm, timbre, texture.

Interlude

- Which instrument is featured in a free improvisation during this interlude?
- At the end of the interlude, which instrument plays a partly chromatic rising scale?

Verse 3

- This verse is 8 bars long. In which bars do the pitches of the vocal line *not* match the beginning of verse 1 (printed above)?

Chorus 3

● Although no vocal is involved, the music is based upon the same chord pattern as the previous choruses, repeated as an ostinato:

How many times is this chord pattern played before there is any change?

● Which of the instruments is featured solo, throughout this chorus?

Coda

● How is the tension and excitement, built up during chorus 3, released in the coda?

Linked listening

Chromatic

Bach: Chromatic Fantasy and Fugue in D minor
Mozart: Piano Concerto No. 24 in C minor (K491) – opening theme
Chopin: Nocturne No. 3 in B major
Wagner: Prelude to *Tristan and Isolde* (see pages 222–3)
Schoenberg: *Verklärte Nacht* (Transfigured night)
Louis Armstrong: *West End Blues* – Armstrong's brilliantly improvised solo introduction includes all twelve notes of the chromatic scale
Billy Strayhorn: *Take the 'A' Train*
Duke Ellington: *Caravan,* and *Mood Indigo*

Whole-tone

Debussy: *Cloches à travers les feuilles* (Bells heard through the leaves (from *Images* Book 2), and *Reflets dans l'eau* (*Images* Book 1) – whole-tone scale in the bass at about $2\frac{1}{4}$ minutes
Bach: Chorale, *Es ist genug*, from Cantata No. 60 – the chorale opens with whole tones; Alban Berg uses this chorale in the fourth movement of his Violin Concerto, and includes the whole-note motive in the note row on which the work is based (see page 228)
Bartók: *Whole-tone Scale*, Piece No. 136 from *Mikrokosmos* Book 5

Modal

Plainchant: *Alleluia: Pascha nostrum* (recorded on 'Enjoying Early Music' cassette) – Mixolydian mode
Christmas carol: *God Rest You Merry, Gentlemen* – Aeolian mode
Neidhart von Reuental: *Winder wie ist nu dein Kraft* (recorded on 'Enjoying Early Music' cassette) – Dorian mode
Gabrieli: *Canzon 13* (see pages 214 and 216) – the piece opens in the Mixolydian mode
Vaughan Williams: *Fantasia on 'Greensleeves'* – based on two folk-tunes, *Greensleeves* and *Lovely Joan*, both in the Dorian mode; and *Fantasia on a Theme by Thomas Tallis* – Tallis's melody is in the Phrygian mode
Simon and Garfunkel: *Scarborough Fair* – Dorian mode transposed onto E
Black Sabbath: *Paranoid* – Aeolian mode transposed onto E, and harmonized with three chords: E minor, D major, and C major
Bananarama: *Na Na Hey Hey Kiss Him Goodbye* – chorus is in the Dorian mode transposed onto C (and is sometimes sung in canon)
Miles Davis: *Kind of Blue* – jazz pieces based on modes; e.g. in *Flamenco Sketches* – a fusion of jazz and Spanish music – the soloists (including Davis, trumpet, and John Coltrane, saxophone) base their improvisations upon a pre-agreed series of five different modes

CHAPTER 26

Timbre (3) – exploring the voice

Listening

Listen to these two extracts of vocal music which make different uses of the soprano voice. The music is printed for the first half of the first extract, and the whole of the second.

The first extract is the beginning of Rachmaninov's *Vocalise* for soprano and piano. (A **vocalise** is a wordless composition, or section of a composition, which is sung to one or more vowel sounds (for example, 'Ah').

The second extract is the opening of Act III Scene 1 of Berg's opera, *Wozzeck*. Here, Berg contrasts normal singing with passages using the technique of **Sprechgesang** ('speech-song'). This is a style of vocal performance which is midway between speaking and singing. Each note is printed with pitch and duration, but with a cross on its stem. The singer approximates the pitch of each note, rather than pitching it precisely.

Listen to the two extracts again. Notice:

- how these different uses of the voice create different moods;
- (in the second extract) the expressive effect of the Sprechgesang contrasted with normal singing;
- also, in each extract, the effect made by the accompaniment.

A vast range of other, extremely varied, kinds of vocal sound have been explored by composers in the second half of the 20th century. These include;

humming	shrieking	sustained/fragmented	clicks made with
sighing	laughing	singing of vowels	back of tongue
moaning	crying	fast articulation of	closed mouth
speaking	gasping	consonants	half-closed mouth
whispering	hissing	vibrato, shakes and	hand over mouth
shouting	muttering	trilling effects	

All these can be transformed, in various ways, by means of electronics. For some of these 'new' vocal sounds, composers have had to devise new notations. A selection of these is given on the opposite page. However, not all of these have gained worldwide acceptance – many composers prefer to invent their own individual symbols.

Listening

Investigate the opening of Luciano Berio's *Sequenza III* (1966) for female voice. Berio composed this for Cathy Berberian, to whom he was married from 1950 to 1966. The piece is based on this short poem:

> Give me a few words
> for a woman to sing
> a truth allowing us
> to build a house
> before night comes

Berio does not set this poem line for line. He treats the words simply as *sounds*. He selects individual words, sometimes splitting them into separate syllables or even separate letters (vowels, or consonants). For instance, the piece opens with rapid repetitions, but in changing order, of: 'to, co, us, for, be'. And then 'sing to me, sing to me ...'.

   Throughout the music, Berio provides the singer with 'mood cues' (often abruptly changing) such as: 'tense', 'urgent', 'distant and dreamy', 'witty', 'nervous'.

Listen to the extract from *Sequenza III*, two or three times. Which of the various kinds of vocal sound, shown on the opposite page, do you hear included in this music?

Performing/Composing

Here are two lines from a poem:

> What beckoning ghost along the moonlight shade
> invites my steps, and points to yonder glade?

Try a performance of the setting, below, of the first line (all the notation is included on the chart, opposite). Then compose your own setting of the second line.

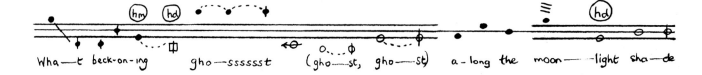

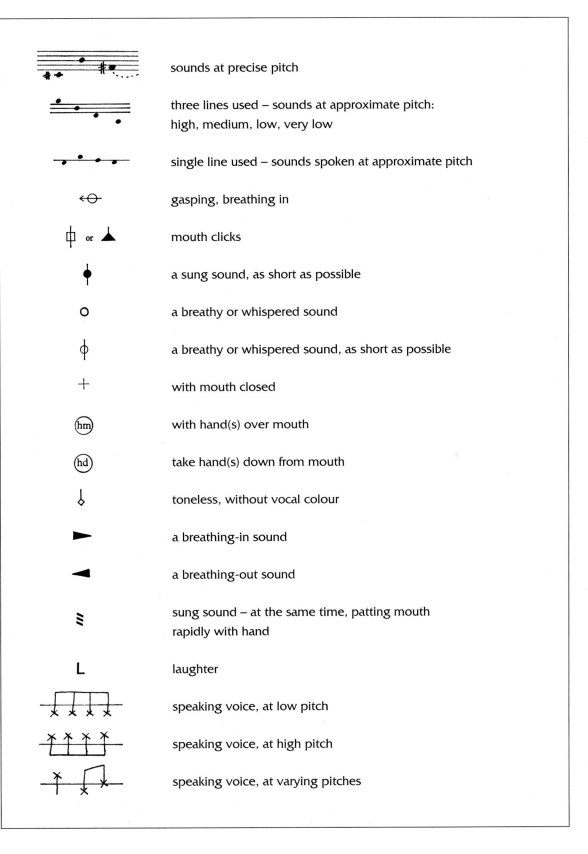

	sounds at precise pitch
	three lines used — sounds at approximate pitch: high, medium, low, very low
	single line used — sounds spoken at approximate pitch
	gasping, breathing in
	mouth clicks
	a sung sound, as short as possible
	a breathy or whispered sound
	a breathy or whispered sound, as short as possible
	with mouth closed
	with hand(s) over mouth
	take hand(s) down from mouth
	toneless, without vocal colour
	a breathing-in sound
	a breathing-out sound
	sung sound — at the same time, patting mouth rapidly with hand
	laughter
	speaking voice, at low pitch
	speaking voice, at high pitch
	speaking voice, at varying pitches

Listening

Now listen to a song called *¿De dónde vienes, amor, mi niño?* (Where do you come from, my love, my child?). This is the third of five songs from *Ancient Voices of Children*, a work by the American composer George Crumb. All five songs are settings of texts by the Spanish poet Federico García Lorca.

The song is in the form of a dialogue between a mother (soprano) and her unborn child (boy soprano, singing off-stage). Accompanying these two voices are an electrically-amplified piano, harp, mandolin (intentionally mistuned, and played with a metal plectrum), and percussion – tam-tams, tenor drum, timbale (single-headed cylindrical drum), pedal-tuned kettledrum, suspended cymbals, and two mounted glockenspiel plates (played by the soprano).

The song opens with an unaccompanied *vocalise* for the soprano. She sings this facing into the strings of the piano. The pianist keeps the sustaining (right) pedal down, so that the strings are free to vibrate in a soft, shimmering haze of echoes in response to the soprano's voice. Her *vocalise* consists mainly of changing vowel sounds, often articulated with the consonants 'k' or 't'. Also included are flutter-tonguing (trilled 'r' sound) and laughter. At the end, as she shouts '¡mi niño!' (my child!), there are strokes on tam-tams and the pianist reaches into the piano and plays fingernail glissandos across the lower strings.

Then, very softly, the three percussionists begin a Spanish bolero rhythm (exactly the same rhythm as in the famous *Boléro* by Ravel). This will continue as an exciting rhythmic *ostinato* (which Crumb calls the 'Dance of the Sacred Life-Cycle') until the end of the song. On certain notes, two of the percussionists whisper the sounds *kai!*, *ko!* or *ku!* The soprano and boy soprano begin their dialogue, at first in *Sprechgesang* style.

The percussionists make a gradual crescendo to the mid-point of the song, and then a gradual diminuendo – the whispers gradually changing to shouts, then back to whispers.

The song ends with a vivid explosion of sounds.

On the opposite page is a plan showing the main musical events of the first part of the song, with a translation of the Spanish words.

First listening

Follow the plan as you listen – continuing to listen when the plan ends, and identifying the main musical events taking place.

Second listening

This time, concentrate your listening on the different vocal styles being used, and all the different types, colours and qualities of vocal sound.

Third listening

There are many colourful *contrasts* in this music. But do you hear any *repetition* of musical events (besides the repetitions of the ostinato bolero rhythm)?

What do you like or dislike about this music?

1	**Soprano**	Vocalise...
		My child!
		↙
		(tam-tam strokes, glissandos on piano strings)
2		(percussionists quietly begin bolero rhythm ...)
	Soprano (eager, exuberant)	*Where do you come from, my love, my child?*
	Boy soprano (metallic, hard)	*From the crest of the cruel frost.*
	Soprano	*What do you need, my love, my child?*
	Boy soprano	*The warmth of the woven cloth of your dress.*
3		(oboe solo)
4	**Soprano** (joyously!)	*How the branches rustle in the sunlight and the fountains leap all around!*
		(piano, harp and mandolin join in)
5	**Boy soprano** (speaking, in a very dramatic style)	*In the courtyard the dog is barking, in the trees the wind is singing.*
		The oxen bellow at the drover, and the moonlight curls my hair.
6		(pianist plays glissando across strings, drums on low strings, in clusters, with fingertips)

Composing

Try one or more of these ideas:

1   Compose a *vocalise* for a solo voice – with or without an accompaniment.

2   Form a group of musicians. Compose/improvise an atmospheric piece consisting of vocal sounds, based on one of these themes (alternatively, think up a theme of your own).

> Hauntings
> Storm and sunrise
> Tropical forest
> Antarctica
> Star clusters
> Dream machine

3   Set the following lines of verse (or write some of your own) for solo voice using Sprechgesang. Add an effective backing for a group of voices, using some of the other vocal sounds and techniques mentioned during this chapter. Also experiment, and discover/create some of your own.

Consider: duration of sounds and pauses in the Sprechgesang, varying textures and vocal timbres, changes of pace and dynamics.

Decide: whether or not any instrumental sounds should also be involved.

> The wine that only eyes can drink,
> at nightfall pours from the moon in waves,
> and a spring-tide gushes forth
> and floods the distant, still horizon.
>
> Desires and longings, ghastly sweet,
> come swimming through the silver floods ...
> The wine that only eyes can drink,
> at nightfall pours from the moon in waves.

Notate a score for your piece. Add an explanatory key to your score, clearly explaining the notational symbols you have used so that performers will understand how to interpret them. If necessary, also add any verbal instructions.

Performing

Whichever of these three composing ideas you try, organize a performance of your piece, and make a recording of it. Consider the use of 'echo' (if this recording facility is available to you) to enhance any parts of your music. Afterwards, listen back, and assess the effectiveness of your piece.

Linked listening

Varied uses of the voice

Ravel: *Vocalise en forme de habanera*

Delius: *To Be Sung of a Summer Night on the Water* – two unaccompanied, wordless part-songs for mixed voices

Villa-Lobos: first movement from *Bachianas brasileiras* No. 5 for soprano and eight cellos – in ternary form, A^1 B A^2, with the melody vocalized in A^1 and hummed in A^2

Nielsen: *Andante pastorale* from Symphony No. 3 ('Expansiva') – during the last third of this movement, solo tenor and solo soprano weave *vocalises*

Glière: Concerto for coloratura soprano and orchestra

Stravinsky: *Pastorale* – a *vocalise* for soprano and piano (later arranged for soprano, oboe, cor anglais, clarinet and bassoon)

Schoenberg: examples of Sprechgesang from the song-cycle *Pierrot lunaire* (see also page 225) and from the opera *Moses and Aaron* (the part of Moses is sung in Sprechgesang)

Berg: Act 3 Scene 4 from the opera *Wozzeck* (Sprechgesang)

Penderecki: *Stabat Mater* for three mixed choirs (described in 'Enjoying Modern Music') – includes, besides normal singing, reciting, whispering, muttering, chanting, anguished cries

Ligeti: *Aventures*, a 'comic entertainment' for three singers (soprano, alto, baritone) and seven instrumentalists (flute, horn, cello, double bass, percussion, piano, harpsichord) – for this piece, instead of using words, Ligeti invented an alphabet of 112 sounds

Berio: *Circles,* setting three poems by e. e. cummings, for female voice, harp and two percussionists (composed for Cathy Berberian)

Berio: second movement from *Sinfonia* for eight voices and orchestra – disconnected vowels and consonants are pieced together by the voices until they eventually form the words 'O Martin Luther King' (the black civil rights leader, assassinated in 1968)

Cathy Berberian: *Stripsody* for female voice – a rhapsody based on a comic strip score, creating a fantasy world: part music, part noise, part drama

Stockhausen: *Stimmung* (Tuning) – six singers, using varied vocal techniques and changing tone-colours, sing the notes of a single chord (B♭ F B♭ D A♭ C); from time to time, one or another introduces a poem or calls out a 'magic name' which is then taken up by the others

Nono: *Coma una ola de fuerza y luz* (Like a wave of force and light) – in this atmospheric work, a soprano, piano and orchestra perform 'live' in combination with a tape presenting electronic sounds and the electronically modified sounds, previously recorded, of the soprano, piano, and a choir of women's voices

Examples of jazz scat singing (in which nonsense words and syllables and improvised sounds are used instead of normal words) – Louis Armstrong (e.g. *Hotter Than That; Heebie Jeebies*), also Ella Fitzgerald, Sarah Vaughan, Cab Calloway, Cleo Laine, the Swingle Singers

Examples of vocal styles and timbres of various musical traditions and cultures – for example: Chinese (Peking) opera; Japanese Noh drama, Kabuki theatre (which has been described as 'the Italian opera of Japan') and Bunraku puppet theatre; chanting of Tibetan Lamaist/Buddhist monks; Indian folk-songs, chanted poetry (words as sounds), a vocal raga; the Balinese *Kecak* dance; Spanish flamenco; reggae toasting

CHAPTER 27

Making use of physical space

Some composers have written pieces which rely upon placing the performers in a particular arrangement within the performing area, in order to create various **musical and spatial effects**. These effects may exploit a 'stereo spread' of sounds, left to right in front of the listener; or an impression of distance by placing some performers further away than others; or both.

Listening

Berlioz, in his Requiem Mass, uses a very large orchestra and more than two hundred voices. One of Berlioz's aims in composing this work was to create massed sounds suited to performance in a very large space. At certain points in the music he adds four separate brass groups, positioned at the four corners of the chorus and orchestra.

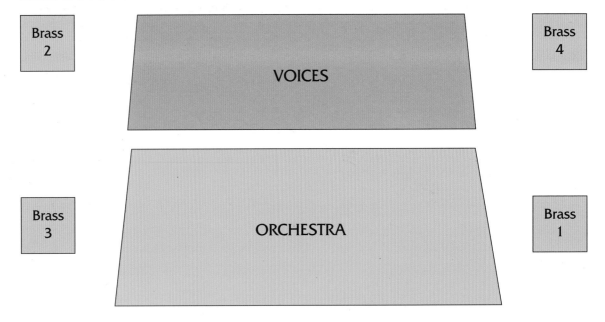

Listen to the massive effect created in the *Tuba mirum* section ('A trumpet, spreading wondrous sound'), which also includes the thunderous roar of two tenor drums and eight pairs of kettledrums.

The four brass groups join together in playing a *fortissimo* chord. Then they enter one by one. Which of the following descriptions matches the rhythm and the melodic lines during the first minute or so of the music?

rhythm:	even, smooth, unchanging	varying, and with some syncopation
melodic lines:	melodious, song-like	fanfare-like motives

When the kettledrums crash in, which of the following is true?

1   the drums all sound the same note, E♭;

2   the drums sound several notes, forming a single chord throughout;

3   the drums sound various notes which form different, changing chords.

An interesting way of making use of physical space is to create **echo effects**. The effect of natural echo is imitated in the music by the softer repetition of a phrase or part of a phrase. Besides being quieter, the echo effect may be enhanced in various ways. For example:

● by giving the repeated (echo) portions to a smaller group of performers;

● by spatially separating the groups – perhaps placing the echoing group to the side of the main group, or behind it so that the echoes come from a distance;

● by contrasting the sounds of the two groups – perhaps in pitch (lower/higher), or in timbre (brighter/mellower).

Listening

Listen to the Echo Chorus, *In Our Deep-vaulted Cell*, from Purcell's opera *Dido and Aeneas*. The scene is the dank and gloomy cave of an evil Sorceress. She summons her witches to her aid, and they plot to separate the lovers, Dido and Aeneas, and bring about the destruction of Carthage. Throwing vile ingredients into a huge cauldron, they cast a spell . . .

The chorus of witches on stage is echoed by a second chorus behind the scenes. Sometimes a whole musical phrase is echoed, sometimes only part of a phrase.

Main chorus	**Chorus behind the scenes**
In our deep-vaulted cell	
the charm we'll prepare,	*-ed cell,*
too dreadful a practice,	*prepare,*
too dreadful	*too dreadful a practice,*
a practice	*too dreadful*
for this open air.	*a practice*
In our deep-vaulted cell	*for this open air.*
the charm we'll prepare,	*-ed cell,*
too dreadful a practice	*prepare,*
for this open air	*too dreadful a practice*
	for this open air.

Listen again, answering these questions.

1   Give three ways in which the echoes are made to sound effective.

2   Why, do you think, did Purcell decide to set these words as an 'echo chorus'?

Listening

Another piece which exploits echo effects is Mozart's *Notturno* ('night music') in D major, K286. Mozart writes the music for four orchestras. Each is made up of two horns and strings (first violins, second violins, violas, cellos and double basses).

Investigate the melody-line score, printed opposite. This is the opening of the first movement, and the score shows the first two sets of echoes (A and B) and the beginning of the third (C).

Sometimes Orchestra 2 echoes the complete phrase presented by Orchestra 1, sometimes only part of it.

Orchestra 3 usually adds a briefer echo, and Orchestra 4 a briefer echo still.

Usually (but not always) Mozart *overlaps* the echoes – Orchestra 2 begins to echo before Orchestra 1 has quite completed its phrase, and the same with Orchestras 3 and 4.

The producer of this recording carefully worked out the most effective 'stereo placement' of the four orchestras in relation to the microphones, so that the listener can locate each separate orchestra in space: left to right, and also front to back (near and far).

Orchestra 1 is spread across centre front. Orchestra 2 is a little farther back and to the right. Orchestra 3 is to the left and farther away still. And Orchestra 4 is again on the right, and the farthest away of all.

Listen to the recording two or three times, following the melody-line score. When the printed music ends, the recording continues. Discover:

- when an echo repeats the whole of the music just heard – and when only a fragment is echoed;
- when an echo overlaps the end of the preceding phrase – and when there is no overlapping.

Composing

Compose an 'echo piece' for two performers – either two instruments, or two voices, or one of each. If there will be a noticeable difference in timbre, decide which of the two performers will provide the most suitable sound for the echoes.

In building up your echo piece, consider:

- whether an echo should softly repeat the whole of a preceding phrase, or only half of it, or just the last fragment;
- whether an echo should overlap a preceding phrase, by coming in before it is quite completed (as often happens in Mozart's *Notturno*) – or follow on without any overlapping (as in Purcell's Echo Chorus, described on page 211).

Performing

When you have finished your piece, practise performing it with a partner. Then make a stereo recording of it. Consider carefully the stereo placement of the two performers in relation to the microphones – left and right, near and far. You may find it best first to record just the opening part of the piece, then listen back – and if necessary, experiment with the positionings to achieve the best possible echo effect.

The use of spatial effects is especially associated with the music of composers working in Venice towards the end of the 16th century (the end of the Renaissance period). The Venetians loved colour and contrast in their music. Many of their compositions are for two or more groups of musicians – and in performance, these groups are widely spaced apart. Within a group, the timbres might be blended. But there are contrasts of timbre, and perhaps also of pitch, *between* the groups.

During the music, the groups alternate, respond to each other, and combine together to produce a rich and sonorous effect. A musical idea presented by a group on the left is answered by the same, or perhaps a different, idea from a group on the right. This passing to and fro of musical ideas between the groups – often with the effect of challenge, or opposition – is called **antiphony** (meaning 'sound against sound').

Listening

Investigate a piece in antiphonal style by the Venetian composer Giovanni Gabrieli. His *Canzon 13* (1597) is for three contrasting groups of instruments. The diagram below shows the placings of the instruments you will hear.

Group 1 consists of bowed string instruments. Group 2 has plucked strings and woodwind. Group 3 is made up of wind instruments and double-bass viol.

Descriptions of several of the instruments are given on the opposite page. All of them were made in various sizes.

GROUP 2

harpsichord   4 lutes

bassoon

3 recorders

GROUP 1

2 bass viols

5 violins

GROUP 3

double-bass viol   organ

2 sackbuts

cornett   shawm

First listening

Listen to Gabrieli's *Canzon 13*, picking out the varied timbres of the three contrasting groups, and the location (placement) of the instruments: left, centre back, and right.

Second listening

Listen for entries of the main themes (several are printed on page 216), and for antiphonal effects between the groups as they take up the themes.

Third and fourth listenings

As you listen, answer the questions on page 216.

Some Renaissance instruments

Renaissance lute

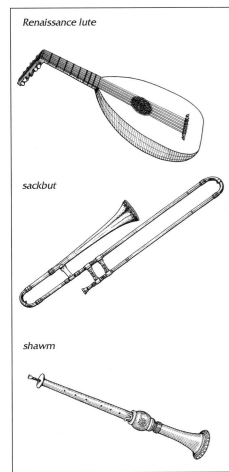

sackbut

shawm

bass viol

cornett

The Renaissance **lute** had a rounded back, and was shaped like half a pear. The pegbox was bent back at an angle, and the fingerboard had frets (like those on a guitar). The strings, which were plucked, often numbered eleven – ten of them tuned in pairs, plus a single top string.

Viols had sloping shoulders and flat backs, and the fingerboard was fretted. A viol was held upright in front of the player, rather than being tucked under the chin, and its six strings were played with a bow. The largest viol, the double-bass viol, was the direct ancestor of the modern double bass.

Sackbut was the name given to the early form of trombone. The bell was less flared, giving a softer, rounder, more mellow tone than the modern trombone.

The **cornett** was made of wood or ivory. It had a cup-shaped mouthpiece, like a trumpet, and finger-holes, like a recorder. In ensemble music, cornetts were often combined with sackbuts. Because of its cup-shaped mouthpiece, the cornett was classed as a 'brass' instrument.

The **shawm** (an ancestor of the oboe) had a double reed and a flaring bell, giving it a brilliant and penetrating tone. It was brought to Europe from the Middle East at the time of the Crusades.

St Mark's Cathedral, Venice, where Giovanni Gabrieli was in charge of music for many years

1 Suggest a word to describe the mood or character of the music at the beginning of this piece.

2 Which of the three groups includes the highest-sounding instrument?

3 Which group includes the lowest-sounding instrument?

4 Do the melodic lines in this music move mainly by step, or mainly by leap?

5 Which group of instruments contains the brightest timbres?

6 Which group contains the darkest timbres?

7 How does theme G provide musical contrast?

8 The section of music beginning with G contains three phrases. Then Gabrieli balances the structure of his piece by bringing back some of the themes heard earlier. Which are they?

9 In some themes, the entries of the groups overlap – creating *imitation*. Mention two themes where this sounds most noticeable.

10 Throughout this piece, Gabrieli constantly varies the musical texture. How does he achieve this?

Listening

Now listen to a jazzy arrangement by Bob Sharples of the pop song *Singing the Blues*. Sharples took great care in working out the stereo placement of the instruments he chose, drawing up a diagram to show their positions in relation to the microphones.

Two main groups – each including saxophones, brass and percussion – are placed left and right. In the centre are double bass, jazz drum kit and more percussion, with 'jangle box' to one side and electric guitar to the other.

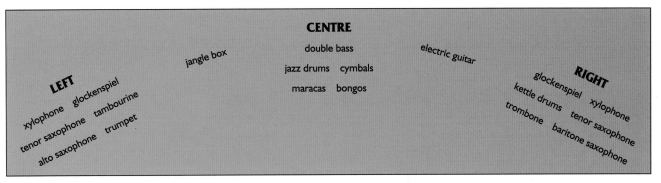

In his arrangement, Sharples explores spatial effects, and colourful combinations of timbres. As you listen to the recording, spot examples of the following:

- blending of timbres, and contrasting of timbres – within a group, and between groups;
- 'duetting' – pairing up of instruments, sometimes within a group (left, or right), sometimes from opposite groups;
- an instrument from one side playing a solo, while another from the opposite side provides an accompaniment figure;
- instruments from left and right groups joining together in harmony (chordal passages);
- brief 'comments' or responses made by instruments during, or between, phrases played by other instruments.

Composing

Form an ensemble consisting of a conductor and several performers divided into two antiphonal, contrasting groups – spaced apart to left and to right. The contrasts might be between brighter/darker timbres, high/low-pitched instruments, wind/strings, and so on.

The aim is to construct an experimental piece which explores spatial effects and antiphony between the two groups.

Each performer selects six different notes or sounds, and notates (writes down) this 'note-bank' in any suitable way.

For example:

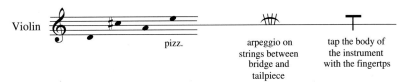

If any percussion players are included, select at least three (if possible, more) different types or qualities of sound.

In building up the music, performers might:

- play self-chosen notes from their 'bank', forming chords or note-clusters;
- at certain points, improvise patterns, using just a few of their notes or sounds – slowly or swiftly, rhythmically or freely, keeping the same order of sounds or varying the order;
- create melodic lines, using any or all of their notes.

During performance, it will be the conductor's responsibility to decide and control dynamics and expression, and to contrast and balance the sounds and timbres. The conductor should sometimes alternate the two groups – so that they respond to each other, or oppose and challenge each other – and sometimes combine the groups.

It is also the conductor's responsibility to build and shape the climax of the piece, and decide how it will end.

Here are some ways in which the antiphonal effects might be created:

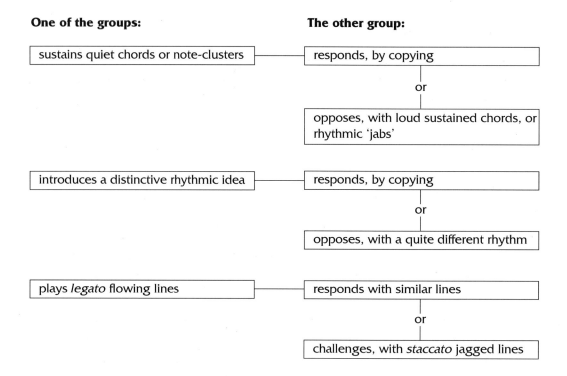

One of the groups:

| sustains quiet chords or note-clusters |

The other group:

| responds, by copying |

or

| opposes, with loud sustained chords, or rhythmic 'jabs' |

| introduces a distinctive rhythmic idea |

| responds, by copying |

or

| opposes, with a quite different rhythm |

| plays *legato* flowing lines |

| responds with similar lines |

or

| challenges, with *staccato* jagged lines |

Try these – and also discover other ways of your own.

Then discuss, and decide:

- exactly which ideas, or events, you will use in your piece;
- the order in which they will be presented by the groups;
- what 'signals' or 'cues' the conductor will use, in performance, to make clear when, and how, performers will contribute – either as a group, or individually.

Performing

Perform your piece for two antiphonal groups, making a stereo recording of it. Then listen to it and discuss it. For example, how effective are:

the contrasts in timbre;

the antiphony between the two groups;

the use of dynamics, expression, and tempo;

the textures;

the shape of the piece – especially the climax, and the ending?

Is there unity – a consistency of musical style throughout the piece? Is there continuity? Are there always gaps between entries of the two groups when they respond/oppose in antiphonal style? Would it be more effective (sometimes, at least) if the sounds overlapped in some way?

Linked listening

More pieces which in some way exploit physical space

Giovanni Gabrieli: *Sonata pian' e forte* for two instrumental groups (this was the very first instrumental composition to have markings on the music indicating *piano* and *forte* – when each group plays alone, the marking is *piano*; when the groups combine, the marking is *forte*)

Vivaldi: third movement from Concerto in A (RV552/P222) 'for solo violin and strings, and with another violin playing echoes in the distance'

Mozart: *Serenata Notturna*, for two small orchestras: (1) two violins, viola, and double bass; (2) first violins, second violins, viola(s), cello(s), and kettledrums

Bliss: *Antiphonal Fanfare* for three brass choirs – Bliss, as Master of the Queen's Music (1953–75), composed this fanfare for the investiture of the Prince of Wales

Mátyás Seiber/John Dankworth: *Improvisations*, for jazz band and symphony orchestra

Panufnik: *Vision 1* from *Sinfonia sacra* – played by four trumpets 'placed as widely separated as possible at the four corners of the orchestra'

Stockhausen, in particular, has exploited spatial effects in several of his compositions, often incorporating electronics. In some pieces, the sounds are intended to surround the listener on three sides, or even completely. Sounds may be *rotated* through space, so that they swing from sound-source to sound-source, sometimes looping back and forth. Although only a 'live' performance can create the true spatial effects, stereo (two-channel) recordings can produce an effective approximation. Some examples are:

Gruppen (Groups) for three equal orchestras, widely separated, and surrounding the audience on three sides

Carré (Square) for four orchestras, each with a mixed chorus of 8–12 singers

Kontakte (Contacts) for widely separated percussionist and pianist (who also plays certain percussion instruments), and electronic four-channel tape fed through four speakers set at points completely surrounding the audience (this piece is described in 'Enjoying Music' Book 3)

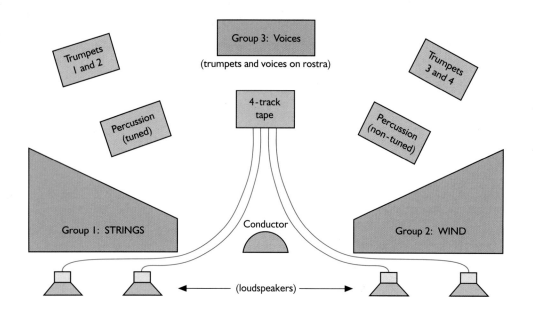

By the black moon
of the highwaymen
the spurs sing.

Little black horse.
Where are you carrying your dead rider?

... The harsh spurs
of the motionless bandit
who lost his reins.

Little cold horse.
What a perfume of knife-blossom!

[Federico García Lorca

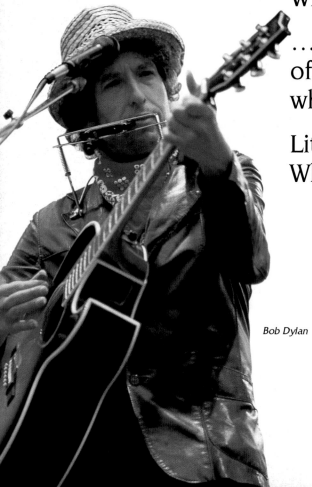

Bob Dylan

The double helix structure of
DNA (deoxyribonucleic acid)

Cathy Berberian – vocal artiste extraordinaire

CHAPTER 28

Tonal and atonal

Play or listen to this music by Beethoven – the opening of the slow movement of his Violin Sonata No. 9 in A major (the 'Kreutzer' Sonata), composed in 1802–3.

In spite of the discords (especially in bar 4) this music is quite definitely in a key – the key of F major. The sounds form a particular relationship with each other. Certain notes assume greater importance than others, and the ear senses a strong 'pull' towards the most important note of the key – the **tonic** note or **keynote**, F. The next most important note is the **dominant, C**, which Beethoven uses as a dominant pedal at the beginning of the music. (A **pedal**, or **pedal point**, is a note which is sustained or continuously repeated, most often in the bass, against changing harmonies.)

The music is **tonal**, 'in a key', and the **tonality** (key) is F major. This is clinched by the perfect cadence at bar 8, with its dominant to tonic (V^7-I) harmonic relationship.

In bar 4, Beethoven uses two chromatic discords, bringing in notes from outside the key of F major (E♭, F♯, G♯) to 'colour' the harmonies. But these discords are used within a clear sense of key. Later Romantic composers – Wagner in particular – made more frequent and more powerful use of chromatic discords, often resulting in an intense expression of moods and emotions.

Listening

Listen to the opening of the Prelude to Wagner's opera *Tristan and Isolde*, completed in 1865, and based upon an ancient saga which relates one of the world's greatest love stories. The music is printed opposite in an arrangement for piano.

Wagner creates a mood of passionate yearning by:

- the persistent use of chromatic dissonances;
- frequent movement by semitone;
- discords merging into further discords (instead of resolving onto expected concords);
- continual, and adventurous, modulation (change of key).

The result of all this is to weaken the sense of tonality, so that at times it is difficult, if not impossible, to say exactly which key the music is in. Often, just as the listener feels that the music is moving in a certain direction, it takes another direction instead.

The opening idea – one of the most famous in all music – combines two important motives, representing Tristan and Isolde:

Tristan

Isolde

Tristan's motive begins with a leap of a 6th, then the notes fall by semitone. In Isolde's motive, the notes rise by semitone. The first chord (a discord), at bar 2, is known as the 'Tristan' chord.

As you listen to the extract, following the score below, use your eyes and ears to notice chromatic discords, and movement by semitone. Also notice, in the first fifteen bars, Wagner's expressive use of silence.

Listen to another extract from later on in the Prelude to *Tristan and Isolde*. How does Wagner create restlessness and tension in this music?

During the twentieth century, some composers have used the technique of **polytonality** – the use of two, or more, keys *simultaneously*, so that they sharply contrast against each other. (If two keys only are used, it is sometimes called **bitonality**, 'two tonalities'.)

In **polytonal** music:

- the melody may be in one key, and the accompaniment in another – e.g. melody in D major and accompaniment in D minor, or melody in A major with accompaniment in B♭ major;
- two or more melodic lines may weave along together in counterpoint, each line in its own distinct and separate key.

Using polytonality, a composer can create considerable tension as dissonances are produced by the conflicting keys – especially if they are a semitone or a tritone (augmented 4th) apart.

Listening

Listen to the *Cortège* (Procession) from *King David* by Honegger. Follow the plan below, which shows the structure of the music, the instrumentation, and the keys which are used in this polytonal piece. Harp, cellos and double basses play continuously throughout.

1	2	3	4	5	6	7
	horn, D minor			2 horns, D minor		4 horns, D minor
2 trumpets, E minor		2 trumpets, E minor			2 trumpets, E minor	2 trumpets, E minor
			trombone, F♯ major	2 trombones, F♯ major	3 trombones, F♯ major	3 trombones, F♯ major
harp, cellos and double basses, F minor						

Listen to *Cortège* again, especially noticing the dissonances caused by the conflicting tonalities (keys). Then listen once or twice more.

1 What do you notice about the bass-line of this piece?
2 How does Honegger vary the timbre of the trumpets?
3 Of the keys Honegger uses, which are a semitone apart?

Composing

Compose some polytonal music. You could try any of the ideas presented on this page. For instance, you could try:

- a melody + accompaniment – perhaps made up of broken chords;
- two melodic lines weaving along in counterpoint (try imitation, or canon);
- (like Honegger) a melodic ostinato in the bass, with fanfare-like motives above, in different keys.

Choose your conflicting keys carefully – experiment and judge the effects, the amount of dissonance.

Make a recording of your polytonal piece, perhaps with the help of others. Then listen to it, and assess its effectiveness.

In tonal music – music in a key – the ear senses a strong pull towards the tonic, or keynote. The next most important note is the dominant. Towards the end of the 19th century, composers were bringing in chromaticisms (notes from 'outside the key') to such an extent that tonality – the major/minor key system – weakened, and began to crumble.

The next logical step was towards **atonality** – meaning total absence of tonality, or key. **Atonal** music makes free use of all the notes of the chromatic scale, and considers all twelve of these notes to be of *equal* importance. In this way, there can be no pull towards any definite tonic. And so in atonal music there is no sense of tonality, or key, whatsoever.

The central figure in the exploration of atonality was the Austrian composer Arnold Schoenberg.

Listening

Listen to one of the twenty-one songs from Schoenberg's song-cycle *Pierrot lunaire* (Pierrot by Moonlight, or Moonstruck Pierrot), composed in 1912. The poems are set for female 'singing narrator' and five instrumentalists using eight instruments. No two songs use the same combination of instruments.

The singer must use the technique of Sprechgesang ('speech-song'). This is a style of vocal perform-ance which is midway between speech and song. Each note is printed with pitch and duration, but with a cross on its stem. The singer approximates the pitch of each note, rather than pitching it precisely.

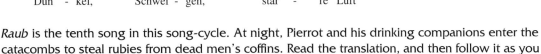

Dun - kel,   Schwei - gen,   star - re Luft

Raub is the tenth song in this song-cycle. At night, Pierrot and his drinking companions enter the catacombs to steal rubies from dead men's coffins. Read the translation, and then follow it as you listen to this atonal piece – in which there is no key, no tonality.

Raub (Robbery)

Red and glowing princely rubies,
bloody drops of ancient glory,
slumber in the bone-filled coffins,
deep down in the gloomy vaults.

Now, with his drinking companions,
comes Pierrot by night – to steal those
red and glowing princely rubies,
bloody drops of ancient glory.

But! – their hair stands up on end,
pallid fear roots them to the spot;
through the dark and gloom – like eyes! –
staring from the bone-filled coffins:
red and glowing princely rubies.

Welsh mezzo-soprano Mary Thomas
performing Pierrot lunaire

Listen two or three times more to *Raub*, answering these questions:

1   Identify the four instruments which play the accompaniment in this song.

2   Mention some of the ways in which the string instruments are being played, to give colour and atmosphere to this atonal music.

3   Do you think the vocal style of Sprechgesang suits the mood and meaning of the poem? Give a reason for your answer.

Schoenberg came to realize that, having abandoned tonality in writing atonal music, a new procedure in composing was needed to bring structure, unity and coherence to an atonal composition. His solution was what is known as **twelve-note technique,** or **serialism.**

In a twelve-note or serial composition, all twelve notes of the chromatic scale are of equal importance:

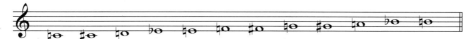

(Notes may appear in different guises – G♯, for instance, may appear as A♭, E♭ may appear as D♯ and so on.)

1   To begin, the composer arranges the twelve notes in a chosen order. This becomes the **note row,** or **basic series,** on which the entire composition will be based. The row printed below, labelled O (for 'original'), is the basic series which Schoenberg constructed for his Fourth String Quartet (1936).

2   The notes of the *original* form of the basic series are then written in reverse order – note 12 becomes note 1, note 11 becomes note 2, and so on. This 'backwards' form of the series is called **retrograde** (R, below).

3   The original form of the series is then turned upside down – called **inversion** (I, below). Intervals which rise in the original, now fall by exactly the same amount, and vice versa. A falling major 3rd becomes a rising major 3rd, a rising perfect 5th becomes a falling perfect 5th, and so on (compare I with O).

4   A fourth form of the series is called **retrograde inversion** (RI). The notes of the inversion are written in reverse order, so that this form presents the series backwards *and* upside down at the same time.

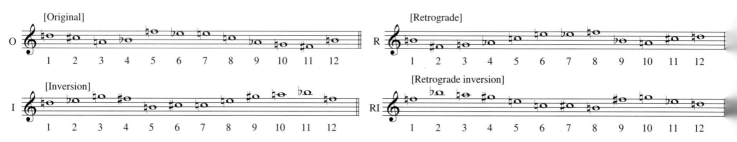

Any of these four forms of the series may be transposed (raised or lowered in pitch) to begin on any of the twelve notes of the chromatic scale. This gives 48 possible versions of the series. The composer can use any of the versions:

● *horizontally,* to shape melodies – two or more of which may weave along together in counterpoint;

● *vertically,* stacking notes on top of each other to structure chords to serve as supporting harmonies (the chords below are built from the original form of the series).

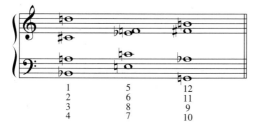

During the composing of the music, any notes of the series may be used at any octave – higher or lower. As all twelve notes are equally important, none of them should appear 'out of turn' – though a note may be *immediately* repeated. It is important to remember that any of the versions of the series merely offers the composer *basic* musical material – a series of notes. The composer must use skill and musicianship, imagination and sensitivity, in:

- shaping melodic lines;
- devising rhythms, to bring life to the music;
- taking decisions on tempo, dynamics, repetition, contrast;
- choosing timbres;
- structuring chords/harmonies;
- creating textures;
- building up a convincing and coherent structure.

Listening

Investigate this short serial piece for a solo instrument. It is based upon the series shown on page 226. The forms of the series are used in the order: original; inversion; retrograde; retrograde inversion; retrograde; inversion. Why, do you think, in bar 14 is the last note of the retrograde form omitted?

First and second listenings
Listen for repetition of rhythmic patterns and melodic shapes.

Third and fourth listenings

1   Identify the instrument which plays this serial piece.

2   Do the phrases of the music always match with the entries of the various versions of the series?

3   In what ways do the last four bars match and balance the first four bars?

4   Describe the overall mood of this music.

If possible, try your own performance of this serial piece – aiming to bring out the mood you have described.

Anton Webern and Alban Berg, Schoenberg's two most important pupils, also took up serialism. Webern followed Schoenberg's 'rules' very closely. Berg used a much freer approach, often breaking the rules if that suited his structural and expressive purposes. He often uses notes of the series out of turn, and may mix serial technique with harmonies that, at times, suggest the music is *tonal* – 'in a key'.

Here is the series which Berg devised for his Violin Concerto (1935). Play each of the four forms of the series.

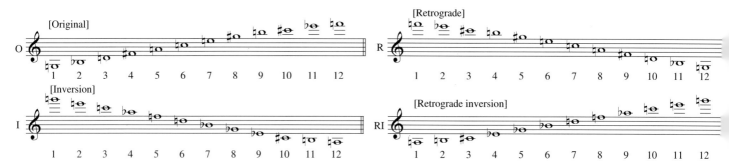

In constructing this series, Berg has arranged the twelve notes of the chromatic scale in this particular order for special reasons. The first nine notes rise in intervals of a 3rd. Notes 1 2 3 give a chord of G minor, while 5 6 7 make A minor. Notes 3 4 5 give D major, and 7 8 9 offer E major. Notes 9 to 12 are part of a whole-tone scale, each note being a whole tone away from its neighbour.

Listening

Investigate the score on the next two pages which shows the essential musical information of the opening of Berg's Violin Concerto.

In the introduction (bars 1–10) the series is treated very freely, with arpeggios shaped from selected notes from the original form of the series (harp and clarinets are given a transposed version, beginning on B♭).

At bar 11, the original form of the series is used to structure chords in a syncopated rhythm, with some notes repeated. Then at bar 15, the solo violin presents the original form of the series, ending with a leap downwards which suggests a musical 'sigh'. The violin plays the inverted form of the series at bar 24.

Then follow other appearances of the series. Most of them are in incomplete form, and all are transposed versions. For example, in bars 34–37 both the original and the inverted forms of the series are transposed down a semitone.

First and second listenings
Follow the score as the recording is played.

Third and fourth listenings
1 Describe the mood set in the introduction (bars 1–10).
2 Which bars especially, in this extract, strike you as being *tonal*, rather than *atonal*?

Fifth listening
Listen, this time, without looking at the score. Spot appearances of the series in its original form (rising), and in inversion (falling). You will need to concentrate your listening over the whole pitch range (the bass of the musical texture, as well as the treble).

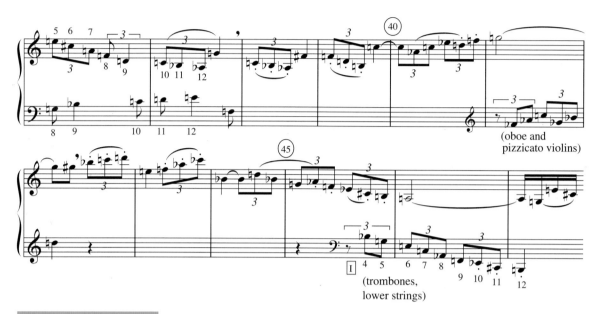

(oboe and
pizzicato violins)

(trombones,
lower strings)

Composing

Create a short serial composition. Choose one of the twelve-note series printed on page 233.

Compose a melody, which will move at a moderate or slowish tempo. Use the four forms of the series in this order:

original;   inversion;   retrograde;   retrograde inversion.

All the time you are working, carefully consider:

- the rhythm – a very important element in serial composition;
- the shape (contour), balance, and range of your melodic line – remember: any notes of the series may be used at any octave;
- repetition and contrast;
- dynamics, expression, and any fluctuations of tempo.

At all times, use your ears – and assess the musical effectiveness of the sounds you are creating.

A portrait of Berg, painted in oils by his composition teacher – Arnold Schoenberg

Having completed your melody, you could add a simple accompaniment by adding supporting chords, structured from the notes of the series.

Performing

When you have finished your serial composition, organize a performance of it – if necessary, asking others to help you. As you listen to the serial compositions of others, assess the musical effectiveness of: the melodic line, the rhythm, the use of dynamics and expression.

Now try this...

Construct your own basic series for a serial composition.

First, write out the chromatic scale (as on page 226). Then select notes in turn, and write them down to form your series. Think about the intervals the notes will make, and the order of the intervals. (Cross off each note, as you use it, from your chromatic scale.)

You will now have the *original* form of your series. Label it, with its name (Original), and number the notes.

Perform your series, and judge its effect. Make adjustments, if necessary (but make sure that your finished series includes each of the twelve pitches, once only).

Next, write out the remaining three forms of your series (follow steps 2, 3 and 4 on page 226). Label each form with its name, and number the notes.

Now use your series to create and develop a serial composition. First, though, it would be a good idea to have in mind who will perform your finished composition. Perhaps you yourself (possibly with the help of others), or a singer or instrumentalist that you know, or perhaps a visiting instrumental teacher.

Make your own decision about what kind of piece you will create – or use one of the following suggestions:

- a single melodic line, for instrument or voice;
- a march, or a dance (for instance, a waltz) for melody instrument plus keyboard accompaniment;
- a two-part piece – for two instruments, or voice and instrument (perhaps making use of imitation, or canon).

When you have completed your serial composition, organize a performance of it, and record it. Afterwards, listen to the recording, and discuss it.

Total serialism, or integral serialism

Since the late 1940s, various composers have extended Schoenberg's ideas. They have composed works in which not only the twelve notes of the chromatic scale, but also twelve-element series of durations (note-values), dynamics, attack (touch, or articulation), and timbre, may be totally controlled by Schoenberg's principles of serialism.

Here is the twelve-element series of dynamics which Boulez devised for the first section of his *Structures*, Book 1, for two pianos:

1	2	3	4	5	6	7	8	9	10	11	12
pppp	ppp	pp	p	quasi p	mp	mf	quasi f	f	ff	fff	ffff

Linked listening

Polytonality

Ravel: *Valses nobles et sentimentales,* No. 6 – opening with high woodwinds in D major, violins and horns in B major, bass instruments in C major (all simultaneously)

Ravel: *Boléro,* third playing of the melody – first piccolo plays in E major, second piccolo in G major, horn and celesta in C major

Ives: *Putnam's Camp* from *Three Places in New England* – an impression of marching bands competing in different keys

Milhaud: Overture to *La création du monde* – solo saxophone in D minor, accompaniment sometimes in D major, sometimes in other keys

Atonality

Schoenberg: String Quartet No. 2 (1907–8), last movement (with soprano)

Schoenberg: *Five Pieces for Orchestra,* Opus 16

Schoenberg: other songs from *Pierrot lunaire*

Berg: *Three Pieces for Orchestra,* Opus 6

Berg: *Wozzeck* – especially Act 1 Scene 3, Act 3 Scene 2

Webern: *Five Movements for Strings,* Opus 5

Webern: *Five Pieces for Orchestra,* Opus 10

Also, pieces in the jazz style known as 'free jazz' or 'free-form jazz' involving elaborate collective improvisation on a theme against complex harmonies, often crossing the border from tonality into atonality (e.g. by Ornette Coleman, John Coltrane – also listen, if possible, to Coltrane's version of *My Favourite Things,* based on lengthy pedal points)

Serialism/Twelve-note technique

Schoenberg: Piano Suite, Opus 25 – the first work to be composed entirely in serial technique

Schoenberg: Wind Quintet, Opus 26

Schoenberg: *Variations for Orchestra,* Opus 31 (the Theme and Variations 1–3 are described in 'Enjoying Modern Music')

Schoenberg: Piano Concerto, Opus 42

Berg: *Lyric Suite* for string quartet

Berg: *Der Wein* (The wine), concert aria for soprano and orchestra

Berg: Violin Concerto – complete (described in 'Enjoying Modern Music')

Webern: Symphony, Opus 21

Webern: Quartet for clarinet, tenor saxophone, violin and piano

Webern: Cantata No. 2, Opus 31

Seiber: the second of *Three Fragments from 'A Portrait of the Artist as a Young Man'* for speaker, chorus and instrumental ensemble

Elisabeth Lutyens: String Quartet No. 6

Milton Babbitt: *All Set* for jazz ensemble

Total serialism

Boulez: first section of *Structures,* Book 1, for two pianos (serialism applied to twelve-element series of pitches, durations, dynamics, and attack)

Stockhausen: *Kreuzspiel* for oboe, bass clarinet, piano, and three percussionists (serialism applied to pitches, durations, dynamics)

Stockhausen: *Gruppen* for three orchestras (pitches and tempi)

Stockhausen: *Gesang der Jünglinge,* electronic (pitches, durations, dynamics, textural densities, stereo placements – left, right, close, distant)

Nono: *Il canto sospeso* for soprano, mezzo-soprano, tenor, chorus and orchestra (pitches, durations, registers and, to some extent, dynamics)

Here are the basic series, or note rows, of some of the serial compositions mentioned on the opposite page:

Schoenberg: Piano Concerto

Berg: *Lyric Suite**

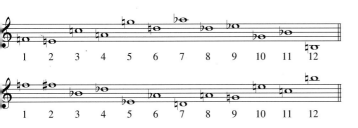

Berg: *Der Wein*

Webern: Cantata No. 2

*Berg used this same note row in his song *Schliesse mir die Augen beide* (1925); in the voice part, the note row (in the original version only) is presented five times in succession.

CHAPTER 29

Chance and choice – aleatory music

Improvising

Using voice or any suitable instrument, experiment and find your own solutions to the following.

1   Create a melodic line to fit this rhythm. Choose a suitable tempo, and add dynamics and expression.

2   Add your own rhythm to these given pitches.

3   Choose any four notes, in any order, and add rhythm to create an ostinato which repeats for 15 seconds.

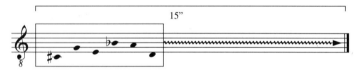

4   Improvise a free, floating melodic line, filling in the gaps between the given pitches.

5   Turn these graphics into sounds.

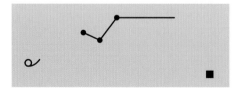

6   Perform any three, or all, of these fragments, joining them in any order of your choice, repeating
     any of them at will.

Perform your solutions to other people – and listen to theirs. Discuss the differences in the results.

In the six items opposite, some musical elements had been determined in advance, by the composer,
but other elements (for example, pitch, duration/rhythm, timbre) were undetermined, and were left to
you, the performer. Choices involving creative decisions and considerable invention had to be made.
And so the results (as far as the composer is concerned) are unpredictable.

Music which involves elements of chance, choice, unpredictability, or indeterminacy – either in the
way it is composed, or performed, or both – is called **aleatory music** (from the Latin word *alea*,
meaning 'a dice').

   Here are some examples of aleatory devices or procedures, several of which you have just
experienced:

- a performer may be asked to choose between two or more alternatives, such as which notes
  or which sections of music to perform – and, perhaps, in which order to perform them;

- a performer may need to make choices or decisions about tempo, timbre, dynamics,
  expression, musical nuances;

- the pitch of notes may be given – but not their duration;

- note-durations/rhythm may be given – but the performer is left to decide upon pitches;

- pitch and duration may be suggested – but only approximately;

- performers may be given the choice of *when* to perform notes, or note-groups, within a given
  time-span;

- performers may be asked to provide some notes of their own choice, by improvising – or to
  improvise upon given materials;

- in some aleatory scores, no conventional notes are provided at all – instead, a collection of
  graphic symbols, a diagram, a drawing, a text, or simply a basic idea, to be interpreted very
  freely and imaginatively; other aleatory scores mix graphic symbols and conventional
  notation;

- during the composing process, the composer may take decisions about which notes to use
  and how to use them by throwing a dice, tossing coins, or by other chance operations.

When 'chance-choice' elements such as these are used, no two performances of the piece can be
exactly alike.

On the next two pages are printed some of the notational symbols you may find in aleatory scores, or
in scores which include certain aleatory aspects – especially when pitch and duration are treated
freely. Several are based on staff notation symbols, which have been adjusted or extended. Some
have become more widely accepted than others. Many composers devise their own symbols – in
some instances, for a single composition.

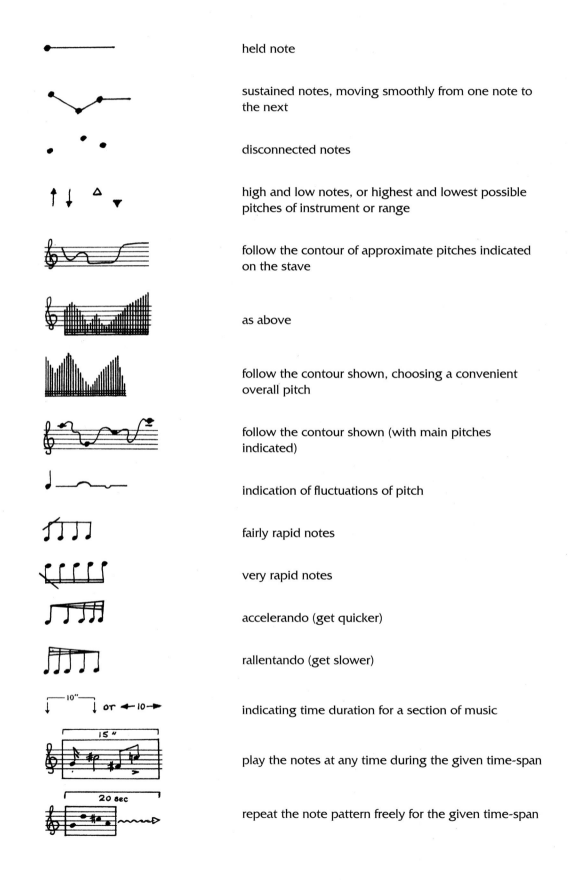

held note

sustained notes, moving smoothly from one note to the next

disconnected notes

high and low notes, or highest and lowest possible pitches of instrument or range

follow the contour of approximate pitches indicated on the stave

as above

follow the contour shown, choosing a convenient overall pitch

follow the contour shown (with main pitches indicated)

indication of fluctuations of pitch

fairly rapid notes

very rapid notes

accelerando (get quicker)

rallentando (get slower)

indicating time duration for a section of music

play the notes at any time during the given time-span

repeat the note pattern freely for the given time-span

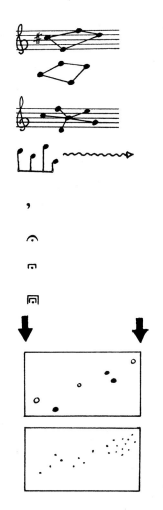

repeat the notes freely, beginning and ending on any one

as above, but precise pitches not indicated

alternate the central note with one, or more, of the others

repeat the pattern of approximate pitches for the duration indicated by the arrow

brief pause

normal pause

long pause

very long pause

indicating conductor's section down-beats

indicating notes to be played at approximate pitch, grouped and timed according to the duration of the box; the height of the box represents the total range of the instrument

random staccato or light and delicate sounds at approximate pitch

Listening

Investigate the aleatory score on pages 238 and 239, which includes some of the notations explained on these two pages. The music is for three instrumentalists: A, using soprano range; B, using mezzo-soprano or alto range; and C, using bass range.

The piece is structured in a number of brief sections. Any timings indicated are approximate. In some of the sections, precise pitches are indicated on five-line staves. In the others, the height of each box represents the total range of each performer.

Match the notations used in the score with the explanations given on these two pages. Then listen to the interpretation of this aleatory score, recorded on the CD.

Performing

Now form a group of three performers plus a conductor, and try your own performance of the score. Make a recording of it, and then listen to it. Compare your interpretation of the score with the performance on the CD.

Mosaics

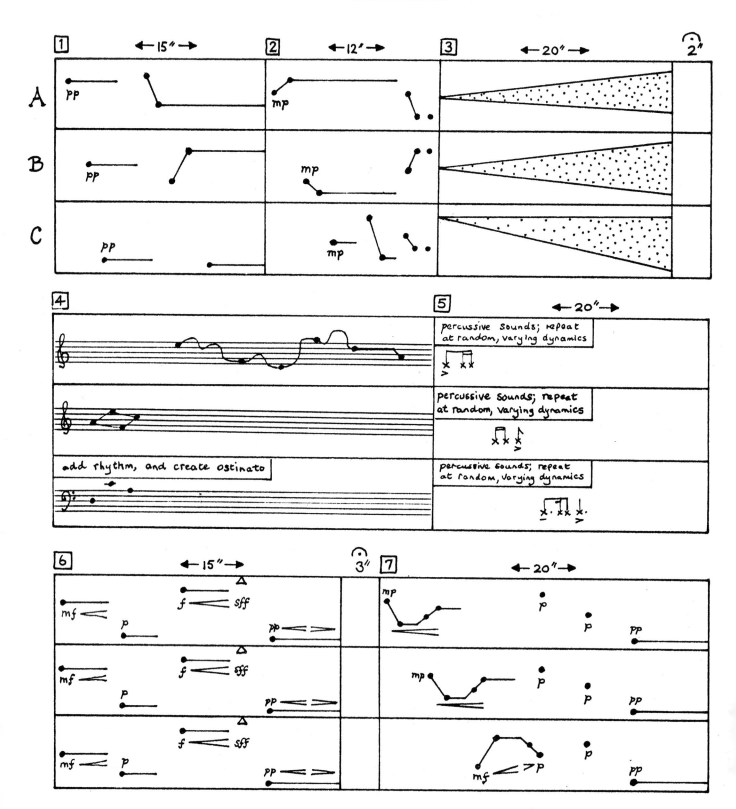

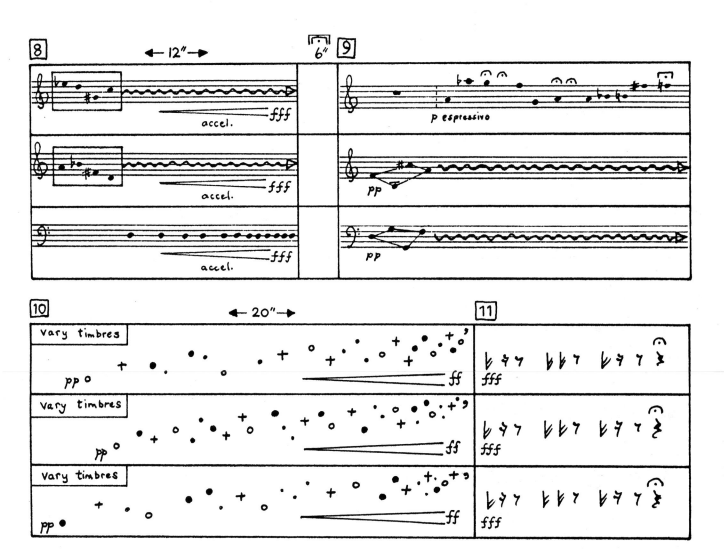

Now try this...

With a partner, investigate the score, printed on the next two pages, of music called *The Voyage* by Jim Northfield. The upper half of each box in the score is a graphic representation of taped electronic sounds, recorded on the CD. Two musicians are necessary for this piece:

● a performer (using any instrument) whose part is written in the lower half of each box; and

● an 'engineer' who pauses the recording when indicated, and then judges exactly when to press 'Play' – also, if you think necessary, control and alter the volume (loudness).

The main aim is that the performer responds to, reacts to, and interracts with, the recorded electronic sounds and the cues in the score with imagination, musicianship – and enjoyment!

First listen to the recording on the CD of the electronics part. Then try a performance.

Record your performance – then listen back, and evaluate the result. Judge whether you can improve or refine it in any way. If so: re-record, play back, and assess.

Afterwards, swap parts (the new performer using a different kind of instrument if you like). Record, and listen back. Compare, discuss, and evaluate your two different versions.

The Voyage

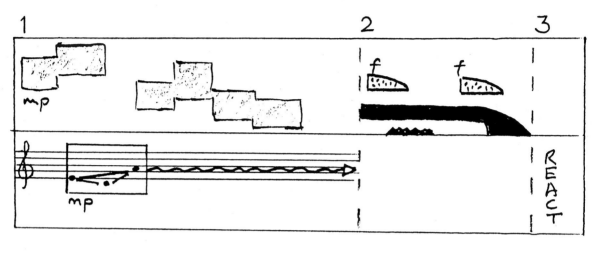

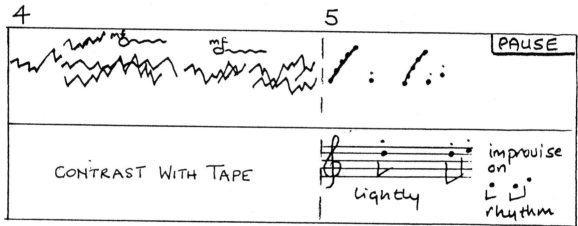

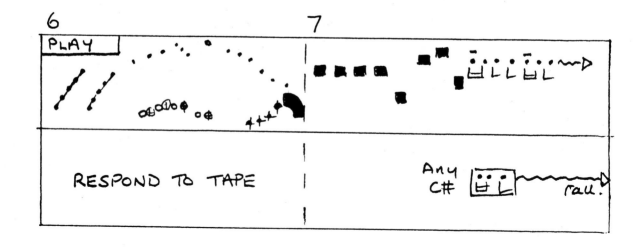

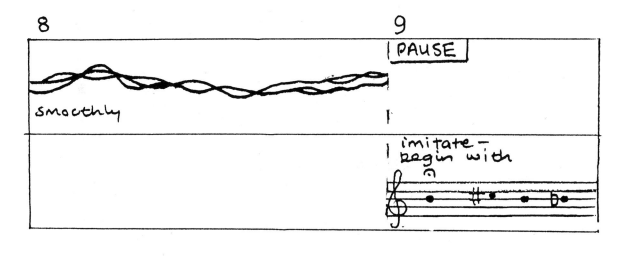

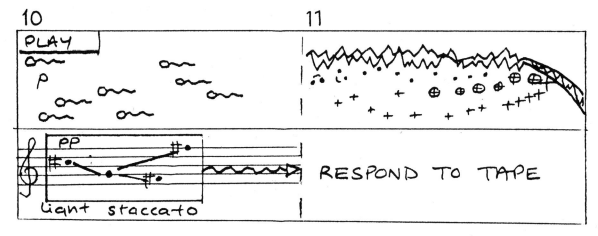

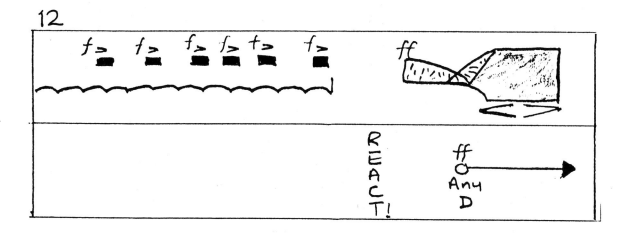

Composing

Compose your own aleatory piece for voice(s) and/or instrument(s). Decide whether you want to include elements of chance, or choice, or both – and how you will do this. Make use of any of the aleatory ideas and notations included anywhere in this chapter, if they suit your purpose – and/or devise others of your own.

When you have decided upon your ideas, notate a score for your piece. Work out the most suitable way of indicating the durations of the various events or sections of music. Add an explanatory key to your score, clearly explaining the notational symbols and graphics you have used so that the performer(s) will understand how to interpret them. If necessary, also add any verbal instructions.

When you have completed the score of your aleatory piece, exchange scores with someone else – and prepare and re-create each other's pieces.

Listen to the performance of your piece. How similar were the results to what you expected? How different were they?

Linked listening

Examples of aleatory or indeterminate compositions

Stockhausen: *Piano Piece IX* (1956), consisting of 19 fragments of music, any of which the pianist may select and play in any order. At the end of each fragment are printed markings of speed, loudness and touch, which must be applied to whichever fragment the pianist chooses to play next. Any fragment may be played twice (the second time, an octave higher or lower than the first) and the piece ends once any fragment has been chosen and played for a third time. (When the actual order of musical events – sections of music, perhaps pages of score – is left to the performer(s), the composition is said to be in 'open form' or 'mobile form'.)

Stockhausen: *Mixtur* (1964), another work in open form, consisting of 20 *moments*, or pieces, for five orchestral groups (percussion, woodwind, brass, pizzicato strings, bowed strings) and live electronics (four sine-wave generators and four ring modulators). There are many aleatory or indeterminate aspects involved in *Mixtur* (described in detail in 'Enjoying Modern Music').

John Cage: *4'33"* (1952) for any instrument or group of instruments. In this piece, no one plays a note! The 'music' consists of whatever environmental sounds and audience reactions occur during the 'performance', which lasts for precisely 4 minutes and 33 seconds. A recording of this piece by the Hungarian ensemble Amadinda brings in the sounds of birdsong, church bells and distant voices.

John Cage: *Concert* (1957–8) for piano and orchestra (any number of players) – may be performed, in whole or in part, any duration, as a solo, chamber ensemble piece, symphony, aria (with soprano), or piano concerto. The players, who should be separated in space as widely as possible, choose to play, in any order, any number of pages from their parts. Co-ordination is by elapsed time, the conductor using gestures 'to represent a chronometer of variable speed'. Cage has commented: 'harmonious fusion of sound is not an objective.'

Earle Brown: *Available Forms 1* (1961) for eighteen performers, including two percussionists. Another piece in open form, printed in a mixture of conventional and graphic notation on six loose pages, with four or five musical 'events' on each page. The conductor decides the actual succession of the events, also choosing to combine, repeat or omit any of them.

Ligeti: *Volumina* (1961–2) for organ – printed as a graphic score in which pitches and durations are indeterminate. There are three performers, two of them controlling the organ stops and couplers as the organist plays changing note-clusters, of varying density and dynamics, with each hand and also on the pedals.

Davidovsky: *Synchronisms No. 1* (1962) for flute and electronic sounds. In creating this piece, the composer found two problems: 'proper synchronization (a) of rhythm and (b) of pitch. During the shorter episodes where both electronic and conventional instruments are playing, rather strict timing is maintained. However, in the more extended episodes of this type, an element of chance is introduced to allow for the inevitable time discrepancies between the live performer and the constant-speed tape recorder.'

Tim Souster: *The Transistor Radio of St Narcissus* (1982–3) for flugelhorn, live electronics and tape. Certain aleatory factors are involved – for example, the flugelhorn player is at times instructed to improvise and imitate the sounds on the tape, and occasionally, although pitches are precisely notated, the player is given freedom and choice concerning durations.

'Convergence' (1952) by the American artist Jackson Pollock, who aimed to create 'an indeterminate painting by allowing colours to drip freely onto the canvas'

CHAPTER 30

Mixed media, and the theatre element

In November 1967, in Illinois, the American composer John Cage organized a 'mixed media event', an 'environmental extravaganza', which he entitled *Musicircus*. **Mixed media** is a term used to describe a work (not counting opera or ballet) in which music is merged with other arts or media. (**Multimedia** means the same thing.) Some possible ingredients in a mixed media piece are given in the box below.

For *Musicircus*, Cage assembled various performers in different media and from different cultures and traditions. The event took place in the Stock Pavilion, a huge building used for showing cattle, and consisted of simultaneous performances of jazz, rock, electronic, piano and vocal music, dance and mime. There were also films, slides, and coloured lighting effects. Each artist or group had a platform, and spectators were free to wander around and also make sounds on a large metallic structure in the centre of the arena.

Listening

The effect, for spectators wandering around the area, would have been similar to the extract recorded on the CD. As you listen, identify the different types and styles of music. Also, visualize what spectators may have *seen*.

Ingredients which might be merged in a mixed media piece

- music – played and/or sung
- movement
- dance
- mime, gesture
- speaking, chanting, narration, poetry
- actions, drama
- costume, masks
- ritual, incantation
- pre-recorded tape
- electronic sounds
- setting, background, décor, scenery, props
- lighting effects
- film, slides, video
- 'stereo placement' – spatial effects
- often, an aleatory ('chance' or 'choice') element
- sometimes, audience participation

Another of Cage's mixed media pieces is *HPSCHD*, which he composed in collaboration with Lejaren Hiller. The title is the word 'harpsichord' reduced to the computer's six-letter word limit.

HPSCHD was first performed in May 1969 in the huge Assembly Hall of Illinois University, and included 7 amplified harpsichords and 51 computer-generated sound-tapes, all relayed over 58 loudspeakers. All this was accompanied by coloured lighting effects and films and slides projected onto huge sheets in the centre of the performing area and onto a screen running around the rim of the vast ceiling. Also involved in the lengthy performance was an 'audience' of several thousand spectators who could come and go at will, and freely wander around and also through the performing area.

Later, a stereo recording was made. This included an edited assembly of the 51 electronic tapes, and three of the harpsichords: *Solo I*, recorded on both channels; *Solo II*, left channel; and *Solo VI*, right channel. (Cage had said that a performance for 1–51 tapes and 1–7 harpsichords was perfectly valid.)

The tapes Each of the 51 computer-generated tapes uses its own range of pitches, dividing the octave equally into a different number – from 5 to 56. Each tape is composed according to a series of programs – for example, ranging from repetitive notes and silences to non-repetitive notes and very varied gaps. Other programs intermix note orders, time and durations, volume and dynamics.

The harpsichords The music of *Solo I* is computer-composed according to the same programs used for the 51 tapes, with the octave divided into twelve equal intervals (semitones).

The music of *Solo II* is based on Mozart's *Musikalisches Würfelspiel* (Musical dice game) – an 'introduction to composing minuets by means of dice'. The player is offered a 32-bar structure. Bars 8, 16, 24, and 32 are fixed. But Mozart offers ready-composed alternatives for the remaining empty bars, which the player determines by throwing dice. *Solo II* consists of 20 minuets 'composed' in this way.

The music of *Solo VI* begins with a realization of Mozart's dice game. This is continually repeated – but the performer gradually replaces bars with any passages from piano works by Beethoven, Chopin, Schumann, Gottschalk, Busoni, Schoenberg, Cage, and Hiller.

Listening

If possible, listen to the first four minutes of *HPSCHD*.

First listening
Cage expects us to be selective in our listening. (The human ear tends to be selective anyway – each time we listen to a piece, the attention may focus on different details.) As you listen for the first time, concentrate on *Solo II* (left channel) playing minuets composed by throwing dice.

Second listening
Concentrate on *Solo VI* (right channel) which begins with another dice-composed minuet. Soon the player begins to substitute fragments from Beethoven's *Appassionata* Sonata. For example, this at 1′ 16″:

And this at 1′ 41″:

Third listening

Concentrate on the electronic sounds, and *Solo I* (both channels).

Fourth listening

Select (disentangle) from the texture any material you choose.

At the first performance, for spectators wandering round and through the performing area, the perspective and balance of the sounds were constantly changing. Cage suggests that listeners to the recording may care to achieve similar changes by adjusting volume and/or balance control (perhaps even eliminating one channel altogether). You could also stroll around the room as you listen. Assess how the perspective and balance of sounds change according to where you move.

A public performance of *Musicircus*, or *HPSCHD*, will included elements of **theatre** – Cage once said: 'theatre is seeing and hearing'. Many composers since the early 1960s have included theatre elements in their pieces (also called **music theatre**). For example, singers, and also instrumentalists, may be required to move, gesture, act or mime, wear costume. *Seeing* becomes important, as well as hearing.

A good example of music theatre is Peter Maxwell Davies's *Revelation and Fall*, composed in 1966 for soprano and sixteen instrumentalists. The soprano, who appears as a nun in vivid scarlet habit, must vary her vocal style from normal singing, through Sprechgesang, to screaming terrifyingly through a loudhailer.

Luciano Berio has often included theatre elements in his compositions. *Sequenza V* (1966) for solo trombone was composed with memories in mind of the famous clown Grock, who was once Berio's neighbour. He remembers seeing one of Grock's performances. At times, between the jokes and antics, the clown would look at the audience and ask: 'Why?'. Berio describes *Sequenza V* as a developing of 'Why?'. The trombonist must make use of new sounds and techniques (see page 125) and also make gestures and vocalize.

Listening

Listen to the first four minutes or so of *Sequenza V*. Berio requests that for the first part of the piece, the performer (wearing white tie, lit by a spotlight from above) should strike the pose of 'a variety showman about to sing an old favourite'.

1   For each of the opening isolated sounds, the performer raises the trombone and then lowers it again.

2   Later, he begins to interject vocal sounds. Sometimes the trombone imitates these; sometimes the voice imitates the sound of the instrument.

3   Eventually, after agitated breathy sounds, the performer utters a bewildered 'Why?' – then immediately sits down.

4   He must perform the rest of the piece 'as though rehearsing in an empty hall'. He often sings while playing. Sometimes the pitches of voice and trombone match; sometimes they are different. Throughout *Sequenza V*, the player uses a plunger mute which he opens and closes and sometimes rattles inside the bell of the trombone.

Composing

Create a mixed media piece, combining aural and visual ingredients. It could be fairly simple – for example, suitable music to enhance or to interact with movement, dance, a sequence of slides. Or it could be more complex and combine a wider variety of ingredients.

Use entirely your own ideas, or choose one of the suggestions for a theme in the box below. You may find you can build upon ideas from the pieces in the linked listening list on the next two pages.

- The Dawn of Creation
- Dreamscape
- Night-Spell
- Space
- The Enchanted Island
- The Four Elements – earth, air, fire, water
- Seasons
- an environmental issue
- local history or legend
- a scene from a mumming play or folk legend
- a comic or humorous theme

Consider using (if available):

- coloured lighting effects;
- costume, masks;
- rostra, and steps;
- slides, and/or a specially-prepared video, as 'background';
- overhead projector with transparencies throwing coloured images onto a white wall or large screen.

(You may find other ingredients mentioned in the box on page 244 are also suitable.)

Also consider:

- preparing a tape of electronic, computer-generated, or natural sounds and using it with, or without, live music;
- including dramatic effects, such as sudden silence after aggressive sound, violent sounds after silence, sudden stillness after vigorous movement, dynamic movement after stillness, sudden change of lighting.

'We have made pieces by working together. You get together with an idea. You describe the idea, and everybody talks about it, and then we try to work it out. When a piece gets to a certain point, you know that it is in at least good enough form to show to an audience...'

(A member of the 1960s ONCE group – an ensemble of musicians, dancers, designers, and artists, based in Ann Arbor, Michigan)

Performing

When you have worked out your ideas, rehearse and refine your mixed media piece. Then organize a presentation of it – perhaps to an invited audience. If at all possible, make a video recording of it.

Afterwards, discuss and assess the effectiveness and impact of the presentation of your piece.

Linked listening

You will, of course, need to make use of your visual imagination while listening to recordings of any of these pieces!

Scriabin: *Prometheus, the Poem of Fire* (1911) for piano, orchestra and wordless chorus – Scriabin intended the music to be accompanied by colour, and notated a part for 'colour keyboard' which, as it was played, would bring floods of coloured light streaming into the concert hall (e.g. vivid red for note C, orange-rose for G, green for A, brilliant yellow for D)

Varèse: *Poème électronique,* composed for the Brussels Exposition of 1958 – for three-track tape, including electronic sounds, bells, drums, organ, and voices, electronically transformed. It was relayed over a network of 425 loudspeakers throughout the Philips Pavilion and accompanied by lighting and other visual effects devised by the pavilion's architect, Le Corbusier.

Cage: *Theatre Piece* (1960) for 1–8 performers (musicians, dancers, singers, etc.) choosing actions from a list of twenty nouns and verbs. The music consists of Cage's tape montage *Fontana Mix.*

Stockhausen: *Sternklang* (Star-sound) (1971) for five groups widely separated across a public park on a warm, clear, summer night. The music, co-ordinated by signalling and torch-carrying runners, is based on the patterns of stars and constellations, whose names are now and then called out in an incantatory manner.

Stockhausen: *Trans* (1971) – the string players of the orchestra, seated in two rows across the concert platform and bathed in a reddish-violet light, play long-held notes in clusters while the amplified sounds of winds and percussion come from behind. The music is punctuated at varying intervals by the sliding-clacking sound of a wooden weaving shuttle heard from loudspeakers. Other 'events' include string solo cadenzas, trumpet fanfare-like passages and jazzy muted brass gestures. Stockhausen said that the whole idea, and the music, came to him in a dream.

Stockhausen: *Inori* (Adorations) (1974) – one or two solo mime artists, on a raised platform above the orchestra, perform ritual gestures of prayer from various cultures. The music develops a melodic formula through stages centring on rhythm, dynamics, melody, harmony, and polyphony.

Kagel: *Match* (1964) – a 'musical duel' for two cellists and a percussionist (this piece is described on page 99)

Peter Maxwell Davies: *Vesalii icones* (1969) for male dancer (who also plays a honky-tonk piano), solo cellist, and instrumental ensemble

Peter Maxwell Davies: *Eight Songs for a Mad King* (1969) for male voice and instrumental ensemble – the instrumentalists, performing in huge cages, symbolize the birds of the (costumed) mad king (George III) who raves and gestures around them

George Crumb: *Ancient Voices of Children* (see page 206) – Crumb suggests that the work 'could be adapted to theatre presentation involving dance and, perhaps, mime', but even in an unstaged performance there are certain elements of theatre. The soprano at times sings 'into the piano' then 'reverts to normal position, facing the audience'. The boy soprano sings off-stage until the last song. Both, at times, sing or whisper through a 'cardboard speaking tube'. In the third song (page 206) the drumming and vocal sounds of the percussionists provide a powerful theatre element. During the last song, the oboist walks slowly off-stage and plays, then 'moves to a more remote off-stage position'. Towards the end, the boy soprano walks slowly on-stage and takes position near the piano.

Berio: *Recital I* (1972) – a music theatre piece tracing the mental breakdown of a concert singer

Jean Michel Jarre has achieved much success with 'music/laser/video extravaganzas'. On 14 July 1979, in La Place de la Concorde in Paris, he organized a spectacular event based on his synthesizer compositions *Oxygène* and *Équinoxe*, experienced by one million spectators and 100 million television viewers across the world.

Birtwistle: *Verses for Ensembles* (1969), and *Secret Theatre* (1984) – in both these works, certain players at various times move to different positions on the concert platform to play. *Verses for Ensembles* is for brass quartet, two woodwind quintets (one higher in pitch than the other), and two percussion ensembles (one of pitched instruments, the other unpitched). *Secret Theatre* is for chamber orchestra divided into two groups: 'Cantus', playing chant-like melodic lines in unison, rhythmic unison, or heterophony; and 'Continuum', playing ostinatos (sometimes interlocking, sometimes superimposed) to form block-like harmonies.

Mike Westbrook: *Pier Rides* (1986) – based on the nine Muses (goddesses, in Greek mythology, of individual arts and sciences) and incorporating dance, costume, theatre, lighting, music (jazz), and song

'Pomegranate', a mobile by Alexander Calder